SOCIAL CHANGE, SOCIAL POLICY AND SOCIAL WORK IN THE NEW EUROPE

Social Change, Social Policy and Social Work in the New Europe

Edited by
ANNA KWAK
ROBERT DINGWALL

LONDON AND NEW YORK

First published 1998 by Ashgate Publishing

Reissued 2018 by Routledge
2 Park Square, Milton Park, Abingdon, Oxon, OX14 4RN
711 Third Avenue, New York, NY 10017, USA

Routledge is an imprint of the Taylor & Francis Group, an informa business

Copyright © Anna Kwak and Robert Dingwall 1998

All rights reserved. No part of this book may be reprinted or reproduced or utilised in any form or by any electronic, mechanical, or other means, now known or hereafter invented, including photocopying and recording, or in any information storage or retrieval system, without permission in writing from the publishers.

Notice:
Product or corporate names may be trademarks or registered trademarks, and are used only for identification and explanation without intent to infringe.

Publisher's Note
The publisher has gone to great lengths to ensure the quality of this reprint but points out that some imperfections in the original copies may be apparent.

Disclaimer
The publisher has made every effort to trace copyright holders and welcomes correspondence from those they have been unable to contact.

A Library of Congress record exists under LC control number: 98071970

ISBN 13: 978-1-138-34337-5 (hbk)
ISBN 13: 978-1-138-34340-5 (pbk)
ISBN 13: 978-0-429-43917-9 (ebk)

Contents

List of Contributors   vii

Introduction   1
Robert Dingwall and Anna Kwak

Part I: Social Policy and Social Change

1. From Socialist to Liberal Utopia: Changes in Poland's Social Policy since 1989   9
   Józefina Hrynkiewicz

2. Politics and Social Policy in the New Poland   29
   Fred Powell

3. Current Trends in Family Policy: European Union Countries and Poland   43
   Marek Rymsza

4. Family Policy and Family Life in Poland   59
   Anna Kwak

5. Social Policy and the Family in the United Kingdom   73
   Gillian Pascall

6. Changes in Prison Policy as a Part of Political and Economic Transformation in Poland   85
   Andrzej Mościskier

7. Recent Trends in English Penal Policy   97
   Paul Roberts

vi *Social Change, Social Policy and Social Work in the New Europe*

Part II: Social Policy and Economic Change

8   Higher Education and the Labour Market in Britain   121
    Daniel Lawrence

9   Trends of the 1990s in Swedish Welfare Policy -   141
    Implications for Social Work Education
    Lennart Nygren

10 The Prevention and Relief of Unemployment in Britain   153
    Paul Ransome

11 Changes in the Polish Labour Market During the Period   161
    of Transformation
    Ewa Giermanowska and Józefina Hrynkiewicz

Part III: Social Work in the New Europe

12 The Irish Model of Social Work   183
    Fionnuala Lordan and Izabela Rybka

13 The Development of Social Work in Britain 1869-1996   199
    Mark Lymbery

14 The History of Social Work in Sweden   213
    Staffan Öberg

15 Social Work Education in Britain   221
    Mark Lymbery

16 Delivering Social Work Education in Partnership in   233
    Britain
    Tina Eadie

17 The Development of Social Welfare in Poland   245
    Izabela Rybka

List of Contributors

Robert Dingwall is Professor of Sociology in the School of Sociology and Social Policy at the University of Nottingham.
Tina Eadie is a Lecturer in the Centre for Social Work, School of Sociology and Social Policy at the University of Nottingham.
Ewa Giermanowska is an Assistant in the Centre of Youth Studies, Institute of Applied Social Sciences, University of Warsaw.
Józefina Hrynkiewicz is a Professor in the Department of Social Policy, Institute of Applied Social Sciences, University of Warsaw.
Anna Kwak is a Professor in the Department of Social Pathology, Institute of Applied Social Sciences, University of Warsaw.
Daniel Lawrence has recently retired as a Senior Lecturer in the School of Sociology and Social Policy at the University of Nottingham.
Fionnuala Lordan is a Lecturer in the Department of Applied Social Studies at the National University of Ireland, Cork.
Mark Lymbery is a Lecturer in the Centre for Social Work, School of Sociology and Social Policy at the University of Nottingham.
Andrzej Mościskier is an Assistant Professor in the Department of Social Pathology, Institute of Applied Social Sciences, University of Warsaw.
Lennart Nygren is Professor of Social Work in the Department of Social Welfare at the University of Umeå.
Staffan Öberg is a Lecturer in the Department of Social Welfare at the University of Umeå.
Gillian Pascall is a Senior Lecturer in the School of Sociology and Social Policy at the University of Nottingham.
Fred Powell is Professor of Applied Social Studies at the National University of Ireland, Cork.
Paul Ransome was formerly a Lecturer in the School of Sociology and Social Policy at the University of Nottingham and is now a Lecturer in the Department of Sociology and Anthropology at the University of Wales, Swansea.

Paul Roberts is a Lecturer in the Department of Law at the University of Nottingham.

Izabela Rybka is an Assistant in the Department of Social Policy, Institute of Applied Social Sciences, University of Warsaw.

Marek Rymsza is an Assistant in the Department of Social Policy, Institute of Applied Social Sciences, University of Warsaw.

Introduction
Robert Dingwall
Anna Kwak

This book brings together a selection of papers produced as a result of the collaboration of the Universities of Warsaw, Nottingham, Cork and Umea in a programme of work funded by the EU TEMPUS programme between 1992 and 1997. The objective of the programme was to improve the preparation of social welfare professionals by the University of Warsaw for employment in the new market-oriented society that was being created in Poland after the end of 'real socialism' in 1989. The programme had several components intended to develop the curriculum and pedagogy of the Institute of Applied Social Sciences in Warsaw and to improve its resource base. Its philosophy was not one of exporting West European models of economic and social organization, but of creating opportunities for colleagues from the different institutions to share their experiences. The Polish partners would then consider what to adopt and what to discard in the light of their local situation. Most of the papers in this volume were produced as part of a series of workshops to support curriculum development and were previously published in Polish in one or other of two collections, *Wybrane problemy pacy socjalnej* [Selected Problems of Social Welfare], edited by Anna Kwak, and *Edukacja do pracy socjalnej* [Education for Social Welfare], edited by Anna Kwak and Andrzej Mościskier. All of them have been revised and updated for the present volume and some additional material has been commissioned to provide a fuller context.

Why do the participants in this programme want to share their experience more widely? What is the justification for this collection? We believe that there are two elements which should make this work of general interest to anyone who is interested in social policy and social work in any European or European-style society. As the programme developed the participants found themselves in the middle of two debates which are currently being conducted in most developed countries. The first is over the nature and purpose of university education and its relation to the labour market. Should universities worry about the employment of their graduates and the skills that are needed by the wider economy and society or should they simply concern themselves with their own mission to transmit advanced learning? The second is over the modernization of the welfare state. Despite the very different experiences of the four countries in the programme, the participants came to a common analysis of the failures of the approaches to welfare which had been dominant over the post-war period. The Polish experience, and the Western partners' reaction to it, provided a particularly good case study. The abruptness of change in Poland and the explicit choices faced by that society since 1989 revealed the extent to which Western Europe had either avoided these issues or had produced evolutionary responses which had had a larger cumulative impact than had often been acknowledged.

The Nature and Purpose of Universities

In the days of 'real socialism', universities had played a rather marginal role in Polish society. The 'workers' state' did not attach a high value to non-manual forms of work (see chapters by Hrynkiewicz and Rymsza) and the universities were assigned a minor role in the production of certain kinds of professional and as bearers of the national culture in literature, humanities and so on. Given the troubled history of the Polish nation, and the extent to which culture rather than territory, had often been its defining characteristic during periods of foreign occupation, the latter was not a trivial matter. However, the graduates fed mainly into a small intellectual class whose importance often seemed greater outside Poland than inside. Provided that the universities did not cause trouble for the regime, and there were various mechanisms in place to ensure this, they were treated largely with a kind of benign neglect. They became conservative and inward-looking institutions, whose agenda was largely defined by those who worked in them, where the organization often encouraged patronage and nepotism and where the limited resources and prestige system favoured theoretical over practical studies.

The events of 1989 brought two consequences. In the short-term, Polish universities seized the opportunity to claim and legalize the kind of autonomy which they believed to exist in Western Europe. Various barriers to state intervention were erected and faculty democracy was written into statute as a basis of university organization. Unfortunately, as the chapters by Nygren and Lawrence illustrate, these moves had mistaken the rhetoric of Western Europe for its forms. Although West European countries were moving at different rates, their universities were becoming much more actively *managed* institutions: although the fictions of university democracy might be maintained, they were accompanied by the development of a culture of accountability and responsibility. Although, as Lawrence's paper suggests, this may have reached a pathological level in the United Kingdom, faculty autonomy is less and less absolute and faculty democracy is balanced against a requirement to show that its results are efficient, effective and in the wider public interest.

This has emerged as a problem in Poland with the other result of the transformation, namely the desire to modernize the economy and the consequent need to raise the general level of skills and education. As Hrynkiewicz's chapters bring out, the educational system inherited by the democratic state is wholly inadequate to support a modern European economy. Too many children are being educated to too low a level. This perception is widely shared: the years since 1989 have seen a dramatic upsurge in the demand for higher education, even though only a small percentage of the school-leaving population have been educated on tracks that feed into it. But it needs to be the right kind of education. Both Polish and international companies are suspicious of the traditional highly-theoretical, culturally-oriented education which has dominated in the university faculties of humanities and social sciences.

The Institute of Applied Social Sciences was created in 1990 as a partial response to these developments. It was intended to offer students a new kind of education aimed towards employment in the social welfare sector, broadly defined, of the new society and economy. An important part of the TEMPUS programme was devoted to encouraging IASS faculty to adopt more interdisciplinary approaches to the curriculum, to integrate practice-based learning and to become involved in dialogue with employers. This part of the programme drew heavily on the experience of social work education in Ireland, Sweden and the United Kingdom. The papers by Lordan, Rybka, Lymbery, Eadie and Öberg in Part Three, explore the reasons why such an approach came to be regarded as essential for work in this profession and the methods by which it has been institutionalized in their respective countries. It should be stressed, however, that the IASS was not exclusively concerned with the education of social workers and that this experience was seen as a wider source of possible models for collaboration between universities and any type of employer in the social welfare sector.

As the programme developed, it became clear that the slower pace of change in Western Europe had made it possible to accomodate the notion of partnership between universities and the wider society more easily than was the case in Poland. Although there were differences between the participants over the extent to which people outside the universities should become involved in their activities, no-one felt that a system which depended upon a mixture of public funds and student fees could afford to ignore the views of governments or of the employers on whom the students' prospects of paying off their debts would depend. This remained contentious in Poland, with academics from the pre-1989 culture, even those who had opposed the former regime, continuing to assert the traditional mission of the university to offer only theoretical instruction through authoritarian forms of pedagogy. Since this generation have been able to trade on their prestige from the years of opposition to dominate elected offices, whose associated patronage has not been effectively checked by a new culture or organization, it has been difficult to sustain progress without the resource leverage that the TEMPUS programme offered. It seems unlikely that the situation will change further without government intervention, which would face major legal and constitutional difficulties. The West European partners noted the growth of private sector higher education in Poland as a warning to themselves: when public universities ignore changes in the world around them, they must expect that other institutions will develop to fill the gaps.

The Future of State Welfare

The second area which the participants in the programme debated was the future model of the welfare state. There was an understandable tendency on the part of the Polish participants to stress the uniqueness of their post-war experience. 'Real socialism' had certainly represented an extreme form of a dependency-generating culture, where an individual's effort, reflected in their wage earnings, played only a small part in determining their standard of living. In effect, as both Hrynkiewicz and Rymsza suggest, the scale of state subsidies for most necessities, made employment necessary only as a means of avoiding the social and legal disadvantages of being unemployed in a society where this status had been abolished! The result, they argue, was an attitude to work which had little concern for effort or quality. Merely spending time in the workplace was enough. Unfortunately, the social and economic transformation of 1989 had not been matched by a cultural transformation. People had assumed that market capitalism would deliver the prosperity that 'real socialism' had failed to bring them. Successive governments had failed to explain that market capitalism would also require important changes in their attitudes and behaviour. Capitalism was a state of mind as well as a method of

Introduction 5

organizing economic activity. Giermanowska and Hrynkiewicz bring this out very clearly in their analysis of Polish unemployment policies since 1989 and the movement away from a system that simply paid benefits to one that tied these to active job search. The habit of the past, that the state would deliver employment without any effort on the individual's part, could not be sustained in the new society.

As the papers by Ransome and Nygren imply, however, Poland may simply have represented an extreme and pathological form of the social democratic welfare state that was created in Sweden during the 1930s and in the United Kingdom after World War II. Both had focussed on the support of people without work and asked for little in return. Both had come into question during the 1980s and 1990s over their effectiveness in reducing unemployment as opposed to sustaining the unemployed. Both had now begun to place much more emphasis on the accountability of the unemployed for their receipt of benefit. Benefit was something to sustain re-entry to the labour market rather than a long-term subsidy and the unemployed had an obligation to co-operate with state agencies acting to facilitate their employment. Some of these issues are also touched upon by Kwak and by Pascall in their discussions of family and gender issues. Pascall, in particular, points to the impact of the New Labour 'Welfare to Work' policies on women, particularly those who are lone parents. In effect, the option of being a full-time parent on state benefit is being withdrawn. The state may organize child care facilities but women should look to the labour market as their source of economic support.

One area in which there is a striking contrast, however, is penal policy. Mościskier's account of the attempt to develop a more positive approach to penality in Poland since 1989 makes particularly instructive reading alongside Roberts's depressing discussion of English penal policy over the same period. In contrast to its higher education policy, the 'Imagined Europe' which has shaped Polish criminal justice has brought radical changes. Prison has become much less central to the societal response to crime and alternatives are being actively developed. The prison population has been falling steadily and, despite rise in violent crime, there is little evidence of any demand to reverse this trend. In England, the policy has been dominated by a bipartisan 'Prison Works' philosophy, whose main achievement has been a boom in the construction industry and the wanton destruction of the much-admired probation service. Reading these papers, one is tempted to wonder which country actually has the deeper democratic tradition.

Many other issues are, of course, opened up in this collection. Lordan and Rybka examine the important role of NGOs in more plural approaches to welfare provision. This paper, together with those of Powell and Rymsza, also touch on the question of Church/State relations which are a critical dimension of social policy in many European states but are not well represented in the Anglophone literature. Nevertheless, the impact of, for example, Catholic social teaching on 'subsidiarity' is likely to be felt increasingly as the European Union moves towards harmonization in this sphere under the Treaty of Amsterdam. The struggles of these four countries to find a proper balance between states, markets and individual actions as sources of welfare will be reproduced across the continent as the new millennium opens.

Acknowledgements

A programme of work like this is, of course, the result of many people's time and goodwill. Our first thanks must naturally go to the EU TEMPUS programme and the matching support from Sweden, whose financial contributions made the work possible. We cannot thank every participant by name. However, we would particularly like to acknowledge the contributions of Professor Torsten Åström, Chair of the Department of Social Welfare at the University of Umea who was a constant source of encouragement and inspiration to all of us, and Nuala Lordan, from the Department of Applied Social Studies, National University of Ireland, Cork, whose unfailing cheerfulness, optimism and people-management skills kept us going at many difficult moments. We should also like to thank David Ward, now Professor at De Montfort University, for introducing Cork to the emerging partnership and for his assistance in the early development of the programme while Director of Social Work Studies at Nottingham, and Alan Aldridge, also from Nottingham, for his diplomatic contribution to the establishment of the relationship with Warsaw. The objectivity and constructive criticism brought by Lydia Sapouna, the programme evaluator from Cork, were constantly valued, even if sometimes uncomfortable! Finally, we should acknowledge the vital work of our administrative back-up teams - Ros Kirk, Nicola Hopcroft and Jude Jones in Nottingham, Tamara Adamowicz and Sylwia Salamon in Warsaw.

PART I
SOCIAL POLICY AND SOCIAL CHANGE

1 From Socialist to Liberal Utopia: Changes in Poland's Social Policy since 1989
Józefina Hrynkiewicz

Polish Social Policy 1945-89 - The Utopia of Socialism

After 1945, Polish social policy took its inspiration from the communist social utopia where everyone is entitled to everything and the state is the exclusive distributor of goods and services in accordance with needs of citizens. Equality, elevated to the status of a constitutional principle, was the basic expressed value of social policy. The 1952 Constitution guaranteed everyone equal access to all goods and services and obliged the state to provide them as needed. This concept of social policy defines the state as a philanthropist with unlimited ability to meet constantly growing needs.

The implementation of this principle was obviously impossible. The obligations contained in the Constitution could not be fulfilled even by the richest country. From 1945-89, the ideal was acknowledged but its full implementation was postponed into an indefinite future. In the meantime, access to social goods was distributed in relation to the value attached to different groups within the society.[1] In principle, everyone was entitled to everything: in practice, those who were thought to be most important for the preservation of the communist political and economic order had priority claims on goods and services.

The result was the development of a culture where it was assumed that the state *gave* everything, including a job, income, vacations, education, lodging, retirement pensions, benefits, scholarships, cheap books, medical care, etc. The state decided arbitrarily about what and how much, when and under which conditions it might give. Thereby, the state controlled citizens, since it not only decided the principles of distribution, but itself carried them out. The control of citizens went even deeper, as most goods and services were available almost exclusively within the state controlled (rationed) distribution system. During the 1980s (the years of martial law and after) strict control was imposed upon distribution of all goods ('coupon sale').

Access to goods and services was closely connected to employment, since work was not only a right, but also an obligation of a citizen. Apart from their economic or administrative functions, state workplaces - the only kind which existed - organized social services and distributed social goods and benefits. They built houses and allocated them; organized, and controlled access to, vacation facilities for employees and their families. They built stadiums and physical recreation centres (sports fields and halls) and organized services in the fields of health protection and care, education and child care, recreation, leisure, and culture. They engaged themselves in social welfare activities. Workplaces shared out the most desired goods and services, which were permanently in short supply - dwellings, cars, household equipment, opportunities for tourism and so on. This mechanism for distribution was essential, since wages were low and the production or supply of all goods and services was nationalized. For more than 45 years wages were merely a supplement to goods, benefits and social services allocated by the state. A long-term low-wage policy tied the living standards of citizens to the benefits allocated by the state and deprived them of any opportunity to prosper from their own activity, far-sightedness and providence. It also denied them responsibility for their own social security and well-being.

In its programmatic statements, the state repeatedly declared its commitment to satisfying the increasing needs of employees and their families. It was the state's role to decide which needs were important, which were growing faster (or slower) and whose needs, when and to what extent, should be satisfied. Workplaces and sectors of the economy which were of particular significance to the state were given numerous privileges. These included relatively high wages, easier access to rationed goods and services, longer vacations and retirement privileges (shorter contribution periods and supplements to retirement pensions).

The communist authorities considered the most important sectors to be mining, heavy and military industries. Generous privileges were granted to the army, special services, militia, top political party functionaries and central administration officials. Other sectors, such as the textile industry, construction, communications and agriculture, were less important to the government, so their employees enjoyed fewer privileges. Social service workers (including education and health protection personnel) were treated as the lowest rank of employees, regarded by the authorities as non-productive and, hence, deprived of most privileges.

The state was not able to fulfil its self-declared obligations and had no intention of doing so. Different groups struggled for influence in order to secure for themselves the highest possible volume of goods, services and social privileges. This conflict was the result of the unstable, vague and secret principles regulating access to goods and services. The lack of transparent distributional principles gave the state authorities the ability to control citizens' living conditions and to manipulate different groups - setting them against each other. Among the demands voiced during the workers revolts in 1956, 1970, 1976 and the *Solidarity* protest of 1980, there was always a call for full disclosure of group privileges and the principles by which the authorities justified them.

The unstable, vague and secret principles for dividing rights, services, benefits and goods created conditions for bribery and corruption, particularly in institutions providing services vital for citizens like health care, housing, public administration and commerce. The complete nationalization of these social services resulted in limited supplies, a lack of competitive pressures and low quality. Their quality was be so bad that it simply nullified their supposed functions. The fact that such goods appeared at all was enough (either no alternative was available or else it was completely unaffordable by the average member of the population).

The social policy established by 'real socialism' functioned in practice as an ideological manoeuvre aimed at manipulating the granting and concealing of privileges and handicaps. From 1945 to 1989 Polish social policy referred, in its declarations, to the paramount values and ideological goals of justice, equality, universal well-being, full and rational employment, and the satisfaction of needs at the highest level. However, in its practice, only emergency and special actions were performed in order to stabilize the totalitarian order imposed as a result of the partition of Europe after World War II. Under the slogans of social equality, divisions were introduced into Polish society between those groups enjoying numerous privileges and goods and those completely disadvantaged, groups with a high consumption standard and those located on the margin, with permanently unmet needs (even of a basic character, e.g. food, shelter or clothes). This situation persisted because of a complete prohibition against any form of social dialogue or self-organization. There was no pressure from public opinion, mostly because of the lack of freedom of the media. Instead, there existed political police and effective oppression.

Social consent for the existence of the rationing system for 45 years was 'acquired' by regulating consumption. The majority of the population was always held at a very low level, which was further reduced at times of social distress and conflict, leading ultimately, in the 1980s, to the introduction of administrative control over the distribution of all goods and services. The lack of democratic mechanisms for elections, negotiations and control and of opportunities to include, articulate and adjust interests within the decision-making system led to mass workers' revolts (i.e. in 1956, 1970, 1976 and 1981) bloodily suppressed by the authorities. Mass worker protests brought only short-lived and emergency changes in the distribution of income and privileges. They also led to intensified control and surveillance, which often applied the methods of political terror, including the elimination of those thought to have inspired or led the rebellions.

The pursuit of the state's social policy - designed to implement a universal distribution of goods and services, and committed to ensuring that all the increasing needs of everyone would be met in a country with a low level of per capita GDP[2] - inevitably led to:

- deepening disparities in the material situation and social status of various social and occupational groups and local communities;
- the formation of numerous social communities and groups living at the margin of social life;
- concealment not only of the unmet basic needs of these marginalized groups (e.g the disabled, families in difficult living situations, the homeless) but also of their very existence;
- concealment of many difficult social problems, such as poverty, hidden unemployment, social pathology (crime, drug and alcohol abuse, bribery, social exclusion of weaker groups);
- the encouragement of demanding attitudes by citizens towards the state, since they had no right of independent action to change their situation;
- the development of a culture of dependency as a result of almost half a century of State philanthropy where helplessness rather than action was rewarded;
- the decay of civic initiative and social self-organization;
- the loosening and breaking of social ties and community self-help;
- an Orwellian confusion and demoralization as a result of the perversion of the basic language of welfare.

From Socialist to Liberal Social Utopia

The proposals for changes in social policy presented to the communist authorities by their opponents never contained any programme for a comprehensive change in the system. Demands were made to improve the access of certain particularly disadvantaged social or occupational groups to goods and services and to give them priority when deciding on the grant of privileges - or to deprive some particularly privileged groups. This approach to social policy has continued since the communist period. After 1989 the fight for one's own privilege (or for one's group) has proved effective in creating separate and preferential systems of retirement pensions for the army, special services, prison management and police in 1994/95, and for judges in 1997. This method was also applied to maintain a separate system of health care designed exclusively for top state officials and established under communist rule. These systems are funded by public money, but provide higher standards of benefits and services than those available to the public. There is still a demand for the state to 'give to us' or maybe to 'take away from them'.

It is difficult to distinguish stages of change in Polish social policy since 1989.[3] An analysis of the programmes of the successive governments allows us only to distinguish trends which are broadly social-democratic, conservative and liberal. It is not easy to identify any consistent orientation: the ideological declarations made by ruling parties have differed from their actual implementation. For example, a party declaring its commitment to social-democratic reforms carried out an extremely liberal programme.[4] This analysis, then, focusses on the general direction of the changes which have occurred, rather than attributing them to particular parties or coalitions.

Is it Possible to Give Up the Socialist Social Utopia?

It has proved to be very difficult for the state to give up its guarantee to provide all citizens with goods and services in accordance with their needs. Deeply rooted in public consciousness is the idea that the change initiated in 1989 not only confirmed the state's promise but would lead to a more diligent effort to fulfil it. Even the popular feeling of successive generations, that such promises are completely unenforceable, has not made it possible to renounce the intention 'to satisfy steadily growing social needs at the highest level' (as the documents of the old communist party used to declare). It did not matter that an overwhelming majority of citizens had not benefited from them, and never had any chance to do so. State provision was an *entitlement*. Being conscious of this potential right, people did not want to lose it. This problem became particularly evident in 1994-97 when a new Constitution was being drafted. The post-communist parties justified it by reference to its maintenance of many previous social rights.

In the public mind 'deprivation' of rights - to work, housing, education, leisure, health care and cultural services - was a matter of one's own individual situation. By giving up these rights, even if they were unreal and had never been implemented, both individuals and social groups would lose hope that their unmet needs might yet be satisfied. Many Poles, seeing their rights guaranteed by the Constitution, have hoped (or deceived themselves) that, at some time, they might possibly enjoy those rights.

These hopes and illusions are invoked in election campaigns by many politicians belonging to post-communist parties. This promise was an important factor in the electoral success of the post-communists in 1993 (when they regained power) and their strong showing in 1997. It does not matter that their declarations have been different from their actions in office. In election campaigns, they assure their electorate that all social guarantees from the previous period have been continued and that all errors and defects in implementation will be eliminated.

As yet, there has been no research and analysis to explain the persistence of behaviours and attitudes established in the socialist social utopia. Arguably, the declarations of social rights are the last consolation for many Poles in their current difficult situation. If they have no work, no qualifications, no housing, no regular income, no opportunity to start a family and ensure its subsistence, they still have a theoretical entitlement to all of these things.

With this, the question arises: are these attitudes a threat to the stability of the new situation in Poland? The declining participation rate in elections suggests that increasing numbers of citizens are refusing to take part in this fundamental act of democratic citizenship: in 1997, only 47.9 per cent of those eligible to vote did so compared with 62 per cent in the elections of 1989. The falling confidence in the socialist social utopia, has not been matched by a simultaneous growth of confidence in a market economy and liberal democracy. The proportion of the population who do not support any political party or published election programme is rising. Surveys made before and after elections characteristically show that the proportion of the population intending to vote ranges from 68 to 75 per cent, while actual voting is typically about one-third lower. This suggests that a significant part of the population is afraid to declare publicly its refusal to participate in elections in case this leads to a negative evaluation of them.

What is the Alternative to the Socialist Social Utopia?

Social policy has not changed because of a failure to spell out and agree with the society the changed role of both central and local government. The process of 'depriving' citizens of their illusions - and their so-called rights are no more than this - has proved to be more difficult than expected. After 8 years of transformation, we might think that public consent to change would have been possible in 1989 when the 'non-communist' government was elected. At that time, however, there was no consciousness among the ruling elite that a programme of change in social policy was as important as a programme of change in the economic system. Arguably, the politicians have no will to change social policy, since the 'non-communist' government was formed with participation of the communists who maintained all social privileges.

The correction of the socialist social utopia is the acid test of change in published programmes for social policy since 1989. The first election manifesto of *Solidarity* failed this test. It declared the establishment of a new social policy aimed at providing the population with suitable living conditions. This would ensure full and rational employment, adequate wages, work safety, universal access to housing, protection of the environment, improvement of health care, new opportunities for young people and the elimination of all everyday troubles. Since 1989 there have only been small changes in particular fields of social policy and no government has accepted the challenge of reforming the system as a whole. Even the latest government, formed in September 1997, declared its general commitment to 'a state responsible for creating a safe framework of individual and collective existence'.[5]

The 1989 government established the view that a market economy and political democracy would make it possible to solve all the problems of the society. The existence of social problems was treated as a consequence of the totalitarian system and the centrally planned economy, state control over the activities of citizens, as well as their lack of adjustment to the rules of a market economy. All of these problems would be solved by the invisible hand of *laissez faire*. The residual social problems have a temporary character and result from continued limitations on the operation of market mechanisms. These problems would disappear when the market became fully operational and covered not only the economic, but also the social sphere of life. To reduce resistance to these changes a wide range of social policy benefits was introduced. Compared with previous times, there was actually a steady increase in the share of social benefits in the structure of income of the population. The proportion of people receiving income other than from gainful employment also increased (up to one-third of the total population).[6]

A Reactive Approach to Social Policy

An analysis of changes in social policy since 1989 shows the dominance of a reactive approach. Social policy has responded to problems rather than tried to solve them. There has been no approach to producing a long-term settlement or to the construction of a particular kind of social order. The liberal governments were opposed to such an idea, believing that all problems would be solved by the market. At the beginning of 1992 there was an attempt to formulate programmes attempting to address specific problems including health care, unemployment and education. However, these were only general statements which did not lead to actions based on a coherent combination of values, objectives, means and methods of solving particular problems.[7]

This reactive strategy has led to constant difficulties, reflected in deteriorating quality of, and access to, services like health care and child care, including day nurseries and services for children with physical or learning disabilities. The level of benefits has been reduced, affecting family allowances, unemployment benefit, social benefits and housing allowances. The underfunding of basic social services has worsened the material conditions for those working in them and brought conflicts with their personnel, mostly in health and education.[8]

The deterioration in public finances, beginning at the end of the 1970s and deepening since 1989, has forced a constant fall in expenditure on most spheres of social policy. The authorities have adjusted their activities to the level of funds available for social purposes in this economic crisis, even during a slight recovery from 1993. Only the most urgent tasks (the so-called economy programmes) could be carried out. At the same time, the unmet needs and unsolved problems of education, health care and social insurance imposed growing liabilities on the system with increasing numbers of beneficiaries and a deterioration in the living standards of the most vulnerable groups.

The unrealistic character of the social programmes presented by both liberal and socialist policy options has obstructed - and still obstructs - the initiation of a general discussion about the objectives, principles and means of social policy.

From Socialist to Liberal Utopia: Poland's Social Policy since 1989 17

Laissez Faire and Philanthropy - Attempts at Liberal Changes in the System of Social Policy and their Effects

Polish society has not accepted, and does not accept individualized liberal solutions because they are perceived as a threat to the existence of the poorest and a considerable deterioration in the living conditions of a majority of the population. There is, however, acceptance for solutions of a conservative character, based on social solidarity (similar to those used in Germany). In Poland, such solutions have been applied after World War II and, thus, they are well known and positively evaluated.

Following the 1993 election, the post-communists - who promised a return to the socialist social utopia in social policy - came to power. In practice, they pursued an extremely liberal programme of changes in social insurance, social welfare, health care, systems of education and culture, assistance for the unemployed and housing.

Since 1989, the liberal approach to social policy has been one of the main political forces. Liberal solutions were considered as an effective method of introducing rationalization of state expenditure on social services and benefits. The market economy was assumed to help achieve higher quality of services, more efficient use of material resources, lower employment in the service sector and, finally, limited powers for state bureaucrats. The allocation of benefits would be targeted on those in the most pressing need.

The liberal approach was also expected to achieve a substantial reduction in public expenditure for social purposes and to force the users of social services to make rational use of them. The costs of services - education, health protection - still declared as free, would be shared. There would be more pressure for economy in the services themselves. This assumed, of course, that funds to support improved quality and access would be available to the households which needed and used the services.

The liberal strategy for rationalizing social services involved a massive transfer of their costs to users. This has been implemented at a time not only of steadily decreasing real incomes in the general population, but also of increasing inequality. Real wages fell until 1995, when they rose by 3 per cent compared with the previous year. Wage increases (although relatively small) were observed mostly in higher paid groups and professions, starting from a very low level. The liberal approach resulted in a situation where a permanent deficit in services was replaced by a surplus, resulting from a dramatic decrease in the number of users (e.g. in pre-school, dental, educational, cultural and leisure services) as low-income families could no longer afford them.

Commercial principles were introduced to pre-school and after-school care, to specialized diagnostic services and costly medical treatment as well as dental services. Cultural services, including those for children, have also been commercialized.[9] In higher education, part-time students were obliged to pay for their education provided in public universities.[10] The introduction of fees has not led to any improvement in study conditions as the revenue is only used to cover the shortfall in state funding. As a consequence of insufficient funds, the state has cut expenditure on the infrastructure of social services (education, health care, culture, recreation, child care). Its funds are mostly used to pay wages and other current operating costs.

The introduction of a market mechanism to social services provided by public institutions has made it possible to charge users for part of their costs, thereby limiting their accessibility to the low-income population. Although the principle of free access remains intact, the scope of free services has been limited. The shortfall in free social services is filled by services provided by the public sector on a commercial basis. Although the provision of such services has not been prohibited, their true costs are not known and the fees are calculated arbitrarily by the providers who retain the profits.

The commercialization of social services provided by public institutions has encouraged an informal or black market. This exists with the tacit consent of the authorities, as it mitigates pay claims from the employees. Some influential categories of public employees in social services (mostly, but exclusively, in health care and higher education) are also interested in the continuation of the black market. This enables them to make large non-taxable profits without outlays, risk or responsibility. All the costs of the infrastructure, equipment and labour are met from public funds but the profits are privately appropriated. The authorities accept the situation because it is less costly, both economically and politically, to maintain it than to eliminate it by reforms which would depart from the popular fiction of free social services and cause dissatisfaction among the potential, and influential, losers. They have established strong lobbying groups which have obstructed all reforms of health care and higher education and which have now gained seats in parliament.[11] A competitive market in social services also requires powerful consumer protection institutions. The consumer movement is poorly organized and lacks influence to balance that of producers.

There is still no stable legal, material, professional or financial basis for the development of private sector social services. This development is obstructed by insufficient funds, staff, infrastructure etc. and faces unfair competition from the grey or black market supply from the public sector. The lack of clarity about ownership and professional ethics in social services is producing a deepening crisis of bribery, corruption, inequality in access, and demoralization of staff.

The responsibility for providing social services is now beginning to be transferred to local governments (communes). This is not, however, being matched by a transfer of funds. In 1995, communes were entrusted with the obligation to administer and manage primary schools. However, the situation in schools has not improved as communes have not received sufficient money from the state budget for such purposes. As a result, communes perform the most urgent tasks (education) and give lower priority to others such as child care. Poorer communes (particularly in rural areas or those affected by structural unemployment) have no money to improve the material conditions of education and have received no funds for such purpose from the national budget. The process of such transfers is extremely complex, because the cost of services cannot be calculated and settled. Another obstacle is the huge overhang of debt incurred by institutions of health care and education.

Policy Changes and their Results

Standards of Living

Political freedoms (including the elimination of censorship and state control over citizens' foreign travel, freedom of expression, the end of political terror, free and democratic elections) achieved through the transformation processes were soon treated as their natural consequences. More difficult problems resulted from Poland's underdevelopment as a result of 50 years of communist rule. Under communist rule, Polish society was characterized by widespread material poverty. Therefore, the effects of the transformation have been evaluated by most people not simply in political terms but also by reference to their living standards. Poles expected that their democratic government, with the introduction of a market economy would contribute to the improvement of their material existence. This change to better living standards was expected not in the perspective of the next generation, as the communists promised, but more or less immediately. Indeed the first non-communist government predicted only short-term (18 months) and temporary difficulties.

Given these expectations, the least anticipated outcome of the transformation was a rapid increase in poverty. According to different estimates, this now affects from 5.5 million to 7.5 million people, or 15-20 per cent of the total population. A particular effect of this change is reflected in income inequality. In 1996, the richest 8 per cent (1 million) of households received about one quarter of total income and owned about one-third of property assets: at the bottom, 13 per cent (1.5 million) of households received 4 per cent of total income and owned 5 per cent of property assets. Since 1990, income inequality has risen rapidly. In 1991 the richest fifth of families had incomes three times those of the poorest fifth, rising to a fourfold gap in 1992. In 1993 the richest 10 per cent of families had incomes eight times those of the poorest 10 per cent.

According to public opinion surveys conducted by CBOS in 1994, 60 per cent of the respondents considered the disparities in income to be too large, and 21 per cent felt that there was a conflict between the rich and the poor in Poland. In surveys conducted by CBOS in 1995, 69 per cent of respondents thought that their existence was worse than 8 years before, and only 19 per cent assessed it as better. According to the results of a 1996 survey made by the Central Statistical Office, only 13 per cent of respondents considered their situation to be very good or fairly good, 56 per cent as not bad, and 31 per cent as bad or very bad. Satisfaction with one's own situation was most often expressed by self-employed people (36 per cent) and least often by farmers (8 per cent). Dissatisfaction was most often expressed by recipients of social benefits (79 per cent) and pensioners (34 per cent).

The situation of the most seriously distressed households has not changed. These are mostly the households of the unemployed, single-parent families and those with many children, as well as farmers and pensioners families. Almost one-third of all children under 18 are growing up in families with many children or single-parent families, low-income families or those affected by poverty. In 1994, more than 43 per cent of families received incomes below the social minimum level (89 per cent of families of the recipients of social benefits and 51 per cent of farmers' families). A typical feature of Poland's poverty is its persistence in families with many children, those with low levels of education, living in rural areas or long-term unemployed. The situation of families of the beneficiaries of social welfare system and families of the unemployed is particularly difficult (and sometimes desperate). Despite an economic recovery since 1994-95, the real incomes of workers, farmers and social welfare beneficiaries have been decreasing.

The most difficult issue is the poor housing situation. 42 per cent of town residents and 70 per cent of those in rural areas live in unsatisfactory and overcrowded conditions. Decreasing incomes, high inflation rates and lack of consistent state policy have led to a serious housing crisis. The number of completed housing units has been falling since 1978. Current building is about one-third of the 1989 level, with an enormous increase in costs: in 1997 1 square metre of a completed housing unit cost an equivalent of 2-3 months pay for someone on an average wage.

The structure of households expenditure shows that a high per centage goes on food and housing - two-thirds of the total expenditure in low-income families. There has been a rapid growth of expenditure on housing, which now accounts for 20-30 per cent of total expenditures. Low-income families consume some 20 per cent less food, of lower nutritional value, than medium-income families.

The surveys concerning living conditions and consumption level indicate that the costs of the transformation were mostly born by economically and socially weaker groups, including workers, farmers, public sector employees, families with many children, single mothers, low-educated and low-skilled persons, and the residents of economically disadvantaged - mostly rural - areas.

The divergence of consumption levels and living conditions does not necessarily mean that the policies of income distribution and consumption are incorrect. However, distributional policy during the period of transformation has faced problems including the growth of poverty, growing income inequality - the poor become poorer, a lack of effective means of combatting poverty especially among the unemployed and families with children. Poverty is more often inherited in low-income families which are malnourished and have limited access to education and health care. They have no way to break the cycle of disadvantage.

Unemployment, poverty and the increasing number of socially excluded families and other groups can be considered to be the main social cost of the Polish transformation since 1989. Their situation has been aggravated by the limitations introduced in 1996 and 1997 on the eligibility of the unemployed to apply for social welfare benefits. These were imposed on the recommendation of the World Bank and applied a so-called 'scale of income equivalency' to test the living standards of families. After the introduction of this scale, in the Act of 1997 on Social Welfare, the number of low-income people with the right to apply for social welfare benefit was reduced by almost half.[12] The use of such a scale in Poland seems to be unjustified, since the level and structure of expenditure and the living standards in the country are not comparable with those which apply the scale. However, the introduction of this scale enabled considerable reductions of expenditure from public funds on social welfare.

Social Security

In 1990-91, the social security system (retirement and disability pensions, benefits) served as an important buffer protecting against possible social unrest and conflicts as a consequence of the radical changes being effected in Poland. These were leading to the closure of working establishments and dramatically growing unemployment.[13] In the first year of the transformation, the number unemployed increased by 50,000 every month (reaching 3 million in 1990-93, with an unemployment rate of around 17 per cent). These figures only refer to registered unemployment and do not take into account the unemployed hidden on early retirement and disability pensions. At the initial stage of the transformation, benefits for the out-of-work and unemployed were granted generously. The criteria of eligibility for benefit were easily satisfied. This policy met with public criticism, providing a basis for future limitations. Unfriendly public attitudes to benefit recipients, encouraged by the authorities and the media, served to justify the rejection of applications for benefits and further limitations on their levels and accessibility.

In 1990, the Act on Social Welfare was adopted. This Act was passed in circumstances of rising unemployment, poverty and decreasing real incomes. Its purpose was to provide social protection for the groups threatened by loss of their jobs and incomes as a consequence of the transformations. The number of people covered by social welfare was growing (from 799,000 in 1989 to 1,645,000 in 1990, and around 3 million in 1992). Almost one fifth of the Polish population were receiving benefits. In 1994 the number of recipients began to fall, mostly due to changes in the principles governing the granting of assistance (withdrawal of housing assistance, reduction in the real value of welfare benefits). However, the number of people finding themselves benefiting from social welfare remained unchanged at around 7.5 million, still over 20 per cent of the Polish population. This figure does not include families and individuals supported by non-public organizations like the Roman Catholic Church.

The introduction of the scale of equivalency and other amendments in 1997 removed the right to social welfare benefit from almost everyone with any permanent source of income, however inadequate. This included lone-parent families, families with many children, disabled people and people receiving the lowest retirement or disability pensions. Only a person without any permanent income may be a client of the social welfare system. At the same time, many families lost their right to family allowance (whose real value decreased) and were deprived of social assistance for housing costs. Social assistance for school children was limited and the entitlement of many unemployed to benefit reduced. Access of children to educational services was limited after the closure of nurseries by those communes which had no funds to operate them.

During the first years of the transformation, the benefits paid by the social welfare system were used to soften public resistance to the changes. Their intention was to convince the society that everything would be as it was before, that its delivery would improve and that benefits would grow. To this end, early retirement of those with longer periods of employment was facilitated. The rules for granting disability pensions were also liberalised. The result was that almost 2.5 million retired in 1990-93 (twice as many as in any comparable period before or since). Initially, i.e. up to 1992, relatively high levels of retirement and disability pensions were maintained in order to promote retirement. Pensions were often equal to, and sometimes even higher than, compensation for work.

The maintenance of such a situation soon proved to be impossible. With a growing number of benefit recipients and an increasing unemployment rate, the only solution was to reduce benefits and limit their accessibility. This process began at the end of 1991 with a reduced indexation of benefits and elimination of supplementary benefits for certain occupational groups. The real value of benefits has systematically decreased, while retirement and disability pensions, and unemployment benefits have become more difficult to obtain.

At first, an attempt was made to apply an insurance principle which linked the level of benefit to the amount of contributions paid and the duration of previous employment.[14] Indexation of benefits was linked to the general level of pay rises. Other benefits which had no social insurance character, like family allowances, care benefits, nursing benefits and benefits for veterans, were separated from the social insurance system. This period of reforms ended in 1994. Since then, the system of indexation of retirement pensions has been adjusted to the condition of public finances. This has led to a gradual decrease in the real value of benefits, reflected in a growing gap between the level of a retirement pension and the level of incomes.

Two substantially different concepts of social insurance reform existed after 1989. The first, dominating up to 1995, assumed the continuation of general social insurance covering almost all citizens, organized in accordance with the principles of reciprocity and solidarity. This covered almost all social risks, including inability to work or gain income due to sickness, old age, disability, occupational injury, occupational disease, death of a breadwinner, maternity, unemployment, bankruptcy of an employer, etc. (moreover, the introduction of prevention and rehabilitation prior to disability pension, as well as training allowance). In 1996, the concept was completely changed under the influence of the World Bank. This introduced private capital, accumulated through targeted and compulsory saving, as the basis of provision for need in old age. Other social risks were *referred* to the social welfare system rather than treated as insurable.

In August 1997, the parliament adopted the legislation which will introduce (from 1999) a new insurance system. The risks of old age will be separated from the social insurance system and met by capitalized contributions paid during a working lifetime. This system will be obligatory for people under the age of 30 (people aged 31-49 may participate on a voluntary basis, and people over 50 cannot participate). Social insurance contributions (45 per cent of pay) will be divided into two parts: one fifth will be capitalized as the basis of a personal pension while the remainder will be used to pay current pensioners and those who will retire in the next 10-15 years and as insurance against other risks such as sickness, inability to work, or the death of a breadwinner, as well as benefits for those who - being in a capital system - lose their ability to work before attaining retirement age.

The payment of benefits in this system will be guaranteed by the State, although at a level lower than that of subsistence (28 per cent of average pay - around 65 per cent of the social minimum for a single pensioner - as calculated in 1997 costs). Upon introduction of the new system, retirement benefits will be some two-thirds lower, relative to wages, than the average retirement pension paid in 1997.[15] Rules similar to those applied to the retirement insurance of persons currently over 50 would determine eligibility for coverage against other risks: inability to work due to sickness, occupational injury, occupational disease or death of a breadwinner.

This reform departs from the previous principles of universality, reciprocity and solidarity in social insurance. It neglects the most expensive social risks like inability to work, death of a breadwinner, occupational injury and chronic disease and concentrates on 'insuring' the young against old age. The German model, which is well known and accepted in Poland is giving way to a Chilean model. The shift from the principles of solidarity, reciprocity and universality to compulsory saving for old-age by the young and the rich will leave the poorer residue of society more dependent on social assistance.[16]

In health care, the system of organization, management and entitlements established at the time of the centrally planned economy has remained unchanged. It is still financed directly from the State budget. The system of management and financing, inadequate to the requirements of a market economy, and inappropriate institutional structures, with growing operating costs and decreasing outputs, are responsible for the low quality of services delivered and the emergence of grey and black zones in health care. In this officially free system, various forms of patient fees have been introduced, limiting access by low-income groups.[17] A 1993 attempt to introduce health insurance, based on a German model, failed due to the dissolution of the parliament. Its successor was not interested in systemic changes and maintained a centralized, bureaucratic and irrational system throughout its 4 year term.[18]

Education

Changes in the education system since 1989 have led to the ending of the state monopoly. Voluntary and religious organization, associations, foundations and individuals, have established new schools at all levels. The share of the non-public sector in primary and secondary education is still very small (4 per cent of the total number of pupils in 1995). However, the share of students in higher non-public schools, providing college-level education, in 1996/97 was 14 per cent. The end of bureaucratic controls on the development of higher education led to a doubling in the number of students, to 900,000 in 1996/97. This increase was achieved without additional public expenditure on higher education, mostly as a result of citizens' initiative and high educational aspirations.

In 1990, the management of nurseries was assigned to local government. As a result the proportion of children aged 3-5 covered by such service decreased, from 34.6 per cent in 1985 to 24.4 per cent in 1994. After taking over the nurseries, communes raised the fees considerably but could not provide assistance for low-income families. Over 28 per cent of families claim that they do not benefit from nursery services because they are too expensive.[19] In 1996 local governments also took over the administration of primary schools.

Over the years, education has been regarded by Poles as a core value. Its importance has also been emphasised by governments in their official declarations concerning Poland's economic and social development.

However, their practice has been quite different. Expenditure on education, science and culture has been maintained at a very low level for many years. Their share of GDP is small and decreasing.[20] It is typical of the Polish situation that each new government comes to power with slogans promising rising expenditure on education, science and culture and does not fulfil these.

Culture

The most important changes in the cultural sphere are the abolition of political control and censorship, and the introduction of market principles. In the first years creative freedom seemed to be sufficient for successful cultural development. However, there has been a considerable reduction in public expenditure on the maintenance of cultural institutions and heritage. This reduction has mostly affected artistic education, particularly activities introducing children and young people to the highest cultural values and the maintenance of libraries and cultural institutions for children and young people. The market has stimulated the development of trade in commercial cultural goods but proved to be harmful to non-commercial goods promoting the highest values. At this time, there is no consistent state policy aiming at protecting these values.

The Political Context of the Changes

In Poland, the principle was applied after 1989 that the transformation would not deprive the functionaries of the old regime of power and influence. They had only to give up their exclusive political power, maintaining - in turn - unlimited access to economic powers. In fact, they have maintained considerable political power, while strengthening their economic position.

In 1993, the post-communists returned to power in democratic parliamentary elections. Their election programme promised a return to the socialist social utopia. However, they actually applied extremely liberal social policies, restricting the access of poorer groups of the population to social services, particularly culture, health care and education. The application of these liberal ideas led to increased income inequality between families and intensified pauperization processes, with the social exclusion of weaker groups (mostly disabled people, families with many children, low-skilled people and the rural population). Systemic reforms were not initiated in any sphere of social policy. Despite economic growth, public expenditures for education, child care, health care, culture, science and housing were reduced. The media created a picture of positive changes in all social areas and statistical indicators were manipulated to emphasize social and political successes.

In 1997 Poland saw a change in government. Following the elections in September, the new administration is a coalition of christian-democratic parties (dominated by Solidarity Trade Union) with the liberal Union for Freedom. The government has announced that it will implement systemic reforms in education, health care and social insurance. Their direction is, however, difficult to foresee, as the government is made up from parties with completely different views on the reform of social policy. The conservative nature of the reforms advocated by Solidarity cannot be reconciled with the radical liberal social and economic order sought by the Union of Freedom, as these approaches originate in completely different value systems and concepts of social order.

Notes

1. I shall not deal with the privileges connected with access to power, prestige and information under a totalitarian regime. This analysis is confined to the explicit mechanisms of distributing such 'social privileges' as were generally accessible under communist rule.
2. The GDP for Poland - calculated per capita, in US$, according to purchasing power parity - amounted to 3,834 US$ in 1980 and 5,114 US$ in 1993.
3. Frequent changes of government (4 times in 1989-93, and 3 times in 1993-97 with maintenance of the existing coalition) make it difficult to assess the results of planned or initiated changes. It is easier to identify trends in the changes brought about by particular groups or ideological currents connected with political parties than to indicate precise stages.
4. This remark refers to the Social Democratic Alliance (SLD), a coalition composed of various groups rooted in the old system and the communist party transformed (according to its members) into social democracy.
5. The new coalition formed after the election of September 1997 has no coherent concept of social policy, as its members represent completely different views not only on the direction of changes in policy, but also on its fundamental aims and values.
6. According to the Central Statistical Office, in 1995, 46.2 per cent of the population were self-employed, and 35.9 per cent maintained themselves from sources other than paid employment.
7. The government, which had proposed systemic changes based on the German model, resigned in June 1992. Its successor returned to liberal solutions.
8. The lack of government response to the indebtedness of the systems of education and health care and the declining real value of the wages paid to their employees has led to regular

protests and strikes. For example, there has been a continuing protest by anaesthesiologists since mid-1996 with a refusal to work on any thing other than life-saving operations.
9. The liberals' argument that parents have no obligation to educate their children and therefore do not benefit from educational services cannot be applied to health care as there is no parent (except in pathological cases) who is not interested in the good health of his or her child.
10. *Editors Note.* Polish universities are funded to teach a controlled number of full-time students without payment of fees but are allowed to recruit a similar number of extramural (part-time) students at whatever rate the market will bear. Since the core funding is inadequate to cover operating costs and staff salaries, extramural students have become an important source of revenue for the universities.
11. The 1993-97 parliament included powerful doctors' and teachers' lobbies which protected their sectors from changes expected by the public, but harmful to their position.
12. The scale of equivalency modified for Poland applies an income coefficient equal to 1 for the first adult member of the household, 0.7 for any other adult member of the household and 0.5 for any child. Poverty rates, calculated on the basis of household budget surveys, amounted to 49.25 per cent in 1995, but fell, with application of this scale, to 26.27 per cent. See: Górecki B. (1996), *Ubóstwo w Polsce 1987-1995*, typescript. In September 1997 the rates were fixed at around 90 US$ for the first adult person, 80 US$ for the second, and around 40 US$ for each child in a family. A complex mechanism of indexation was also established.
13. See Chapter 11.
14. This principle was applied in the Act of 17 October 1991 on the Principles of Indexation of Benefits.
15. In 1997 the average retirement pension represented 68 per cent of average earnings. The legal minimum net retirement or disability pension (after taxation) represented 25 per cent of average earnings or 72.3 per cent of the social minimum calculated for a one-person household. The so-called scale of equivalency, introduced in March 1997, fixed the poverty line at around 65 per cent of the social minimum for the household of a single pensioner.
16. The advertising campaign for insurance reform promises a real growth in retirement pensions and the reduction of contributions. Such promises are unrealistic, but encourage public expectations. Polish society has not realised the possible consequences of the reform. According to opinion polls, everyone favours the reform, but pensioners would like higher pensions and employers want to pay lower contributions. However, the government always refers to the crude results of the polls, according to which everyone is for them.
17. According to 1996 survey data, 27 per cent of respondents in a representative sample of the adult population had paid informal fees for services in public institutions of health care.
18. In October 1997 the new government referred back to the 1993 proposals and declared that a system of sickness insurance would be created.
19. *Potrzeby edukacyjne*, GUS, Badania, 1995.
20. The share of GDP spent on science has fallen from 0.76 per cent in 1991 to 0.54 per cent in 1995. The share for higher education has fallen from 1.05 per cent in 1990 to 0.76 per cent in 1995.

2 Politics and Social Policy in the New Poland
Fred Powell

Poland has played a unique role in forging the New Europe. The images that dominated the media during the 1980s turned the Solidarity movement into a metaphor for the new politics that swept across Eastern Europe. Lech Wałęsa came to personify the Solidarity movement and its fortunes have waxed and waned with his political successes and failures. General Jaruzelski personified the old authoritarian order. Outside Poland, Pope John Paul II 'The Polish Pope' epitomized another side of Polish culture that had become the focus for opposition during the years of communist rule between 1945-89. His brand of unyielding conservative Catholicism, with its austere rejection of liberal values, symbolized the survival of traditional Polish culture. It also signalled deep cultural divisions that have come to dominate the Polish political landscape since the fall of communism.

This chapter sets out to achieve four objectives. First, it outlines the collapse of communism and its implications. Second, it critically appraises post- communist politics, Solidarity's role in constructing a new democracy, the forging of the 1997 constitution, and the new internationalism of NATO and potential European Union membership. Third, it evaluates attempts to create a civil society as a bulwark against state tyranny. Finally, it examines how social policy has evolved in a society that has abandoned a state collectivist model.

The Collapse of Communism

The distinguished historian, Eric Hobsbawm, has observed in his book, *Age of Extremes*, 'politically, Eastern Europe was the Achilles heel of the Soviet system, and Poland its most vulnerable spot'. According to Hobsbawm there was a unique conjuncture of events in Poland 'the country's public opinion was overwhelming united not only by a dislike of the regime but by an anti-

Russian (and anti-Jewish) and consciously Roman Catholic, Polish nationalism; the church retained independent nationwide organization; and its working class had demonstrated its political power by massive strikes at intervals since the middle 1950s' (Hobsbawm, 1995, p.475).

By 1980 mass working class discontent, backed by dissident intellectuals (many ex-Marxists) and an increasingly militant Church (encouraged by the election of Karol Wojtyla as Pope in 1978), led to the formation of the Solidarity movement. Solidarity was a national independent trade union, which by the end of 1980 had 10 million members (60 per cent of the labour force) - at least 1 million had been members of the Communist Party! Lech Wałęsa, who had led the Gdansk strike to a successful conclusion on 31 August 1980, was elected chairman.

Solidarity proved to be the catalyst that pushed Polish society out of quiescence into a spontaneous and active democracy. An independent press flourished and a wide ranging debate about reform commenced. The regime initially responded with repression. On 13 December 1981, General Jaruzelski appeared on television and announced martial law. Strikes were outlawed, censorship introduced and most of the Solidarity leadership were interned, including Wałęsa. Solidarity was formally dissolved in October 1982 and Lech Wałęsa was released from detention. By July 1983, Jaruzelski felt confident enough to end martial law but it was not until 1986 that all political prisoners were released.

Repression simply served to drive Solidarity underground. Resistance to the regime continued and the murder in 1986 of Father Jerzy Popieluszko, a pro-Solidarity priest, brought 200,000 people onto the streets in protest. Jaruzelski gradually moved towards a more conciliatory position and, by the end of the decade, was willing to compromise over the democratization of the system. In April 1989, he reached a round table agreement with the Church and Solidarity that recognized the opposition and allowed it to stand for parliament. After elections in 1989, in which Solidarity gained a large majority in the senate, (65 per cent of seats were reserved for communists in the lower house, the Sejm) a Solidarity Prime Minister, Tadeusz Mazowiecki, was appointed. General Jaruzelski installed himself as President. Mazowiecki was the first non-communist prime minister in Eastern Europe since 1945. Solidarity's democratic success set the stage for the domino-like collapse of Communism throughout Eastern Europe and the emergence of new politics.

Postcommunist Politics

Offe (1996, p.225) has observed:

> Post communist political economies face three problems of transformation: property must be privatised, prices must be liberalised, or "marketised", and the state budget has to be stabilised in order to relieve strong inflationary pressures. Corresponding to these three transformations, and in fact motivating them, are three cost considerations: privatisation is mandated by the consideration that it will reduce production costs; marketisation will reduce transaction costs (including the transaction costs resulting from perverse incentives generated by soft budget constraints); but stabilisation, if strictly pressured, does not economise on costs, but leads to increases of costs of a special kind, namely "transition costs" (comprising the vast devaluation of both physical and human capital, the fiscal crisis ensuing therefrom, and the concomitant pressures on transfer, service and infrastructure budgets), thus generating political resistance to marketisation and privatisation.

Offe's analysis of the political economy challenges facing post communist society helps to contextualize the Polish experience.

The Mazowiecki government introduced a package of economic reforms in January 1990 intended to transform Poland from a command system to a free market economy. It was a shock-therapy transition that allowed prices to rise without government restraint, abolished state subsidies, devalued the zloty in an attempt to make it convertible with Western currencies and sharply controlled the money supply in keeping with the free market economics of the Chicago school. The economy appeared to respond quickly to this treatment. Inflation slowed down and food shortages eased. However, prices began to spiral out of control, rising by 250 per cent in 1990. Meanwhile, real incomes dropped by 40 per cent and unemployment (which was largely unknown in communist times) began to rise sharply.

The political pressures were intense, leading the Solidarity movement to split into two factions. The prime minister, Tadeusz Mazowiecki, led the more intellectual and liberal wing. Lech Wałęsa, who wanted a harder anti-Communist stance, was ideologically closer to the Christian nationalism of the other faction, which had strong working class loyalties. The rivalry between the two Solidarity leaders continued into the Presidential contest in November 1990, from which Wałęsa emerged victorious. The Third Republic was declared and free parliamentary elections followed in 1991. The postcommunist era had truly begun.

However the new Polish parliament was highly factionalized and did not bring political stability. During President Wałęsa's five year term of office Poland had five changes of government. Four of these governments were led by Solidarity and followed a neo-liberal economic discipline. Much of the blame for both the economic hardship and the political instability was attributed to Wałęsa's perceived 'war at the top'. The denouement came in 1993 when President Wałęsa dissolved parliament and called new elections. From Wałęsa's point of view this proved to be a serious political miscalculation.

The 1991-1993 Parliament had been composed of 29 factions, elected from the myriad of would be political groupings that appeared on the political scene, over 300! Many of the groupings lacked any real grass roots support (Wesołowski, 1996, p.120). In 1993 a new requirement was instituted that a party needed to obtain at least 5 per cent of the vote to win seats in the Sejm. This reduced the number of parties represented in the Sejm to seven. The big winners were the postcommunist SLD, which, together with the Peasants Party (PSL), took two-thirds of the seats and formed the Government. In the Presidential elections of 1995 the postcommunists further tightened their grip on power, when Wałęsa was voted out of office and replaced by the postcommunist SLD leader, Aleksander Kwaśnniewski.

Given the decisive defeat of the communist regime in 1989, the election of a postcommunist government would seem to be surprising. However, this political success must be seen in the context of the economic hardship arising from the transition to the market, the political chaos of the 1991-1993 Parliament, disillusion with Solidarity's leadership and the church's theocratic ambitions (discussed below). The postcommunist success must also be viewed in the context of socialism's on-going capacity to contribute to forging a more just social order and to act as a restraining influence on market tyranny. Problems of poverty (greatly exacerbated by marketization) coupled with progressive issues such as gender equality, arguably continue to demand a socialist political response. However, it must be doubtful whether the postcommunists can 'mutate' into a comfortable ally of capital, the traditional enemy of Marxism. Having abandoned the goals of state ownership and full employment, it would seem that support for universal welfare provision coupled with the advocacy of a progressive form of cultural politics is the postcommunists' best hope for political survival.

What is clear is that the new Poland has achieved a measure of political progress, which is embodied in the new constitution signed by President Kwaśniewski on 16 July 1997. The President declared that 'this constitution

Politics and Social Policy in the New Poland 33

opens new prospects and creates a modern state' (*The Warsaw Voice*, 27 July 1997). Eight years after the fall of communism the Poles had finally replaced the Stalinist 1952 constitution with a sophisticated compromise.

The 1997 constitution was agreed by the four main parties in the Sejm, the postcommunists (SLD), the Peasants Party (PSL), the Freedom Union (UW) and the Labour Union (UP). It was opposed by the Christian nationalist parties of the Right. Poles approved it in a referendum. The new constitution simultaneously strengthens government and the rights of citizens to petition over violations of the constitution. The economic rights of private ownership and businesses freedom are also guaranteed. Economic limitations are imposed on government, which is not allowed to let the public debt exceed three-fifths of GDP. Provision is also made for parliament to renounce some aspects of sovereignty in anticipation of NATO membership early in the new millennium.

The surprise victory of the Solidarity movement, in the Polish General Election held on 21 September 1997, had its roots in Solidarity's defeat in 1993. The small Solidarity factions combined in a common front called Solidarity Election Action (AWS). The election of the AWS, led by the populist, Marian Krzaklewski, reintroduces the possibility of political instability. The AWS may seek to overthrow the 1997 constitution, believing that it does not attach sufficient weight to the role of the Roman Catholic Church. Its 'pro-family' stance could result in the imposition of a ban on abortion. Ironically, the AWS is likely to slow down the pace of economic reform, because its largely trade union constituency is wary of the privatization of state-owned industries and marketization. Manifestly, the political progress of recent years is threatened by this new uncertainty in Poland's political direction.

Civil Society and the Solidarity Ethos

In recent years the concept of 'civil society' has enjoyed something of a revival. Politicians and academics in many countries have embraced it as a prescriptive model for the future organization of society. Exponents of civil society present it as a mediating space between the private and public spheres in a pluralist democracy. As Wedel (1994, p.323) has put 'a civil society exists when individuals and groups are free to form organisations that function independently and that can mediate between citizens and the state'.

The French aristocrat, Alexis de Tocqueville, who visited the United States in the 1830s, is widely credited with inventing the concept. Liberal by political persuasion, de Tocqueville is sometimes regarded as having depoliticized the term 'civil society', celebrating any form of associational activity for its own sake in his study, *Democracy in America*, first published in 1835. In fact, de Tocqueville laid considerable stress on participation in local democracy as the best method for ensuring that civil association reinforced and protected democratic politics against tyranny. However, the core of his conception of civil society devolved on the health of intermediate institutions, usually the family, the community and churches. As de Tocqueville (1956, p.202) put it:

> Amongst the laws which rule human societies, there is one which seems to be more precise and clear than all the others. If men are to remain civilised, or to become so the art of associating together must grow and improve in the same ratio in which the equality of conditions is increased.

On the other hand Karl Marx, who, along with a group of fellow German refugees, established the League of the Just (later Communist League) in Paris during the 1830s as a bulwark against capitalism, rejected civil society. Marx regarded 'civil society as an illusion that needs to be unmasked' (Hann and Dunn 1996, p.44). Later Marxists, notably Antonio Gramsci, who struggled against Fascist tyranny in twentieth century Italy, reworked the Marxist position. Gramsci wrote, in his *Prison Notebook*, commenced in 1929 at the beginning of a twenty year prison sentence:

> What we can do, for the moment, is to fix two major superstructural 'levels': the one that can be called 'civil society', and that of 'political society' or the 'State'. These two levels correspond on the one hand to the function of 'hegemony' which the dominant group exercises throughout society, and on the other hand to that of 'direct domination' or rule exercised through the State and the judicial government. (Gramsci, 1971, p.12)

For Gramsci social inequality and class domination was exercised by a variety of cultural institutions that enabled the dominant group to impose its sense of reality upon the rest of society. It was only through addressing this labyrinthine cultural complexity that the oppressed could liberate themselves and wrest control of civil society from the bourgeoisie, which had traditionally opposed popular participation. In Gramscian terms, civil society was conceived as the site of alternative hegemonies.

However, as Hann and Dunn (1996, p.5) observe, 'it is the liberal strand that has become almost hegemonic in most recent debates' about civil society. This is partly due to the political transformation of Eastern Europe. A more profound and subtle influence has been the universalization of Western notions of freely associating individuals in a pluralistic democratic society, that have become the dominant political idiom in postmodern society. Postmodernity represents the replacement of the standardization, nation states and uniformity that characterised the modern era by fragmentation, globalization and the affirmation of individual difference.

While the struggles of Eastern European dissidents, most famously the Czech playwright, Vaclav Havel, highlighted the threat to civil society in state dominated regimes. there is a growing sense of the complexity of the issues in postmodern society. Havel, now installed as the President of the Czech Republic following the 'Velvet Revolution', has argued for 'anti-political politics'. Recently a more sober analysis has emerged out of the tide of change sweeping across Eastern Europe since 1989. Hann and Dunn (1996, p.8) have observed that:

> the recent revolutions in Eastern Europe were the first in human history not to be concerned with establishing some form of rational Utopia. These societies (postcommunist) are seen as characterised by unfettered egoism and consumerism. Only individuals exist, and they are allegedly devoid of significant human relationships.

This assessment does not, however take account of the powerful democratic impulse that led to the fall of communism. Hann and Dunn (1996, p.9) conclude 'civil society is no longer, in the mid 1990s, the emotive slogan that it became for many East European intellectuals in the 1980s'. They cite the iconic figure of Vaclav Havel in support of their case. Havel (1993) has admitted to the existence of 'a post-communist nightmare'. The Hungarian-born philanthropist, George Soros, who financed the movement towards civil society in Eastern Europe during the 1980s, has also been critical of post-communist society (*The Guardian*, 18 January 1997).

Similarly, Anderson (1996, p.99) writing about the 'mythical archetype' Siberia challenges the view 'in both popular thought and in social theory for the complete absence of any kind of autonomously managed or meaningful public space' in Soviet society.

> Unlike the coffee houses or political parties in Euro-American society, civil

society in Siberia was harboured within different 'citizenship regimes', which formed restricted yet significant channels for economic and political practice. The past tense is deliberate: the assault on forms of civic entitlement and participation has never been greater than within the current politics of privatisation (Anderson, 1996, p.100).

The equation of civil society with a generic Euro-American state is clearly an ideological position that has more to do with post-cold war politics than serious social analysis. There are, manifestly, various definitions of civil society and political thought, as outlined above. Western political scientists have tended to dismiss the existence of civil society in Eastern Europe out of hand while, in reality, it 'continued to thrive at grass roots level' (Buchowski, 1996, p.79).

In Poland during the communist era there were a wide variety of voluntary organizations including: peoples' sports clubs, youth associations, women's associations, as well as professional and liberal arts associations (Buchowski, 1996, p.83). Ironically, 'many of these groups, especially professional organisations, transformed themselves into dissident bodies in the 1980s' (Buchowski, 1996, p.84).

Moreover, the Roman Catholic Church was entirely independent of the State in Poland during the communist era. At the end of the 1970s it consisted of 14,000 churches located in 7,000 parishes administered by about 20,000 priests. The Catholic University of Lublin (the only non-statutory university in Eastern Europe) along with theological colleges, provided a focus for intellectual freedom. Furthermore, Catholic newspapers offered a free press to dissidents. The role of the church in opposition to the communist regime was pivotal, as Buchowski (1996, p.86) has observed:

> The church had a stimulating effect throughout society. Deeply embedded in the national tradition and local community life, it represented the interests of various groups at different levels. In other words, the church was itself a major organisation of civic society, and at the same time it provided an infrastructure for other independent groups.

Buchowski (1996, p.87) concluded 'claims denying the existence of civic society in communist Poland cannot be sustained'.

However, the critical limitation on civil society was that it was ultimately under the control of the communist regime, which provided funding, made senior appointments in the secular sphere and ensured overall ideological supervision. The strength of Solidarity was that it sought to create a ethical civil society by providing a holistic critique of the communist regime and an alternative set of principles and programmes for organizing society. This was 'the Solidarity Ethos'. While Solidarity utilized demonstrations and rejected fixed organizational structures, like Western social movements, it differed because it was not a single issue campaign but a general social movement rooted in Polish Romanticism and Christian tradition. It, therefore, offered an alternative world view by elevating society over the state. Solidarity propagated very important aspects of the classical model of civil society, in particular the rule of law, individual freedom of communication and association and public debate (Wesołowski, 1995, p.113). By altering the meaning of civil society in Poland during the 1980s and giving it new ethical basis, the Solidarity movement undermined the communist regime's grip on civil society. The consequences were momentous as Buchowski (1996, p.89) observes:

> The party systematically withdrew from cultural and scientific life and permitted pluralism in these domains. It shifted from a centralised state economy towards a free market, with an increasing role for the private sector.

After the collapse of communism the Solidarity movement fragmented. Many of its principal leaders entered party politics, leaving non-governmental organizations (NGOs) in the hands of second line staff. The bond between civil society and the Solidarity leaders was broken because they were perceived as having deserted their roots. However, latterly members of the Freedom Union have become active again in civil society. The postcommunists have also sought to harness the voluntary sector in combatting social problems, such as poverty. Currently, there are approximately 15,000 NGOs in Poland (Buchowski, 1996, p.91).

In the post transition period differences between the more liberal elements in Solidarity and the Roman Catholic Church began to emerge. While Lech Wałęsa and the Christian nationalist Solidarity Electoral Alliance (AWS) remained staunchly loyal to the Catholic clergy, other former dissidents, notably the Freedom Union (UW), have subscribed to church-state separation and thought that the Roman Catholic church should have no role in political affairs. The Catholic church, on the other hand, argued that it had played a key role in liberating Poland from communism and was consequently entitled to a political reward.

The postcommunists have skilfully sought to present the Catholic church as the enemy of civil liberties in order to garner political support. Abortion has become a major political issue, with strong church-backed attempts to change Poland's liberal abortion legislation now more likely, following the electoral success of the AWS. Another example of Catholic political influence was a decision by the city of Torun, in 1997, to remove posters advertising condoms as a form of AIDS prevention from municipal buildings (*The Warsaw Voice*, 3 August, 1997). The future role of the Catholic church in the political affairs of Poland remains uncertain and but represents a significant challenge to its fledgling democracy.

While the Church has powerful champions among Christian nationalist politicians, it also has severe critics, not just amongst the postcommunists. Szostkiewicz (1992, p.188-92) has alleged that the church is a 'spiritual bureaucracy' ministering to an 'anonymous crowd' of petitioners. In similar vein, Holowka (1992, p.193-204), a former catechism teacher, has denounced the urban parish as a corporate entity differing little from state institutions, such as schools. The Roman Catholic Church, she concludes, blindly enforces a 'collection of prohibitions', and effectively discourages friendships and relationships outside the family. It would seem that the church mirrors the former hegemonic system of control of the Stalinist regime seeking to regulate the most intimate aspects of social life. It is not surprising that more democratically minded Poles fear its influence over the state.

Rollback and Welfare

The American social critic, Noam Chomsky has related changing social policy goals to foreign policy goals in Eastern Europe. Chomsky (1995, p.18) observes 'Rollback meant we undermine and destroy Soviet power as we reach negotiations with a successor state or states'. As part of this process Chomsky sees the renegotiation of the social contract as a strategic goal. The welfare state has become a target for rollback in a new era of market values in which 'the only rights you get are the rights you gain on the labour market' (Chomsky, 1995, p.18). The question, therefore, is: has the welfare state in Poland been subject to rollback since 1989?

Social rights in Poland (like the rest of Eastern Europe) were well developed during the communist era. Offe (1996, p.237-8) has delimited the key elements of social policy in communist society:

- State socialism provided a free and universal system of health,

Politics and Social Policy in the New Poland 39

education, and vocational training to its citizens;
- it also provided heavily subsidized housing, which, however, remained scarce and qualitatively deficient in most places;
- formal unemployment was virtually unknown, an accomplishment that was paid for in terms of vast inefficiencies of production, partly resulting in involuntary (as well as voluntary) 'unemployment on the job';
- childcare services were generously provided in order to free female labour for employment, and also in order to maximize state control over the political socialization of children;
- many mass consumption items were heavily subsidized, again causing vast inefficiencies;
- income inequality was significantly smaller than in market societies, but disposable income was also lower;
- many quality consumption items were unavailable in the market or excessively highly priced or allocated through mechanisms other than prices, such as connections and patronage;
- retirement incomes were extremely low by most Western standards;
- health and other services were of poor quality in many places;
- enforcement of positive rights and claims was difficult, as many of the transfers, services, and benefits were allocated through mechanisms of paternalist managerial, bureaucratic, or professional discretion, while rule-of-law principles remained at best rudimentary.

Offe's analysis indicates the breath of social provision under communism but also its severe deficiencies in terms of quality. There was, however according to its critics, an egalitarianism of underdevelopment. For example, Deacon (1992, p.6) has pointed out:

We are faced with two central conclusions. One is that the positive (from the Western critics' standpoint) features of Eastern European social policy - its formal egalitarianism for example - sit side by side with an underdeveloped and inefficient economy.

Such judgements should be treated with caution, as Wedel (1992) has pointed out in her penetrating book on Poland, *The Unplanned Society*. Wedel (1992, p.1) warns:

The tendency of many in the West to assume one particular outcome of the

Polish 'transition' arises partly from wishful thinking. Before the metamorphoses of 1989 turned Communist steel into scrap the West cast the drama of Communism's failure into rewardingly 'right' and 'wrong' sides. Now equally simplifying and ideologizing phrases without adequate referents .... convey an equally reductionist view.

What is clear is that the four Solidarity governments between 1991-93 sought to renegotiate the social contract. Their liberal market model of society meant that rollback for state welfare was inevitable . But the problem they faced was how to deal with the massive social dislocation arising from the economic transition from a socialized to a market economy. Ironically working class loyalty could only be retained through ensuring a generous system of social benefits for the large and spiralling numbers of unemployed.

Social benefits in Poland during the communist era were mainly provided through the Institiute of Social Insurance known as 'ZUS'. Since there was full employment, policy benefits were geared towards invalidity and retirement, family and child care benefits, food subsidies, rent subsidies, heating allowances as well as expenditure on health, education and culture. There was, in addition, a system of social assistance for the needy, supervised by social workers. As the economy declined during the 1980s, poverty (officially referred to as the 'social minimum') became an increasing problem (Millard, 1992, pp.127-8).

Golinowska (1996, p.69) records a rise in poverty during the transition to democracy. The emergence of endemic poverty in Poland led to changing attitudes towards the poor from the emerging middle classes. It was to prove crucial during the transition era in terms of Solidarity's social policy, which aped the attitudes of neo-conservatives in the West but tempered its disdain for the poor by its fear of the organized working class. Millard (1992, p.130) has commented in this regard:

> The reaction against incompetence, corruption and inefficiency of the ancien regime stimulated an anti-state ethos and a rejection of many social functions of the allegedly 'over-protective state' by a highly influential element of the liberal intelligentsia, now represented in government. A number of them are typical of the emerging entrepreneur, with vested interests in a reduction of the role of the state. Such attitudes are reinforced by a widely shared view that economic crisis prohibits large-scale intervention in the social sphere: Poland cannot afford extensive social policy expenditures.

The accession of Solidarity to power was followed by an immediate narrowing of the scope of social policy. Subsidies were abandoned for food, housing, leisure and culture. The concept of redistributive social justice disappeared from the political agenda. Redistribution was replaced by the idea of 'social protection' against the dislocation caused by the unleashing of free market forces, so that social order would be maintained (Millard, 1992, p.133). The return of the postcommunists to power between 1993-97 represented an attempt to mitigate the worst effects of marketization on society. While it proved to be a capable government, achieving successful economic growth, the SLD government failed to mollify an anxious working-class, which turned its loyalties to the populist Solidarity Electoral Alliance (AWS) in 1997. What kind of social policy an AWS-led government will pursue remains something of a mystery.

Conclusion

Polish politics and social policy have undergone a momentous change since the fall of the communist regime in 1989. While a new democratic society has been forged and civil society destalinized, there remains considerable uncertainty. Solidarity has proven to be politically inept and factionalized. The communists have successfully reinvented themselves as postcommunists, adjusting to the new political realities. However, it remains uncertain whether they can successfully cohabit with market economics. The emergence of cultural politics offers the clearest point of division between the dominant Christian nationalists in the Solidarity political legacy and the more secular minded postcommunists. Social policy in this political ferment has undergone profound change, reflecting Western trends and, in the case of Solidarity-led governments, neo-conservative approaches. It would seem that Poland is seeking to emulate the 'tiger economies' of the Far East with the unleashing of market forces, while simultaneously reacting against the social consequences of this policy. The confusion that has resulted in terms of Poland's future political and social project has the makings of long term uncertainty and an identity crisis.

References

Anderson, D. (1996), 'Bringing Civil Society to an Uncivilized Place', in Hann, C. and Dunn, E. (eds.), *Civil Society*, Routledge: London.

Buchowski, M. (1996), 'The Shifting Meanings of Civil and Civic Society in Poland', in Hann, C. and Dunn, E. (eds.), *Civil Society*, Routledge: London.
Deacon, B. (ed.) (1992), *The New Eastern Europe*, Sage: London.
Gramsci, A. (1971), *Selections from 'Prison Notebooks'* (Hoare, Q. and Howell Smith, G. eds.) Lawrence and Wishart: London.
Golinowska, S. (1996), *Social Policy Toward Poverty*, IPISS, Warsaw.
Hann, C. and Dunn, E. (eds.) (1996), *Civil Society*, Routledge: London.
Havel, V. (1993), 'The Postcommunist Nightmare', *New York Review of Books*, 27 May.
Hobsbawm, E. (1995), *Age of Extremes*, Abacus: London.
Hołowka, T. (1992), 'What Goes on in the Catechism Class', in Wedel, J. (ed.),*The Unplanned Society*, Columbia University Press: New York.
Millard, F. (1992), 'Social Policy in Poland', in Deacon, B.,(ed.) (1992), *The New Eastern Europe*, Sage: London.
Offe, C. (1996), *Modernity and the State*, Polity: Cambridge.
Szostkiewicz, A. (1992), 'A Church Without Laity', in Wedel, J. (ed.),*The Unplanned Society*, Columbia University Press: New York.
Wedel, J. (ed.) (1992), *The Unplanned Society: Poland During & After Communism*, Columbia University Press: New York.
Wedel, J. (1994), 'US Aid to Central & Eastern Europe, 1990-1994', in *East-Central European Economies in Transition*, US Government Printing Office, Washington.
Wesołowski, W. (1995), 'Poland after Solidarity' in Hall, J.A. (ed.),*Civil Society*, Polity: Cambridge.

3 Current Trends in Family Policy: European Union Countries and Poland

Marek Rymsza

Introduction

Family policy is one of those subjects which are currently a matter of particularly heated debate in both the EU countries and in Poland. This is mainly due to the fact that the goals of family policy are, to a large extent, determined socio-culturally. The normative basis of family policy is derived from wider cultural formations and reflects continuing changes in socially accepted values. In democratic countries, for instance, the development of a liberal ideology which promotes the freedom of individuals as the basic social value means that family policy has become less orientated to the family as such than to the individuals within it. Changes in the social structure and in behaviour patterns mean that family policy programmes must also be adjusted. In the EU countries, an increasing number of women seek employment, including those who have small children in their care. This means that family policy directed at children's welfare must be broadened so that the labour market and social infrastructure can be organized in such a way as to make it possible for both parents to combine child rearing with work outside the home.

Family policy may be classified according to a limited number of dimensions. Kamerman (1995) distinguishes between *direct* family policy, having a specific and intended impact on families, and *indirect* family policy, comprising programmes that affect the condition of family life as a side effect of their main goals. Ideologically, family policy can be classified, after Esping-Andersen (1990) into three basic positions: liberal, conservative and social democratic.[1] Liberal conceptions of family policy characteristically emphasize indirect approaches and give little attention to family policy as such. Conservatives prefer direct policy to support the family as a basic social unit. The social democratic conception assumes that the state pursues an active family policy but one which has different goals than that of the conservative, particularly that of greater equality for individuals within the family.

The Traditional Liberal Stance - Marginal Family Policy

This is an important position in Ireland and, to a lesser degree, in the United Kingdom. It has been particularly influential in the United States, where people are generally sceptical towards an expanded role for the state in social policy.

The marginal character of state family policy in liberal thinking has its origin in the conviction that 'there are two natural (or socially given) channels through which an individual's needs are properly met: the private market and the family' (Titmuss, 1974, p.30), and social programmes are justified only if these channels fail. The family has evolved as a natural institution to adjust the allocation of goods made through the free market. It is, therefore, a market actor and not merely an object of policy. The extent of state intervention should be as limited as possible. Universal programmes (e.g. social insurance or family benefits for all families and children) should not be the means of securing the living standards of poor families because obligatory fees and taxes mean restraints on the freedom of self-supporting families to use their own income: 'In a way the welfare state "nationalized" the family because it made itself responsible for providing help in cases formerly taken care of by the family' (Becker, 1997a, p.45). Therefore, social benefits for poor families - if they are necessary - should be selective. Paradoxically, current American critics of the welfare state have argued for cutting means tested (selective) social programmes rather than universal ones. According to Kristol (1995) and Murray (1994), the scale of redistribution through social welfare programmes has become too large and, in consequence, vulnerable families are increasingly being forced onto welfare.[2] Social welfare policy is blamed for the disintegration of family life. If demoralizing benefits are reduced, a strong family will be rebuilt. Nowadays, in the United States, the advocates of such classical liberal solutions are called conservatives, whereas left-wing politicians are called liberals. This reflects the evolution of liberal thought in the United States (and in other Anglo-Saxon countries) in the 20th century (Friedman 1994, pp.18-19).

Liberal-conservative advocates of a minimal role for the state in social policy are also influential in Ireland.[3] Traditionally, NGOs sponsored by the Catholic Church have played a crucial role in Irish social programmes for families. However, in the 1990s, Irish family policy has moved in the direction of a more European, social democratic approach while the United Kingdom, under Thatcherism, significantly shifted towards classical *laissez faire* liberalism.

Generally speaking, Anglo Saxon conservatives (classic liberals) are convinced that the family can adapt itself to post-industrial conditions, but their belief seems problematic. The traditional pattern of family life developed in England and the United States during Victorian times is appropriate for the conditions of a small local community but difficult to carry into effect in urban communities.[4] For this reason, the family policy of most developed countries on the European mainland has always been orientated to counteracting the negative impact of modernization on family life.

Continental Conservatives' Stance - Subsidiary Family Policy

In the tradition of mainland Europe, the principle of social solidarity forms the basis of all social policies (Jordan, 1996). It is assumed that the consolidation of natural social bonds is an essential element in solving social problems. This conception has been influenced by the social thought of the Catholic Church, and this is reflected by the way in which the subsidiary role of the state has often been written into legislation. It has been recognized by Christian social science that industrialization and the accompanying decline of certain functions of the family are irreversible facts. But in some areas, such as the upbringing of children, the family is irreplaceable. State policy should support the family in this, but ought not to relieve it of this function (Sutor, 1994). In many countries, the perception of the socially negative results of industrialization and urbanization was the starting point for a conception of the welfare state as a system of compensation for the victims (Luhmann, 1994). What distinguishes the conservative stance is its recognition that the internal disintegration of the family and the breakdown of its traditional role as the basic social unit are among these negative results. One aim of social policy, therefore, is to help families 'to revive their identity within the industrial society' (Hoffner, 1992, p.103).

In this model, it is the family as a unit which receives social benefits and is the object of policy. The joint taxation of all household income, or at least that received by spouses, is an example of this unitary approach.[5] This, and other elements, of direct family policy are most pronounced in the legislation of Germany and France. Another characteristic feature of social policy in these countries is the dominant role which employee insurance plays in the social security system (Clasen, 1994; Rymsza, 1996b). Families depend upon their employed members for social insurance benefits such as health care.

Some representatives of Christian social science, however, have objections to the structural solutions worked out in the conservative model of family policy which are similar to liberals' objections to the welfare state as such (cf. Novak, 1997; Lecaillon, 1997). According to them, 'socialization' of anti-poverty programmes may have consequences for family life which are as negative as those of nationalization. Lecaillon, for example, objects to social insurance based on Pay As You Go principles, where the payments of today's workers are not used to build up a fund for their future but to pay pensions to current recipients: 'The crux of the matter in this is that intergenerational solidarity has been socialized, the solidarity which, in traditional societies, was realized within the family. An undue extension of the society's competence is a consequence of this socialization quite contrary to the principle of subsidiarity' (Lecaillon, 1997, p.36). While Christian social thought favours many of the social policies adopted by the countries of Continental Europe,[6] its attitude to family policy is very limited.

The Social Democratic Stance - Towards Greater Equality in the Family

The eradication of inequalities between different social groups in their access to broadly understood goods is one of the main goals of social policies as interpreted by social democrats (Ginsburg, 1992). Since the distribution of goods is largely accomplished through the family, the task of family policy is to intervene in the divisions within the family. In such a policy, state activities are aimed not so much at the well-being of the family as a whole, but more at the well-being of particular individuals living in families. The family itself may be perceived as an institution which, through its structure and type of bonds, limits the welfare of some of its members. Violence or merely domination, may be problems requiring state intervention. In social democratic thought, a family with the father as the head and with strong parental authority is a type in which domination is culturally sanctioned. Such a model, called by social democrats 'patriarchal'[7] ought gradually to be transformed into a partnership one. Family policy should serve this goal. Some social democrats even present this goal as a corner stone of the modern welfare state (Hernes, 1992).

Family policy in the social democratic sense should also concentrate on guaranteeing social rights and benefits for all individuals within the family. This is defined by social democrats as a fundamental role for the state. This is well-illustrated by the Scandinavian countries, although, due to their crisis in public finances, social expenditure has been limited and elements of marginal social policy introduced. Swedish social policies of the 1990s may serve as the best example (Stephens, 1996). It is noteworthy that, at present, Scandinavian family policy is definitely focussed on the child. The child's well-being is the main, if not the only, justification of family policy. This orientation seems to be a result of the influence that progressive (leftist) liberals have had on the social programmes of social democratic countries. Their position reflects the challenges of 1960s social movements to the values of traditional family life. At present, one may speak of a social liberal conception of policy towards the family. In practice, as a result of the focus on the child's welfare, contradictions in children's and parents' interests may be exposed and measures weakening legal parental authority may be undertaken. Social democrats' prejudice against the family also finds expression in their promotion of so-called 'alternative models of the family' or 'alternative styles of life'. This promotion adopts pro-family rhetoric and is a typical means of 'softening' public opinion and questioning a broadly accepted definition of the family[8] Radical left-wing social movements, which contest family policy because it consolidates social inequalities, openly attack the family.[9] According to them, the family is an institution which, by its very nature, sets limits to the freedom of individuals.

Trends in the Evolution of Family Policies in the European Union Countries

On the basis of comparative studies (Dumon, 1994; Balcerzak-Paradowska, 1993; Graniewska et al., 1993), it is possible to point to several trends in the evolution of family policy in EU member states. They are as follows:

- A tendency towards eliminating those elements of state policies which in any way discriminate against individuals because of their marital status. Changes in the tax system are a good example here. In many member states, joint taxation of spouses has been replaced by individual taxation. This is definitely a departure from direct family policy and its assumptions that 'the tax capability of spouses is much better reflected by joint

taxation' (Majewicz, 1994, p.20). The individual taxation system is conducive to the individualistic perspective in which marriage and the family are perceived. In this system marriage is treated as a contract between two autonomous individuals.
- Enabling the spouses to reconcile family life with employment is an essential goal of family policy in the EU countries. Dumon (1994) points out that there are two basic approaches to this issue: *segregation* and *integration* strategies. In the former, employment and family life are separated, and a division of roles in marriage follows. One spouse is the breadwinner (usually the man), while the other keeps the home and cares for the children. It is the task of family policy to guarantee that a family with one working parent will be socially secure. This strategy is identified with the notion of the 'family wage' and in measures of redistribution to compensate for loss of income if one parent gives up their job. This function is fulfilled by educational and family benefits. The integration strategy assumes that both parents can, and even should, work. Family policy has a double task of creating the infrastructure for social care of the children and of ensuring that labour law has a social and flexible character. Within this conception there is a fundamental trend that maternity leave should not be granted exclusively to women. Thus one objective of feminist movements has been achieved, namely that of eliminating the division of parental tasks. However, as a result of special legal and social protection for working women, employers may seek to avoid social costs by giving priority to male candidates for jobs. The family policy of EU countries is evolving towards the integration conception even though integrative programmes are supplemented with segregation elements, especially in the sphere of caring for small children.
- The recognition of the child as a separate individual is an important change to the normative assumptions of family policy. A trend to strengthen the legal status of the child within the family is found in the legislation of many states. The position of the child as a separate social and legal subject is reflected in the UN Convention on the Rights of the Child, ratified by all EU member states. It is significant, however, that the convention stresses the parents' responsibility for raising their offspring and defines the state's role as merely ancillary. The Convention on the Rights of the Child seems to be a compromise between conservatives who defend

parental autonomy in child-rearing and progressive liberals who emphasize the autonomy of the child as an individual (Kwak, 1996, pp.132-3). The constitution of the child as a distinct social and legal subject should be seen both as an independent aim of family policy and as an aspect of the trend in family policy towards the general disaggregation of individual rights and interests. The proposition, currently discussed in some EU countries, that benefits paid to families ought to be replaced with benefits paid to children is an element of the above trend. This proposition aims at strengthening the child's position within the family as an individual consumer of social services. It creates a new perspective of perceiving the child as separate from its family (Balcerzak-Paradowska, 1993, p.52). Thus interpreted, policy towards the family is in fact policy towards the child.

- The trend towards replacing insurance benefits to the family with social welfare services or universal benefits financed by the state budget shows that continental conservative solutions are being abandoned in favour of social democratic or liberal ones. Left-wing advocates of these changes argue that systems of employee insurance benefits sustain a traditional model of the family with one working parent because the right to a benefit is derived from other members' dependence on the wage-earner. Nevertheless, private firms are more and more interested in arranging social services for their employees' families. In this way private employers hope to create an image of family-friendliness as part of a wider strategy to create permanent bonds between the firm and its employees. This is undoubtedly a return to corporatist solutions on the continental model, a return all the more significant because it is not inspired by government policies.

- In the EU countries, there is a tendency to decentralize family policy and to transfer some tasks to non-governmental organizations. This policy means that family problems are to be solved at the local level. The trend is consistent with the assumptions of the conservative-continental model of family policy which emphasizes the principle of state subsidiarity. Decentralization is also accompanied by the commercial sector's increased participation in social services. By increasing the number of providers, clients have an opportunity to choose between them. According to the theory of internal markets, individuals and families who choose particular services become consumers assessing the quality of services delivered by particular agencies (Le Grand and Bartlett, 1993). In practice this means that market mechanisms come into play as favoured by liberals. These changes are accompanied by a move away from institutional solutions towards promotion of preventive work, community social work, different forms of family therapy and counselling. The attempt to solve social problems through the public bureaucracies which dominated West European welfare states during what left-wingers call the 'golden age' has proved to be both expensive and ineffective (Esping-Andersen, 1996).

Family Policy in Poland against the Background of the EU Countries

Since the very beginning of the Polish transition from communism, the founding assumptions of family policy have been the subject of heated debate. An analysis of the legislation on social and public policies in the years 1989-1993 has shown that elements of family policy have permeated very widely, although mainly in the fragmented form characteristic of indirect family policy. Only the option for spouses to choose joint taxation and the introduction to Article 1 of the Social Welfare Act (1990), recognising the family as a distinct object of social welfare services are recognizable as direct family policy. The State Office of the Plenipotentiary for the Affairs of Family and Women was created in 1991 but so far, no consistent pro-family policy has been proposed by its staff. The elements of indirect family policy which dominate in Polish legislation are frequently unfavourable to the family. It is generally believed that there is a lack of pro-family solutions in the social security system and in the tax system, and that the state should pursue an active pro-family policy. The lack of pro-family taxation has been highlighted by the Polish Ombudsman (Ombudsman opinion, 1995). However, there is considerable disagreement about the possible aims of a direct family policy and about the means by which it could be operationalized. Different political interests emphasize different elements which are consistent with their general programmes.

A continental-conservative position is represented by the Charter of the Rights of the Family (1983) prepared by the Catholic Church and supported by Polish Christian Democrats. During the 1993-97 parliament, a minority group of MPs from this tendency formed the Parliamentary Group for the Family. After the 1997 election, Christian Democrats became the leading group in both chambers of the Polish parliament. This group has emphasized the need for protective measures against the socially negative effects of the transition: poverty, unemployment and social exclusion.[10] The state should offer support to large families, to families with one or two unemployed parents and to families with special needs (e.g. those expecting a baby, raising a disabled child, etc.). However, institutional help ought to be of a subsidiary character. The intervention of public agencies into family life is justified only in the case of pathological families, and must not lead to limitation of parental authority as such.

The social democratic position, exemplified by the influential Parliamentary Women's Group in the 1993-97 parliament, emphasizes not only a need to assist families in a difficult financial situation but also a necessity to neutralize pathological elements of family life, mainly violence. This is a policy directed not so much towards the family but more towards the individuals within the family (especially children and women). Activists in movements on behalf of children and women represent violence as a common phenomenon of family life in Poland. In the sphere of labour law, social democrats argue that the state ought to make it easier for parents to reconcile duties at home with those at work, and stress the need for men and women to have equal opportunities in the labour market. This influence can be seen in recent change to the labour code (e.g. the introduction in 1996 of the institution of 'parental' leave for child care instead of maternal leave). Some feminists also argue that the retirement age and the right to a dependent's pension should be the same for men and women. Since there is a crisis in insurance finances it is obvious that if these claims are carried into effect, the retirement age for women and the age at which a woman is entitled to a widows pension will be raised. All this will mean renouncing solutions considered 'social gains' in the social democratic stance. These claims reflect a social liberal orientation rather than a social democratic one.

The greatest influence on Polish family policy, however, is the indirect impact of liberal economic legislation, seen, for example, in social insurance reform after 1995.[11] This includes the transfer of family benefits to the tax-supported social welfare system where they will be administered on a selective basis. It contrasts with the hostility to selective programmes during the post-war 'golden age' of West European welfare states, when it was argued that this approach led to the stigmatization and marginalization of benefit recipients. The social democratic goal envisaged replacing selective programmes with universal one.[12] In 1996, Polish legislators transferred these benefits back to the social welfare administration and directed that there should be further moves in this direction.[13] This policy shift seems to have been dictated by a desire to balance insurance finances. The institutional solutions offered by the liberal model of minimal social policy are attractive for anyone looking for budget savings.

To summarize, Polish family policy from 1989 to 1997 can be divided into two basic periods, 1989-93 and 1993-97. The change in policy coincides with a considerable change in the distribution of political power.[14] From 1989 to 1993, during the period of system transformation implemented by Solidarity and its associates, the opposition movement in communist Poland, economic problems dominated and family policy was treated marginally. The Office of the Plenipotentiary for Family and Women's Affairs was created but, due to ideological differences among the Solidarity political elites, this move did not change the situation.

During the 1993-97 period, when a coalition of post-communist parties formed the government, the activities of the Plenipotentiary Office were dominated by women's issues and the family policy was defined in a social democratic mode. This was connected with two factors. Firstly, the Alliance of the Democratic Left (the dominant party of the government coalition) was working on its new image as a party of modern social democracy. Secondly, the Plenipotentiary Office fell under the control of feminist activists. At that time, the government opted for a policy of selective family benefits as one of its four pillars of social security. However, due to a rapidly increasing range of social welfare activities and to the use of more rigorous eligibility criteria, benefits were actually less accessible to certain categories of families, particularly to large ones.

The 1997 elections have opened a third stage in the development of family policy in Poland. Separate standing committees on family matters have been established in both chambers of the Polish Parliament and the Plenipotentiary Office for Family and for Women's Affairs has been replaced by a Plenipotentiary Office for Family Affairs.[15] Analysis of the election manifesto of the Solidarity Election Alliance (AWS) - the strongest partner in the current government coalition - shows that family policy will be shaped in a conservative way. So we can speak about the evolution of family policy in Poland from a liberal conception in the years 1990-93 through a social democratic formulation (1993-97) to a conservative one.

The Dilemma of European and Polish Liberals

When the debate on family policy in EU member states is analysed, it reveals both similarities and differences in the positions of the various interests involved. One element which appears to be common to the discourse, both in Poland and in the EU countries, is the ideal of guaranteeing children the conditions for their most complete development, something which is supported by all three of the ideological options discussed here. In theory, it should be possible to reach a broad consensus on family policy around this proposition.

However, the social policies adopted by many EU member states in the 1980s and 1990s may be defined, after Sullivan (1992), as policies of departure from consensus, connected with deliberate and increasing political polarization. In the case of family policy this polarization corresponds with the Bergers' (Berger and Berger, 1983) description of the American discourse on family policy: a division into two camps - a 'traditional' conservatives' camp and a 'progressive' social democrats' one.[16] The conflict over fundamental values has been demonstrated on a global scale at the last four United Nations population conferences: in Cairo (1994), Beijing (1995), Copenhagen (1995) and, to a lesser extent, in Istanbul (1996).

This division does not map neatly onto the well-established distinction, in the literature on comparative social policy, between protagonists of the minimum state and those of the welfare state, i.e. with the traditional doctrinal controversy: liberalism - socialism revolving round the axis of the permissible degree of state intervention (George and Wilding, 1992). Conflicts over family policy reflect conflicts over the definition of the family itself which, as Berger and Luckmann (1983) demonstrate, can be seen as one of the major symbolic institutions of any society. Protagonists of the policy of subsidiarity traditional in EU countries are led by the social teaching of the Catholic Church, while the 'progressive' camp reflects the radical claims of the New Left. In such a situation the Bergers' definition of the American public debate of the 1970s and 1980s as 'the war over the family' also seems applicable to the political arena of EU member states and of Poland. This kind of polarization has fundamental effects on the political arena, particularly for liberal parties which need new self-identification because they cannot maintain their customary 'pragmatic silence' in the face of a sharpening ideological dispute. Two future scenarios seem possible.

The first assumes an agreement between social democratic and liberal forces, and a new social liberal position. This is not exactly a compromise but rather the simultaneous realization of liberal and social democratic assumptions in different fields.[17] This solution can be seen at the EU level and, especially, in the Council of Europe. The EU conception of the welfare state assumes the construction of a free internal market but allows for legal and administrative intervention aimed at the equalization of opportunities to participate, especially those of men and women. The Council of Europe stance on 'gender equality' reflects the New Left agenda even more directly.[18]

The second scenario assumes an agreement between liberals and conservatives. The consequence of this is a fundamental rejection of the idea of the welfare state not only in the economic but also in the socio-cultural sphere. As a result the family acquires an economic importance in the promotion of human capital investment (Becker, 1997a, b) in addition to its role in promoting basic social values (Whitfield, 1997). Such an agreement has been seen in operation in some EU member states, for instance Italy (Treu, 1997).

Polish liberals face a similar dilemma. The election campaign in September 1997 was the first since 1989 in which family policy was emphasized as important. Family matters were especially prominent in the right wing Solidarity Election Alliance (AWS) manifesto. The Freedom Union, a liberal centrist party stressed strictly economic issues. Currently the leaders of the Union are split between two basic stances. The Christian democratic wing is closer to the conception of a subsidiary family policy, while the social-liberal wing opts for the stance of the New Left. The fact that a government coalition has been created by the Solidarity Election Alliance (AWS) and the Freedom Union makes the second scenario more likely to be carried out in Poland.

Finally, it is worth pointing out that public opinion surveys, both in the EU countries and in Poland, explicitly show that, irrespective of the dominant ideologies in particular societies, the traditional family life is still considered a great value. There is definitely greater tolerance of alternative lifestyles but 'changes in ideas (opinions) about the family and alternative forms are greater than changes in behaviour. This means that the social acceptance of such forms is greater than the readiness to enter into them' (Balcerzak-Paradowska, 1993, p.22), and that the family defined as a triad: mother-father-child (children) remains a dominant cultural pattern (Berger and Berger, 1983). However, if the contemporary nuclear family in developed societies is to carry its fundamental functions, it must be assisted by the state. This is the essential argument for the state to adopt a subsidiary pro-family policy.

Notes

This paper develops an analysis presented in Rymsza (1997a), comparing current trends in EU member states' family policies with the evolution of family policy in Poland since 1989.

1. Esping-Andersen's comparative research on welfare state regimes focuses on social security systems, but the Danish author also underlines family matters as one of the basic differences in the ideological conception of social policies.
2. Kristol and Murray stress especially the disintegration of family life patterns in American black urban areas.
3. Mclaughlin (1993) classifies the Irish model of social policy as 'catholic corporatism' but emphasizes liberal (marginal) approach to the role of the state in solving family problems.
4. Analysis of the Victorian patterns of family life in Popenoe (1996).
5. This approach is still applied by the French legislation which provides for joint taxation of a household (Majewicz, 1994, Czaputowicz, 1995).
6. After World War II, Christian Democrats were architects of social security systems in many countries, especially in postfascist Germany and Italy.
7. Marxists, in particular, promote an extremely broad definition of 'patriarchalism' that covers not only a historical model of family life but all indications of hierarchical relations within the family (see Ginsburg, 1992).
8. Berger and Berger (1983) refer to the triad: mother, father, child (children).
9. See Tong's (1994) analysis of radical feminists.
10. For an analysis of the negative social side-effects of the system transformation in Poland see Hrynkiewicz (1995).
11. For an analysis of the programmes of social insurance reform in Poland see Rymsza (1997b).
12. Such a conception was one of the main elements of the Beveridge Plan of the British social security reform after World War II (Magnuszewska-Otulak, 1992).
13. Act on Family Benefits (1996). All legislative acts on family policy passed by the Polish Parliament in the years 1993-1996 are listed in Balcerzak-Paradowska (1996).
14. See analysis of the Polish political arena in Antoszewski (1994).
15. These are: the Sejm Committee of Family and the Senate Committee of Family and Social Policy.
16. The Bergers use the American term 'liberals' rather than social democrats.
17. See for instance the analysis of British family policy in Maclean (1991).
18. See especially the Council of Europe Publication (1995).

References

Antoszewski, A. (ed.) (1994), *Ewolucja polskiego systemu politycznego po 1989 roku w świetle komparatystycznej teorii polityki*, Wydawnictwo Uniwersytetu Wrocławskiego: Wrocław.

Balcerzak-Paradowska, B. (1993), *Polityka rodzinna w krajach Wspólnoty Europejskiej i jej uwarunkowania*, IPiSS: Warsaw.

Balcerzak-Paradowska, B. (1996), 'Polityka państwa wobec rodziny', in Golinowska, S. (ed.),

Polityka społeczna w latach 1994-1996, IPiSS: Warsaw, pp. 305-30.
Becker, G. (1997a), 'Rodzina jako podstawowa jednostka gospodarcza', *Społeczeństwo*, No 1-2, pp. 51-8.
Becker, G. (1997b), 'Znaczenie kapitału ludzkiego', *Społeczeństwo*, No 1-2, pp. 51-7.
Berger, B. and Berger, P. (1983), *The War over the Family. Capturing the Middle Ground*, Hutchinson: London.
Berger, P. and Luckmann, T. (1983/1966) (Polish edition), *The Social Construction of Reality*. PWN: Warsaw.
Clasen, J. (1994), 'Social security - the core of the German employment-centred social state', in Clasen, J. and Freeman, R. (ed.), *Social Policy in Germany*, Harvester Wheatsheaf: New York, pp. 61-82.
Council of Europe Publishing (1996) (Polish Edition): 'Grupa specjalistów w zakresie równości i demokracji. Końcowy raport z działalności', *Biuletyn Ośrodka Informacji i Dokumentacji Rady Europy*, No 3.
Czaputowicz, J. (1995), 'Jaka polityka prorodzinna?', *Biuletyn OCIPE*, No 1, pp. 1-6.
Dumon, W. (1994), 'National Family Policies in the Member States. Current Trends and Developments', in Dumon, W. (ed.), *Changing Family Policies in the Member States of the European Union*, Commission of the European Communities: Bonn.
Esping-Andersen, G. (1990), *The Three Worlds of Welfare Capitalism*, Polity Press: Cambridge.
Esping-Andersen, G. (1996), 'After the Golden Age? Welfare State Dilemmas in a Global Economy', in Esping-Andersen, G. (ed.), *The Welfare State in Transition. National Adaptations in Global Economies*, Sage: London, pp. 1-31.
Friedman, M (1994/1982), (Polish edition), *Capitalism and Freedom*, Rzeczpospolita: Warsaw.
George, V. and Wilding, P. (1992) *Welfare and Ideology*, Routledge: London.
Ginsburg, N. (1992), *Divisions of Welfare. A Critical Introduction to Comparative Social Policy*, Sage: London.
Graniewska, D., Balcerzak-Paradowska, B., Kołaczek, B. and Staszewska, D. (1993), *Polityka wobec rodziny, kobiet i dzieci*, IPiSS: Warsaw.
Hernes, H. (1994), 'Obywatelstwo kobiet w skandynawskim państwie dobrobytu', in Edvardsen, T. and Hagtvet, B. (ed.), *Nordycki model demokracji i państwa dobrobytu*, PWN: Warsaw, pp. 70-87.
Hernes, H. (1989), *Welfare State and Woman Power. Essays in State Feminism*, Norwegian University Press: Oslo.
Höffner, J. (1992) (Polish edition), *Chrześcijańska nauka społeczna*, WAM: Kraków.
Hrynkiewicz, J. (1995), 'Raport o rozwoju społecznym Polski 1995. Synteza raportu', in *Human Development Report - Poland 1995*, Fundacja Zabezpieczenia Społecznego: Warsaw, pp. 229-52.
Jordan, B. (1996), *A Theory of Poverty and Social Exclusion*, Polity Press: Cambridge.
Kamermann, S. B. (1995), 'Families Overview', *Encyclopedia of Social Work* (19th edition), NAWS Press: Washington, DC, pp. 927-35.
'Karta praw rodziny' [Charter of the Rights of the Family] (1993), *L'Osservatore Romano* [Polish Edition] No. 10, October.
Kristol, I. (1995), *Neoconservatism. The Autobiography of an Idea*, Free Press: New York.
Kurczewski, J. and Maclean, M. (ed.) (1997), *Family Law and Family Policy in the New Europe*, Aldershot: Dartmouth.
Kwak, A. (1996), 'Dziecko i jego prawa w Polsce', in Kwak, A. (ed.), *Wybrane problemy pracy socjalnej*, ISNS UW: Warsaw, pp. 125-34.

Lecaillon, J-D. (1997), 'Społeczne i ekonomiczne znaczenie rodziny', *Społeczeństwo*, No 1-2, pp. 31-8.

Le Grand, J. and Bartlett, W. (1993), *Quasi Markets and Social Policy*, Macmillan: London.

Luhmann, N. (1994) (Polish edition), *Teoria polityczna państwa bezpieczeństwa socjalnego*, PWN: Warsaw.

Maclean, M. (1991), 'Law, Family and Society in the UK: 1989', in Pocar, V. and Ronfani, P. (eds.), *Family, Law and Social Policy*, ONATI Proceedings, No 13, pp. 77-92.

Magnuszewska-Otulak, G. (1992), *Rozwój systemu zabezpieczenia społecznego w Wielkiej Brytanii. Raport Beveridge'a*, IPiSS: Warsaw.

Majewicz, M. (1994), 'Opodatkowanie dochodów rodziny', *Praca i Zabezpieczenie Społeczne*, No 9, pp. 20-7.

Mclaughlin, E. (1993), 'Ireland: Catholic Corporatism', in Cochrane, A. and Clarke, J. (eds.), *Comparing Welfare States. Britain in International Context*, Sage: London, pp. 205-37.

Murray, C. (1994), *Losing Ground. American Social Policy 1950-1980*, Basic Books: New York.

Novak, M. (1997), 'Rodzina i ekonomia w XXI wieku', *Społeczeństwo*, No 1-2, pp. 75-88.

Ombudsman Opinion (1995), *Stanowisko Rzecznika Praw Obywatelskich w sprawie niedostatecznie prorodzinnych rozwiązań w ustawie o podatku dochodowym od osób fizycznych*, Warsaw, typescript.

Popenoe, D. (1996), *Life Without Father*, Free Press: New York.

Rymsza, M. (1997a), 'Socio-Cultural and Ideological Aspects of the Evolution of Family Policies in Liberal Societies', in: Kurczewski, J. and Maclean, M. (eds.), *Family Law and Family Policy in the New Europe*, Aldershot: Dartmouth, pp. 221-46.

Rymsza, M. (1997b), 'Stan i perspektywy reformy ubezpieczeń społecznych w Polsce', *Praca i Zabezpieczenie Społeczne*, No 12, pp. 2-12.

Rymsza, M, (1996), 'Polityka społeczna wobec rodziny w krajach Unii Europejskiej i w Polsce', in Kwak, A. (ed.), *Wybrane problemy pracy socjalnej*, ISNS UW: Warsaw, pp. 149-58.

Stephens, J. (1996), 'The Scandinavian Welfare States: Achievements, Crisis, and Prospects', in Esping-Andersen, G. (ed.), *Welfare State in Transition: National Adaptations in Global Economies*, Sage: London, pp. 32-65.

Sullivan, M. (1992), *The Politics of Social Policy*, Harvester Wheatsheaf: New York.

Sutor, B. (1994), *Etyka polityczna*, Kontrast: Warsaw.

Titmuss, R. (1974), *Social Policy. An Introduction*, Allen and Unwin: London.

Tong, R. (1994), *Feminist Thought. A Comprehensive Introduction*, Routledge: London.

Treu, P. (1997), 'Wspieranie rodziny', *Społeczeństwo*, No 1-2, pp. 227-32.

Whitfield, R. (1997), 'Ekonomiczne i społeczne koszty rozkładu rodziny', *Społeczeństwo*, No 1-2, pp. 85-105.

4 Family Policy and Family Life in Poland
Anna Kwak

Introduction

The Polish family is changing in the same way as the family in all other developed countries. The numbers of marriages and births are declining, while the number of incomplete families, lone mothers and cohabitations is increasing. The only differences are in the speed and intensity of these changes.

Between 1993 and 1995, the marriage rate was steady at 5.4 per 1,000 population 15 years and over, the lowest level since 1946 and down from a peak of 9.7 per 1,000 in 1975. Since 1981, the rate has declined particularly sharply for people under the age of 24, suggesting a growing delay in contracting marriage. The number of live births in Poland has been declining steadily since 1984, especially during the 1990s. In 1995, the number of live births was at its lowest level since the Second World War. Polish demographers are concerned that this level of reproduction is below the replacement rate. In 1995, the rural birth rate fell below that required for replacement for the first time.

The divorce rate has fluctuated. It tended to increase up to 1988 and then declined by about 5 per cent until 1993. In the two following years, the divorce rate increased - in 1994 to 15.2 per cent, and in 1995 to 18.4 per cent of the total number of contracted marriages. This has brought the divorce rate back to the level of the 1980s. Incomplete families are formed as a result of divorce, death of one parent or unmarried motherhood. The number of incomplete families has risen consistently. Most of them are families with lone mothers. In 1995 families with mothers constituted 14.4 per cent and families with fathers 1.4 per cent of the total number of families. For comparison, in 1988, lone mothers accounted for 13.2 per cent of all families and lone fathers 1.2 per cent. The rate of births to unmarried women has increased since 1990 in Poland. This ran consistently at 5 per cent of total live births throughout the period between 1979 and 1985, but rose in 1993 to 8.2 per cent and in 1995 to 9.5 per cent of total live births. However, families with two parents legally married to each other are still the commonest type in Poland. Traditional family life continues to be valued.[1]

The socio-demographic transformation of the family has been accompanied by economic changes. These have had a considerable impact on many Polish families. Poverty and unemployment can seriously destabilize families. Studies conducted in 1993 (CBOP[2] 1993, pp.10-12) showed that the most frequent reason for conflicts in families was financial difficulties (52 per cent). Women respondents from small towns and villages, women with lower levels of education, unskilled female workers, peasant women and unemployed women particularly emphasized this cause of conflicts. Over a quarter of the women respondents believed that conflicts in their families had intensified in recent years as a result of financial difficulties or a family member's loss of employment.

Family policy is the aggregate of the legal and other norms and actions of the state and other institutions intended to define the proper conditions of life in a society and, within these, to promote the development and functioning of families. Its main objective is to establish the general conditions to meet the material and cultural needs of the family, to promote the socialization of children and to secure their opportunities for future participation in the life and economy of the society. The adaptation of families to the new situation of a market economy has not been easy. There are still serious housing problems, high unemployment, shortages in social services, a general decrease in the quality of life and sense of security. How is the family now being assisted in fulfilling its basic function of raising a new generation?

Policy Towards the Family before 1989

An official interest in family life was expressed in the 1952 Polish Constitution in the form of a statement on family protection. Article 79 of the Constitution states that marriage, maternity and family are under the protection of the State. The government is obliged to pay a special attention to families with a larger number of children. In addition, Article 78, which guarantees equality between men and women refers to care for mother and child, protection of pregnancy, paid leave before and after childbirth, development of maternity clinics, day nurseries and nursery schools. Under this constitution, the state was made the main agent for the implementation of social policy, including policy towards the family, through specialized administrative bodies such as central government ministries and their associated institutions. Other social policy actors, like trade unions, social agencies and local government were required to cooperate closely with the state. Their activities had a complementary character.

Over the period from the end of World War II until 1988, there were changes in the State's policy interests towards the family. The degree of activity in family policy reflected the economic, political and social environment. In the early 1950s, for example, women were encouraged to work as part of the general demand for labour to support industrialization and economic development. This was supported by policies which helped women to fulfill both family and working roles. In later years, there was declining interest in finding solutions to the problem of a woman's double career as mother and worker. In the 1980s the government modified some instruments of social policy in relation to the family, mainly in order to seek popular support at a time of rising social discontent.

According to Balcerzak-Paradowska (1995, pp.54-5), there was a strong emphasis until the mid-1950s on encouraging women into the labour force. This led to the development of institutions for child care - day nurseries and preschools. State policy permitted developments in the direction of women's self-realization through work and equality of employment rights. From 1956 until 1969 there was less support for women's employment but their actual labour force participation did not change very much. Men's incomes were simply too low for them to be the sole breadwinners in a family. It became almost universal for both parents to work, although there were severe problems as a result of the inadequate number of places in day nurseries and nursery schools. In that period psychologists also started to raise concerns about the effects of group care on children. In response, there was a policy change in 1968, which gave one year's unpaid leave to working women who had a baby.

The next ten years (1970-1979) saw larger changes in family policy, mainly concentrated in the first part of the period. These enhanced the social benefits available to families by various measures including:

- a new system of family benefits related to the income per person in a family and the number of children;
- a disability living benefit for families with disabled children;
- an equalization of maternity benefits for both white and blue-collar workers;

- a single postnatal benefit for all mothers;
- the extension of unpaid maternity leave to 3 years;
- the establishment of Alimony Funds for families with financial problems as a result of an inability to enforce the payment of child support;
- the development of childcare facilities for 6 year old children through the introduction of compulsory pre-school education;
- the introduction of an attractive loan system to help young families purchase durable goods, with significant assistance from work institutions in repayments;
- the assignment to families of priority in obtaining social services from work institutions, depending on the structure of the family and its financial situation.

Family policy in the years from 1980 to 1988 was marked by the political situation, the growing economic crisis and social discontent, and stronger influence of provisions resulting from international agreements. This meant a rise in level of family benefits, benefits for disabled children and benefits from the Alimony Funds. Mothers' unpaid leaves were linked to opportunities to obtain benefits. In 1985 workplace support for loan repayments by young married couples was withdrawn.

Policy Towards the Family since 1989

Since the transition to democratic government, family policy has been characterized by the decentralization of State responsibilities and the commercialization of services. Local authorities have been made responsible for provisions which frequently proved to be beyond their organizational and financial capacity. Employers have cut back on their welfare activities. Parents have been expected to pay a larger share of the costs of social services. The private sector has been encouraged to play a larger part in organizing social service facilities for families and children. Most of the cash benefits targeted at families have been carried over from the previous socio-economic system with only slight modifications (Graniewska and Balcerzak-Paradowska 1995, Balcerzak-Paradowska 1995). This chapter looks particularly at trends in family policy with regard to maternal and child-care benefits and child-maintenance benefits (Balcerzak-Paradowska 1995, Golinowska and Balcerzak-Paradowska 1995, Report on the situation of

Polish families 1995, Semenowicz and Antoszkiewicz 1996).

Maternity and Child-Care Benefits

These include childbirth benefit, maternity benefit and leave, child-care benefit, child-raising benefit, and benefits for pregnant women.

Childbirth benefit This benefit was introduced in 1974 and has not been changed since. All employed women and women married to employed men are entitled to it upon childbirth. Since 1989, changes have been made in the way this benefit is calculated and it is now, since 1995, equal to 15 per cent of the average industrial wage.

Maternity leave and benefit In 1974, maternity leave was extended from 12 weeks to 16 weeks for the first child, to 18 weeks for the second and subsequent children and to 26 weeks for multiple childbirth. During maternity leave, women are entitled to a benefit equal to 100 per cent of the salary earned for three months prior to the leave. The right to this benefit is granted both to a working mother and to an employed woman who has fostered a child below the age of one and has applied to a court for permission to adopt this child. This principle is still valid, as of 1997.

Child-care benefit This benefit makes it possible for a working mother to look after a sick child under 14 years of age. Since 1974, this benefit has been payable for up to 60 days irrespective of the number of children in the family. It also covers leave from work to care for a healthy child under eight years of age if the child's day nursery, nursery school or school has been closed unexpectedly. In 1974, the benefit was equal to the full wage of the employee but it was reduced in 1995 to 80 per cent of the employee's salary. Under the 1995 Act, however, working fathers and working mothers were granted equal rights to the benefit, although the combined period of entitlement remained at 60 days.

Child-rearing leave and benefit In 1972, unpaid leave for child care was extended from one year to three years. It is available for a child up to three years old, and must be used up by the time that the child is four. This period may, however, be extended by another three years if the child's health demands its mother's individual care (a disabled, chronically ill or mentally retarded child, but only until the child is 18 years old). People who have been in employment for at least 6 months are entitled to child-rearing leave. Since 1981, an employee on child-rearing leave has also been entitled to a *child-rearing benefit*. Since 1992, both child-rearing leave and benefit may be assigned to people other than the child's mother, e.g. to the child's father provided he has the mother's permission and she is not intending to take this leave, and also to a working mother's husband who is not the child's father; to the father or some other member of the family who is looking after the child due to the mother's illness or death. An employee who has taken a child in foster care is also entitled to this leave and benefit. In 1992, the criteria on which benefits are granted were changed. Now, a benefit is granted when a family's per person income does not exceed 25 per cent of the average monthly industrial wage during the preceding year. In the case of lone parents, the threshold for benefit is 40 per cent of the average industrial wage. This benefit is paid for 24 months but in exceptional cases (care for a chronically ill or disabled child or for children from a multiple birth) it can extend for 36 or 72 months.

Benefits for pregnant and child-rearing women These benefits were introduced in 1993. They are available to families where the income per head does not exceed that of the lowest State benefit. A monthly benefit of 28 per cent of the average wage is paid for a period of four months, from the eighth month of pregnancy till the child is two months old. The person entitled has a right to the following:

- a monthly benefit of 28 per cent of the average wage for each child born at this time (women with no income receive a full benefit, but it is adjusted for others to ensure that the total available to the woman does not exceed 28 per cent of the average industrial wage);
- a bonus to buy baby-linen (14 per cent of the average wage);
- a refund of the medical costs of pregnancy, delivery and puerperium, and of treatment in public health care institutions;
- an application for a place in a welfare institution.

Benefits Associated with Child Maintenance

The benefits related to child maintenance include family allowances, nursing benefits, family pensions, and alimony funds.

Family allowance Its role is to supplement the income of a family in which children are being raised and maintained. Family allowance is granted till the child is 16 years old and, provided he continues his education, may be extended until the child is 20 years of age. This allowance is also to granted a spouse caring for a child entitled to a child-care benefit. Since 1995, family allowances have ceased to be social insurance benefits but are paid entirely out of the state budget. From the same date, the right to family allowance (for chidren or for a spouse) has been limited to those families whose per capita income does not exceed 50 per cent of the average industrial wage. Since 1996, these allowances have been revalued annually, in line with the index of price increases for goods and consumer services.

Nursing benefit This benefit is not connected with the family allowance. It is available to families with disabled children and paid at a rate equal to 10 per cent of the average wage. Nursing benefit is paid for a child under 16 if he requires constant nursing care, and regardless of age if his disability is classified as serious.

Family pension Upon the death of his parent a child is granted a dependents' pension until he is 16 years of age or, if he is studying, till the age of 25, and irrespective of age if he had become disabled before he was 16 years of age or during his education before he was 25 years old.

Alimony fund This fund was created in 1974, and the 1991 Act established the value of benefits granted to families in need who are unable to collect child support ordered by the court. This benefit is granted at the value of support currently fixed by the court, less than 30 per cent of the average industrial wage.

Commentators on social policy have concluded that family policy has not been adapted to the new conditions of the market economy in the 1990s (Golinowska 1995; Kurzynowski 1995; Balcerzak-Paradowska, 1995). The activities which were undertaken had a selective character and were not designed to deal with the situation of families in new and difficult socio-economic circumstances. Some of the actions owed less to the practical possibilities of their being implemented than to being symbolic responses to pressure exerted by political groups. For instance, after the anti-abortion bill had been signed into law, provisions for benefits to pregnant women were introduced although there were hardly any resources to pay them. In 1994, 314,291 women were entitled to pregnancy benefits but, by the end of that year, obligations towards 69,442 of them had not been met (Semenowicz and Antoszkiewicz ,1996, p.23).

During the period of transformation after 1989 the family allowances was subject to particular depreciation. Its real value decreased considerably. On the one hand, the category of people entitled to this allowance was extended to include the unemployed and students with children, but, on the other, the allowance for a student child was only paid until the child was 20 years of age (with the exception of disabled children). This allowance had previously been paid for student children until the age of 24 or, for undergraduates during the last year of their studies, even until the age of 25. The weighting of benefits payable in favour of larger families was also abolished and identical allowances fixed for each child. As reported by Golinowska (1995, p.253), in 1993, as compared to 1992, the real value of family allowance decreased by 20 per cent. The real value of the 1993 allowance was only about 60 per cent of that in 1989. The source of financing has also been changed. Family allowance is now paid out of the general state budget and not out of social security funds as was previously the case. Since 1995, families have been entitled to family allowance only if their per capita income is less than 50 per cent of the average industrial wage. Since 1996, allowances have been revalued annually.

A more consistent policy has been followed in the case of child-rearing benefit. The eligibility criteria for this benefit have not been changed and its value has been subject to quarterly indexation to pay levels. During the initial period after 1989, the real value increased (it almost doubled in 1990, and in 1991 it grew by about 30 per cent); later, it became more stable. At present, child-rearing benefit is the main form of support to families with young children. It is received during child-rearing leave for a period of 24 months.

In 1994, a special benefit for families with two unemployed parents was introduced. This benefit is paid until one parent has found work (Golinowska, 1995, p.253).

Family Policy and Family Life

The changes in the Polish economic system have been accompanied by phenomena which have had a negative impact on the functioning of families and on their living conditions. Wage disparities in the society have been growing. There is an increasing group of households whose living standards are very high but many other groups are being pauperized. Many families are losing the feeling of social security.

During the period of transformation, the greatest changes in family policy involved in-kind benefits. Institutions such as day nurseries and pre-schools became the responsibility of local authorities. However, the financial weakness of these bodies led to the closure of some institutions or an increase in fees. The situation was made worse by an obligation to subsidize child-care facilities provided outside the public sector by social organizations, religious groups, private persons and private employers. Since 1992, these preschools have received a subsidy from local authorities equal to half the cost of comparable state provision. The burden of this cost has made it difficult to sustain public facilities but the fees charged by the non-public institutions put them out of reach of parents on average incomes. Between 1990 and 1993, the number of public day nurseries dropped by 50 per cent and of nursery schools by 20 per cent (*Report on the Situation of Polish Families*, 1995, p.125). The closure of institutions was not entirely due to the financial difficulties of local government: there was also a reduced demand for their services. Other factors were operating here, both demographic - a decrease in the number of births - and economic - female unemployment and the impact of increased fees on the family budget. Between 1990 and 1993, the number of children in day nurseries decreased by 50 per cent and in nursery schools by over 10 per cent. Access to child-care facilities became particularly difficult for rural children and for six-year-olds seeking first step education (*Report on the Situation of Polish Families*, 1995, p.125).

The Main Census Bureau (GUS) has reported that, in 1996, as many as 49 per cent of families were living below the then social minimum. In comparison with the 1980s the regression is clearly noticeable. Between 1990 and 1994, the proportion of families living below the minimum was as follows: in 1990 and 1991 - about one-third; in 1992 - over 40 per cent; in 1993 - over 46 per cent; and in 1994 - nearly 50 per cent (Fudała 1996). The change in the socio-economic system in Poland has brought with it a high rate of unemployment. The *Report on the Situation of Polish Families* (1995, pp.22-35) shows that 62.5 per cent of the registered unemployed were in the 18-34 age group, i.e. at an age when people marry and become parents. More than half (54.8 per cent) of all unemployed people are women. The number of families with one or both parents unemployed has also increased. In 1994, more than 70 per cent of the households where one parent was unemployed contained a dependent child under 14 years of age.

The fact that families are living in a deteriorating economic situation is reflected in their debts. Households that had no previous difficulties are now facing problems with rent arrears or the repayment of housing credits and are being forced to move into smaller flats. They have problems satisfying their basic needs and can only purchase the cheapest food and clothing. Expenses on food and clothing have been reduced in 67 per cent of families. More and more families can afford neither holidays (57 per cent of families) nor payable forms of health care. Expenses on culture and education have also been reduced (Kowalska and Witkowski, 1995). The previously unknown phenomenon of child labour has appeared and children's earnings contribute to families' budgets. Polish families living in poverty belong to different categories. In 1994, households living in poverty comprised the following:

- 38.8 per cent of families with 4 or more children;
- 19.7 per cent of rural families;
- 19.3 per cent of families where the main earner was less than 34 years of age;
- 20.8 per cent of families in which the main earner had only elementary education (Fudała, 1996, pp.10-11).

Despite the existing regulations with respect to family policy there are discrepancies between theory and practice. This is particularly true in the case of job protection for women employees during pregnancy, in the period before and after delivery, during maternity leave and child-rearing. In studies carried out in 1996,[3] respondents claimed that, when group dismissals were contemplated, the first to be given notice were women on medical leave to care for their children. When an employer experienced economic difficulties, women on child-rearing leaves were dismissed and no protected work was made available to pregnant women: indeed, it was said, such women were even deliberately given hazardous work to encourage them to leave 'voluntarily'. A considerable number of respondents believed that breaches of women's employment rights were not unusual events (Tryfan, 1997 - research by the Centre for Public Opinion Studies). These findings are confirmed by comparison with earlier studies of women's re-entry into employment after maternity leave. The number of women who take up child-rearing leave is decreasing. In 1994, 60 per cent of mothers availed themselves of such leave, down from more than 83 per cent in 1988 (and 72 per cent in 1991). The reasons lie in the economic situation of families and in increasing uncertainty about the possibilities of re-entry into employment after maternity leave (Kurzynowski, 1995a, p.66). The main motives given for returning to work were economic - fear of losing a job or being compelled to take on a different one. The decision to take up child-rearing leave was mainly influenced by a woman's previous level of earnings and by her education: the lower their wages the more willing were women to take further leave and the higher their education the less willing were women to avail themselves of this right. Child-rearing leave was taken by 49 per cent of mothers with secondary and higher education, by 80 per cent of those with vocational education, and by about 69 per cent of those with elementary education (Kurzynowski, 1995a, p.66).

A 1996 survey of a nationally-representative sample examined attitudes to the current family policy. Only 12 per cent of respondents gave a positive opinion on current provision for families' needs. It should be emphasized, however, that, despite their critical opinion, respondents did not hold the state solely responsible for all difficulties experienced by the modern family. Just over half (57 per cent) divided this responsibility between the state and the family, and 35 per cent of them even believed that families themselves were responsible for their living standards. Just 6 per cent of the respondents said that the state should assume full responsibility. These results seem to reflect a departure in public consciousness from the idea of the welfare state. However, the respondents strongly emphasized their belief that state activities targeted at families in need were necessary. In a list of precedence of those deserving benefits, the first to be mentioned were families with disabled children (98 per cent of respondents); second were families afflicted with poverty, unemployment, diseases (87 per cent of respondents); third were lone-parent families (82 per cent of respondents) and multi-children families; and only then all other families with dependent children (44 per cent). With regard to the last group of families, opinion was split and nearly 50 per cent of the respondents thought that, probably or definitely, the state should not assist such families. In general, the state was expected to support families but not to relieve them of fulfilling their functions. Intervention was expected only in specific situations, e.g. when for external reasons families were unable to cope with their problems. In the opinion of the public, the responsibility for rearing children was the duty of the family. Support should be focussed on families with disabled children, families experiencing difficulties which had economic effects but not economic causes (e.g. sickness), and lone-parent families, especially single mothers. Support for families with larger numbers of children was more controversial (Tryfan, 1997). Respondents endorsed four types of support for families:

- Material help in the form of total or partial coverage of costs of child-

care and child-rearing facilities and opportunities for children to go on summer and winter holidays.
- An increase in family allowances, but related to the specific economic situation of the recipients.
- Support, in the form of cheap credits, to meet housing needs.
- Indirect financial support in the form of tax relief for children and credits for their education (Tryfan, 1995, p.15).

Commentators on social policy have emphasized the need for a proper pro-family policy, but have argued that this should be achieved mainly by increasing employment and ensuring income from this source is sufficient to meet a family's basic needs. Family policy should not take over the responsibility for the living conditions and fate of family members. Nevertheless, some elements of state support for families are not contested. State intervention is required to improve the housing situation, to ensure access to medical care and to ensure that children from less prosperous areas have equal educational opportunities. There is also a need to change the role of social workers and to use their knowledge and competence more effectively in support of families.

Conclusions

The new October 1997 Constitution includes duties on both national and local government to protect families in difficult social and economic situations and to protect the position and interests of motherhood (Article 71). Although the state has not withdrawn from its obligations towards the family, the period of transformation since 1989 has revealed a change in social policy. The state's welfare role has been reduced and more responsibility transferred to adult family members - the people who create a family are responsible for its fate. The 1990 Social Welfare Act emphasizes meeting the needs of the family as a whole and not of its particular members. The Act defines eligibility for benefits in terms of the average income per family member, thus creating a uniform criterion (Kurzynowski, 1995b, p.95). However, it has neither solved the problems of families in the new economic reality nor created a comprehensive family policy.

Writers on social policy (Graniewska and Balcerzak-Paradowska, 1995) assume that the Polish benefit systems in the sphere of maternity leave, childbirth benefits, and child-rearing leave stand out in comparison with other countries. There is little doubt that the introduction of regulations which give both the father and the mother equal rights to avail themselves of child-rearing leave and benefits has been very important. This will allow parents to share caring duties and choose a more advantageous solution. For instance, if child-rearing duties are undertaken by an unemployed father, the mother's salary will remain the same or, if the mother's earnings are higher, the family's income will not be much reduced if a father who earns less avails himself of the rights. Nevertheless, the policy of cash benefits has been directed mainly towards the needs of the poorest households. The economic situation of the country has contributed to the impoverishment of the population, reflected in the widening range of benefits for people on low wages. The proportion of social benefits in employees' incomes has increased and the proportion of family allowances in family incomes has decreased (Kurzynowski 1995b, p.98). The reduction and commercialization of child-care services, education and health care have limited families' possibilities to use these services. Social policy researchers have emphasized the negative impact of these measures on the development of the younger generation, especially on the opportunities for children from poorer families. Facilities such as preschools, day centres and public libraries not only have child-caring and educational functions but also serve to equalize the material and educational level of children from environments of lower economic status. If social policies do not appreciate the important role of the family in the reproduction of the society and take proper account of its needs, they will only reinforce the existing trends towards a reduction in the number of marriages and births.

Notes

1. Source of statistical data: *Statistical Yearbook of Demography*: 1994, pp.87, 142; 1995, p.121; 1996, p.XXXI, 113, 103, 162 - computation by the author. Also - *Raport 1996. Sytuacja demograficzna Polski* pp.27-41.
2. Centre for Public Opinion Studies, October 1993.
3. Surveys by the Centre for Public Opinion Studies - nationally-representative sample of 1097 respondents.

References

Balcerzak-Paradowska, B. (1995), 'Polityka społeczna na rzecz rodziny w Polsce', in Golinowska, S. and Balcerzak-Paradowska, B. (eds.), *Rodziny w Polsce*, IPiSS, Warsaw, pp.51-72.

Fudała, T. (1996), 'Skala polskiego ubóstwa', *Problemy Rodziny*, No 4, pp.9-11.

Golinowska, S. (1995), 'Przemiany w warunkach życia polskich rodzin w okresie transformacji', in Golinowska, S. and Balcerzak-Paradowska, B. (eds.), *Rodziny w Polsce*, IPiSS, Warsaw, pp.243-56.

Graniewska, D. and Balcerzak-Paradowska, B. (1995), 'Świadczenia społeczne dla rodziny', in Kurzynowski, A. (ed.), *Rodzina w okresie transformacji systemowej*, WSP TWP, Warsaw, pp.77-106.

Kowalska, A. and Witkowski, J. (1995), 'Rodziny z osobą bezrobotną', in Golinowska, S and Balcerzak-Paradowska, B. (eds.) *Rodziny w Polsce*, IPiSS, Warsaw, pp.123-32.

Kurzynowski, A. (1995a), 'Sytuacja materialna a bezpieczeństwo ekonomiczne rodzin', in Kurzynowski, A. (ed.), *Rodzina w okresie transformacji systemowej*, WSP TWP, Warsaw, pp.57-76.

Kurzynowski, A. (1995b), 'Polityka rodzinna - stan i potrzeby', in Auleytner, J. (ed.), *Polityka społeczna - stan i perspektywy*, WSP TWP, Warsaw, pp.91-105.

Raport o sytuacji polskich rodzin (1995), Pełnomocnik rządu ds. rodziny i kobiet, Warsaw.

Raport 1996: Sytuacja demograficzna Polski (1996), Rządowa Komisja Ludnościowa, Warsaw.

Semenowicz, A. and Antoszkiewicz, D. (1996), 'Elementy ochrony rodziny w polskim ustawodawstwie', in *Wybrane zagadnienia z zakresu polityki rodzinnej - część I*, Biuro Studiów i Analiz Kancelarii Senatu, Warsaw, No. 308 (R-6/96), pp.11-25.

Statistical Yearbook of Demography (1994, 1995, 1996), Central Statistical Office, Warsaw.

Tradycyjny czy partnerski model rodziny (1993), Centrum Badania Opinii Społecznej, Warsaw, październik 1993.

Tryfan, B. (1997), 'Potrzeby i zagrożenia rodzin w Polsce w okresie transformacji', *Problemy Rodziny*, No 1-2, pp.5-15.

5 Social Policy and the Family in the United Kingdom
Gillian Pascall

New Labour, New Family?

The Labour government elected on 1 May 1997 is the first since 1979. It has called itself 'New Labour' to mark its distance from a collectivist and union-dominated past and the air is full of talk not just of a new Labour but of a new Britain. Will there be anything new about Labour's policy relating to the family?

Since Labour was last in office, families have been changing rapidly. Cohabitation among 18 to 49-year old women has increased three-fold since 1979, reaching a rate of one in ten by 1995/96 (ONS, 1997, p.15). Divorce rates began rising in the 1960s: in 1961 they were 2.1 per thousand married population and during the Thatcher/Major era they became the highest in Europe, reaching 13.4 per thousand (ONS, 1997, Table 1.17; CSO, 1996, Tables 2.16, 2.17). The proportion of children living in lone parent families was rising when Labour went out of office in 1979 and has more than doubled since, to 22 per cent of all children (ONS, 1997, Chart 1.29). These trends have radically reshaped the 'breadwinner model' of the family, in which men's incomes were matched by women's caring responsibilities. While marriage breakdown has put a special strain on this traditional family, demographic change has also added pressure on its capacity to care. Some commentators see these changes as marking an unambiguous decline in the family, although others evaluate them more more ambiguously (Fox Harding 1996). Certainly the implications for different family members are different. Such changes are widespread (Spain and Bianchi 1996, Kwak in this volume), but in the UK these trends are deeper and more established than in many other industrialized countries.

The speed of family change has not been matched by change in the ways social policies relate to the family. Some of these are still recognizable from the immediate post-war era. National Insurance - the centrepiece of the social security system established in the 1940s - continues to assume male breadwinner/female carer families. In this system, women tend to be disadvantaged by contribution rules and earn no pensions or lower pensions. Women's increasing attachment to the labour market did not bring significant policy development in child care under Thatcher or Major governments. Lone parents have been caught between the labour market, caring responsibilities and a benefits system designed for married men. A gap has opened between changes in the family and changes in policies relating to the family, as measures rooted in the 1940s have altered much less than the society to which they relate.

While it is already clear what is new about New Labour in consitutional matters, it is less clear what direction social policies relating to the family might take. There are a number of potential strands of influence. The women's movement is one source of ideas. It has generated new thinking on caring work and parenting, on the division of labour, and on power and violence in marriage and other intimate relationships. It has been a source of political action within the Labour movement. But it is not the only influence on thinking and political action about the family and gender relations. Thatcherism's influence on economic thought has spread tentacles into New Labour, and there is evidence that Thatcherite thinking about the family has also had an impact. Older traditions survive in the Parliamentary Labour Party with continuing support for the collectivist approach of the post-war era. All of these might be expected to lead to a restatement of traditional values and a support for traditional family forms.

This chapter examines the historic shape given to social policy relating to the family at key moments since the Second World War and asks which elements of these traditions are likely to survive and whether new Labour has anything new to offer. Policy relating to lone parents will be treated as a critical case. Lone parents stand outside traditional family patterns, threaten the notion of traditional families, and are growing in number. Britain is also ahead in this field, with more lone parents than other European countries. The response is thus an indicator of family policy in general apart from being a pressing issue in its own right.

The Beveridge Family

The post-war era's influence on British social policy continues, despite half a century of rapid social change. This period saw the foundation of the National

Health Service, universal secondary education, and a comprehensive design for social security. These children of the 1945-51 Labour government have been often reformed but remain recognizable.

Sir William Beveridge made a significant contribution to this project, through his war-time report on social insurance, though he was neither a Labour supporter nor a member of the government which implemented his key proposals. Since Blair claims the Liberal Beveridge as much as the Socialist Bevan among his heroes, his ideas may have a special salience in the New Labour programme. Beveridge drew on principles of self-help and national efficiency, but his view of gender roles in the family was even more deeply inscribed through subsequent social provision. The Beveridge report proposed a social security system with National Insurance at its centre: contributions from employees and employers were to fund benefits in sickness, unemployment and old age. Men contributed on behalf of themselves, their wives and their families. Married women were not expected to earn, and had more important duties: 'In the next thirty years housewives as mothers have vital work to do in ensuring the adequate continuance of the British race and of British ideals in the world' (Beveridge, 1942, p.53). Married women were expected to depend on their husbands for income, housing and National Insurance contributions. The same ideals also underpinned child care policy, as wartime nurseries were closed and mothers assumed to be available to care for children under five and for older children in out-of-school periods.

The assumptions, that married women's paid employment was insignificant and that they could turn to men for support, did not wholly reflect the realities of the 1940s. They reflected family and employment realities ever less as married women joined the labour market, men's employment became less secure and marriage breakdown became more common. By the 1970s Labour governments were making some response to these changes, with equal opportunities and sex discrimination legislation aiming to improve women's position in paid employment. Changes to enhance women's contributory status in National Insurance were a significant feature of social security policy. Old Labour gave some support to women's employment rights but their caring duties remained intact. While Scandinavian and Eastern European countries were developing child care and parental leave policies to support women's paid employment (Leira, 1993, Kwak in this volume), challenging the traditional breadwinner pattern, British social policy clung to the assumptions of two-parent families and women's primary role as mothers. Women's responsibility for care and their status as family members were underlined by the rules for Invalid Care Allowance, which was not available to married women on the grounds that they would be at home anyway (Pascall, 1997a). The main thrust of equal opportunities policy concerned paid work, giving a better deal to women at work, but not challenging the patterns of family responsibility that gave unequal access to the labour market and made them dependent in marriage. By the end of Labour's last period of office it was becoming commonplace to criticize government family policy as assuming and supporting a breadwinner/carer two-parent form which was no longer a social norm.

The underside of this approach was the social exclusion of those whose living arrangements did not conform to the assumed model. Divorce and separation undermined married women's security, but the social security scheme could not cope with them. Unmarried motherhood was a social and economic catastrophe, to be avoided by adoption. Adoptions peaked at 27,000 in 1968, during the 'permissive' sixties, as pregnant women disguised their condition and avoided the economic and social perils of motherhood outside marriage. The situation of lone parents began to improve in the 1970s, when the Finer Committee (1974) was established to investigate their situation - though its proposals were not implemented - and 'unmarried mothers' became 'one parent families'. The Domestic Violence and Homeless Persons' Acts recognised the housing needs of women escaping domestic violence (Morley and Pascall, 1996). Lone mothers' support through means-tested benefits was improved. By the time Margaret Thatcher was elected in 1979, the position of lone mothers had been eased. But they were still outsiders in a social policy system designed for couples with male breadwinners.

The Thatcher/Major Family

The election of the Thatcher government brought a rupture with the assumptions that had been held by other post-war governments: of welfare collectivism and of a very gradual liberalization of the moral climate - with changes in laws relating to homosexuality, divorce, abortion and lone parents. Thatcherism did not bring these trends to an immediate close, but it did announce a reaction to them. It blamed collectivist welfare policies for changes in the moral climate and in the family. Collectivist welfare policies were thought to have removed responsibility from the family, undermining masculinity through undermining male breadwinning. Housing and benefits policies were blamed for the rise in lone parenthood, as it was argued that they encouraged women to seek financial support outside the family by becoming pregnant and living on benefits in public housing (Murray, 1990, Davies, 1993). Lone parents became a focus for anxieties about family change and were blamed for the creation of an 'underclass' (Roseneil and Mann, 1996; Pascall, 1997b).

Thatcherism had two core elements. Hayekian Liberalism led to public expenditure restraint and marketization of a wide array of previously public functions. This economic liberalism was the driving force of Thatcherism. Its critique of public expenditure led to an emphasis on family responsibility as a social safety net. It was combined with a more traditional conservatism which brought a social policy agenda based on 'the patriarchal family as the bedrock of the social order' (Lovenduski and Randall, 1993, p.34). Both were implicated in the famous Thatcher remark that 'there is no such thing as society; there are only individuals, and families'. Mrs Thatcher argued the need to 'strengthen the family' to avoid 'heart-rending social problems which no government could possibly cure' (quoted in Wicks, 1991). John Major followed with his ill-fated 'back to basics' campaign. From 1979 onwards, the UK had seventeen years in which the active restoration of the traditional family in structure, responsibilities and roles, was at the heart of government ideology.

Thatcherite family policy in practice was not always so consistent. Where its economic and social philosophies combined, support for traditional family life was clear. This happened over policies for reducing public expenditure and involvement in health care, for example, where government papers noted a convenient consonance between moral and financial ambitions: 'helping carers to maintain their valuable contribution to the spectrum of care is both right and a sound investment (DoH, 1989). The Child Support Act similarly aimed at 'clarifying and highlighting parental responsibility' for securing children's welfare as it sought to put more of the cost on parents (DSS, 1990, Foreword). But more often the government's aims for the family were undermined by economic policy: women were drawn into paid employment, men's breadwinning security was lost through policies for flexible labour markets, and housing was subjected to extreme market fluctuations. Parents' ability to sustain a secure environment for their children was compromised.

Thatcherite governments sought to sustain traditional families, while their period of office was characterized by family change, especially the growth of lone parent families. One response was to try to recreate traditional responsibilities, with absent parents - mainly fathers - being brought back to their breadwinning role through the Child Support Act. Another was to try to persuade women to avoid lone parenthood, by paring benefits and by reducing access to social housing through the homelessness legislation. In a real break with the past, a third strategy was to encourage lone parents to support themselves and their children through paid employment, by changing the rules for Family Credit (a benefit designed to supplement low wage families) and making it more accessible to parents who combine childcare with paid work. But perhaps the most prominent policy was an ideological attack, blaming lone parents for their own plight as well as for a range of other social ills - young criminality and the creation of an 'underclass' (Murray, 1990). Lone parents were seen as people who made choices - to become pregnant, to keep their babies, to avoid or leave marriages. The solution was to make the lone parent choice as unpalatable as possible by restricting social support and seeking to recreate the stigma of the first thirty post-war years.

The Women's Movement and the Family

The clearest source of radical thinking about the family has been the women's movement. In the 1970s, this focussed on demands for equal pay, equal education and opportunity, child care, free contraception and abortion on demand, financial and legal independence for women, a woman's right to choose her own sexuality, freedom from intimidation by threat or use of violence or sexual coercion (Lovenduski and Randall, 1993). For a brief period, these were claims agreed at national meetings. In the longer term, they have been debated and disputed, but they still form a recognizable agenda for various political groups which have had some allegiance to the women's movement. They have also infiltrated workplace, family, social services and public politics. With its demands for equal pay, education and opportunity, this agenda was partly about women's position in public life. But some demands also represented an attack on the Beveridge family. This was seen as patriarchal, in its assumptions of women's caring responsibilities and structured financial dependence and its emergent dark side of violence against women.

The women's movement had some influence through Labour governments in the 1970s. This was mainly on the public agenda, with legislation on sex discrimination and equal opportunities. The challenge to the Beveridge family was less successful: women were still seen primarily as mothers/caregivers, with minimal state involvement in childcare. But legislation assisting women to escape domestic violence showed that the preservation of the traditional family could take second place to other policy goals and was a direct result of women's movement activism (Morley, 1993).

At this period the labour movement and party were powerfully male

Social Policy and the Family in the United Kingdom 79

dominated. There were never more than 30 women MPs out of around six hundred in any UK parliament until 1987. The substantial increase in women's representation in parliament and government since May 1997 - with now 120 MPs - gives reason to suppose that the influence of the women's movement might be stronger than in the 1970s. Clear evidence that the women's movement has influenced significant Labour politicians and academics comes in publications such as Harman's *The Century Gap*, (1993), Hewitt's (1993) critique of gendered working practices in *About Time* and Tessa Jowell's (1996) *Strategy for Women*, written for the Labour Party.

The Blair Family

How are these histories and ideological currents reflected in New Labour now it is in government? In what measure is Labour looking to its own past, to established Thatcherite policy and practice, and to more radical currents from the women's movement reflected through the significantly increased representation of women in government?

New Labour has learned some lessons from old. Old Labour's position could be encapsulated as actively promoting sex equality in public life while resisting or responding reluctantly to pressures to change private life. New Labour also has an opportunities agenda, seeing employment as vital for both men and women. With one exception - support for child care so that mothers can enter the labour market - it has not yet shown any enthusiasm for policies reflecting family change.

One of Thatcherism's success stories was the infiltration of its ideology about public expenditure and families across the political divide. How does this affect family policy? The Blair government was elected on a promise not to increase taxes. This implies that there will be no shifting back of boundaries between state and family responsibility for a range of areas from nursing care of elderly people to financial responsibility for young people. In particular, the Labour party seems as wary as its predecessors about responsibility for care (Commission for Social Justice, 1994). Thatcherite and Labour governments have been interested in supporting care work where it can be seen to enhance labour market participation: both have adopted policies supporting child care to persuade lone parents to support themselves through paid work. But neither Thatcher nor Blair governments have found resources for supporting care work outside these circumstances.

The Thatcherite critique of lone parents has also had wide support, with ideas promulgated by the Institute of Economic Affairs - a right-wing thinktank - being taken up by the liberal media to ask 'who killed the family?'. Academics who would define themselves as politically left-wing have shared Murray's concern that 'families without fathers produce egoists' (Dennis and Erdos, 1992/3, pp.70-1) and criticized the left for its individualism in relation to the family (Halsey, 1992, pp.xi-xii). Frank Field - now a Labour social security minister - used the underclass language in *Making Welfare Work* (1995) with a section on 'the rise and rise of single parents' expressing special concern about growing numbers of never-married mothers. Field does not go so far as Murray and other IEA writers in describing these women as the engine of an underclass of male crime and violence. Social polarization and the spread of means tests are more central to Field's argument but he adopts a moral tone which echoes Murray, appearing to stigmatize lone mothers as feckless parents:

> What the social and psychological impact is on children spending their leisure hours watching television with a whole sequence of male partners sitting behind them is impossible to judge at this stage (Field 1995, p.111).

Blair claims modernity, recognizing the perils of 'preaching to individuals about their private lives' and stopping short of describing lone parents as the engine of the underclass. But he echoes the Thatcherite critique of lone parents in his account of family crisis in this Labour Party Conference speech, in a passage beginning with teenage pregnancy and moving through a series of social ills. The lack of syntax in the following quotation avoids commitment to the logically connected sequence of the underclass theorists, but the juxtapositions make it hard to avoid the implication that teenage pregnancies have a lot to answer for:

> Nearly 100,000 teenage pregnancies every year; elderly parents with whom families cannot cope; children growing up without role models they can respect and learn from; more and deeper poverty; more crime; more truancy; more neglect of educational opportunities, and above all more unhappiness (Tony Blair's speech to Labour Party Conference, *The Guardian*, 1 October 1997, p.8).

Blair ends this passage professing his desire to support families in terms reminiscent of Mrs Thatcher herself:

> Every area of this government's policy will be scrutinised to see how it

Social Policy and the Family in the United Kingdom 81

affects family life. Every policy examined, every initiative tested, every avenue explored to see how we strengthen our families (Tony Blair's speech to Labour Party Conference, *The Guardian* 1 October 1997, p.8).

Blair does not say which families are to be strengthened.

Some changes to government structures reflect a women's movement agenda, with a Minister for Women, a Cabinet sub-committee for women and a women's unit within the Civil Service. There is a new twist to family policy as child care has, for the first time in UK policy history since World War Two, become a high profile part of the government agenda. The primacy given in Labour party strategy to flexibility of work, parental leave, and child care seems to be a clear result of the increase in women party activists, and the influence of the women's movement. These policies could enable parents - especially lone parents - to combine paid work and family commitments more easily. They have support from lone parents' organizations and more widely. The policies amount to an acceptance that care work can be a significant obstacle to paid employment. Here New Labour accepts a new view of family roles: the long held assumption that women's key roles are as housewives and carers who look to men for economic support has been dislodged. But the driving force behind the change is a desire to increase women's employment as a means of reducing the social security bill for lone parents. In so far as New Labour policies endorse newer family roles they are following well behind established trends, rather than proposing a radical agenda for a new family. The women's movement's critique of women's dependence, of the patriarchal family and of male violence are less in evidence.

Policy relating to lone parents has proved the first divisive issue for the Blair government. At the end of 1997 Ministers decided to carry through benefit cuts planned by the previous administration. Their key defence was that women should support themselves and their children and that they would be helped to do so. Critics argued that the benefit changes hindered this objective, saved little money, and were punitive to mothers and children when paid employment was not a realistic possibility. The critics won the argument but, despite serious rebellion among their own MPs, the government won the vote as mothers stood outside Parliament wearing T-shirts proclaiming 'All mothers are workers'. This was the first serious test of the extent to which the women's movement agenda has permeated New Labour thinking and it became clear that mothers were to be supported as paid workers but not as carers. While this openness to the equal opportunities element of the women's movement agenda echoes earlier Labour administrations, the resistance to acknowledging that motherhood is work goes beyond previous positions and suggests a very limited absorption of the movement's wider agenda.

The lone parent benefit decision was also the first serious test of what the Blair government means by 'supporting families' and it became clear that lone parent families would not be included. These decisions move policy further away from government support for the work of parenthood and towards government support for particular kinds of families. Blair the modernizer is supporting a very traditional idea of the family, owing much to the traditions of the Thatcher/Major era and little to the women's movement.

Conclusion

A Blair government is likely to draw on a range of sources for its ideas about the family and the directions of family policy. The social politics of earlier Labour administrations may not be yet obliterated. Thatcherite economic policies dictate a non-spending policy on care work and the Thatcherite lone parent agenda indicates a desire to strengthen 'traditional' families. A strong women's presence among MPs and, to a lesser extent, ministers may provide a counter to family conservatism. New Labour's seven months of office are not enough for more than a provisional judgement, but how may these influences weigh in the balance?

There is some evidence that the Blair government wants to tap into the change that has been brought about by new social movements such as the women's movement. The moral climate is more forgiving than it was in the post-war or Thatcher/Major eras. The election manifesto acknowledges that not all the changes that have affected families are detrimental or could be reversed:

> The clock should not be turned back. As many women who want to work should be able to do so. More equal relationships between men and women have transformed our lives. Equally, our attitudes to race, sex and sexuality have changed fundamentally (Labour 1997, p.25).

The first few months of the Labour government have faced Blair with choices as a minister and Labour MPs have come out as homosexual and the first marital crisis hit the cabinet. There has been no repeat of Major's mistakes in claiming too much moral high ground. It seems that Blair's modernizing stance will bring some acceptance of family change in place of the search for

'Victorian values'.
Old Labour's policy eased the stringent lot of lone parents. New Labour perceives lone parents both as victims and as generators of social disruption. Lone parenthood may be a little less stigmatized under a modernizing government. Lone parents will be helped - and expected - to help themselves as 'compassion with a hard edge' brings policies for lone parents which add employment duty to family duty. But the manifesto's acceptance of some family change has a counterweight. It describes the task as 'to combine change and social stability' (Labour, 1997, p.25). The inclusion of Beveridge in Blair's pantheon, and the echo of Thatcher in his language of family crisis suggest something other than 'a modern man leading a modern country' in thinking about the family.

The clearest and most critical evidence of the direction of New Labour policy in practice has been offered by the lone parent benefit decision. The surface politics were about turning welfare mothers into paid workers by cutting benefit levels. But, since the policy logic for the proposals did not add up to a genuine encouragement to enter the labour market, it is tempting to detect a family conservatism which would rather deter women from becoming lone mothers than offer state support to those outside traditional families. There is no radical departure here from the Thatcher/Major agenda for family policy but its continuation. The surface of New Labour draws from new social movements and looks towards its new women MPs and ministers for an image of modernity. But the decision to go ahead with cuts to lone parent benefits shows a deeper core of traditional support for traditional families, drawing from Beveridge and the Thatcherite right rather than the women's movement.

References

Beveridge, W. (1942), *Social Insurance and Allied Services*, Cmnd 6404, HMSO: London.
Central Statistical Office (1996), *Social Trends*, HMSO: London.
Commission on Social Justice (1994), *Social Justice: Strategies for National Renewal*, Vintage: London.
Davies, J. (1993), *The Family: Is it just another lifestyle choice?*, Institute of Economic Affairs: London.
Dennis, N. and Erdos, G. (1992/3), *Families without Fatherhood*, Institute of Economic Affairs: London.
Department of Health (1989), *Caring for People - Community Care in the Next Decade and Beyond*, HMSO: London.
Department of Social Security (1990), *Children Come First*, HMSO: London.
Field, F. (1995), *Making Welfare Work*, Institute of Community Studies: London.

Finer, M. (1974), *Report of the Committee on One-Parent Families*, HMSO: London.
Fox Harding, L. (1996), *Family, State and Social Policy*, Macmillan: London.
Halsey, A. H. (1992), 'Foreword', in Dennis, N. and Erdos, G., *Families Without Fatherhood*, Institute of Economic Affairs: London.
Harman, H. (1993), *The Century Gap*, Vermillion: London.
Hewitt, P. (1993), *About Time: The Revolution in Work and Family Life*, Rivers Oram/IPPR: London.
Jowell, T. (1996), *Strategy for Women*, The Labour Party: London.
Labour (1997), *new Labour because Britain deserves better. The Labour Party Manifesto*, The Labour Party: London.
Leira, A. (1993), 'The "Woman-Friendly" Welfare State? The Case of Norway and Sweden', in Lewis, J. (ed.), *Women and Social Policies in Europe: Work, Family and the State*, Edward Elgar: Aldershot.
Lovenduski, J. and Randall, V. (1993), *Contemporary Feminist Politics: Women and Power in Britain*, Oxford University Press: Oxford.
Morley, R. (1993), 'Recent Responses to Domestic Violence against Women: a Feminist Critique', in Page, R. (ed.), *Social Policy Review 5*, Social Policy Association: Canterbury.
Morley, R. and Pascall, G. (1996), 'Women and Homelessness: Proposals from the Department of the Environment II - Domestic Violence', *Journal of Social Welfare and Family Law*, Vol.18, No. 3, pp.327-40.
Murray, C. (1990), *The Emerging British Underclass*, Institute of Economic Affairs: London.
Office of National Statistics (1997), *Social Focus on Families*, The Stationery Office: London.
Pascall, G. (1997a), *Social Policy: A New Feminist Analysis*, Routledge: London.
Pascall, G. (1997b), 'Women and the Family in the British Welfare State: The Thatcher/Major Legacy', *Social Policy and Administration*, Vol. 31, No. 3, pp.290-305.
Roseneil, S. and Mann, K. (1996), 'Unpalatable choices and inadequate families: lone mothers and the underclass debate', in Silva, E.B. (ed.), *Good Enough Mothering? Feminist Perspectives on Lone Motherhood*, Routledge: London.
Spain, D. and Bianchi, S. (1996), *Balancing Act: Motherhood, Marriage, and Employment among American Women*, Russell Sage Foundation: New York.
Wicks, M. (1991), 'Social Politics 1979-1992: Families, Work and Welfare', Unpublished paper presented to Social Policy Association Conference.

6 Changes in Prison Policy as a Part of Political and Economic Transformation in Poland

Andrzej Mościskier

June 1989 is widely believed to have been a turning point in the Polish political situation. Following a spectacular election victory by the Solidarity movement, the first democratic government was formed with Tadeusz Mazowiecki as prime minister and a landslide of political and economic reforms started, marking an unprecedented peaceful transformation from a communist to a democratic political system and from a planned to a market economy. It is interesting that, almost from the beginning of this general transformation, profound changes also took place in the criminal justice system, in general, and the prison system, in particular. This may be understood as a rational phenomenon if one takes into account that the criminal justice system in the communist world played an essential role in the general system of political and social control. Leaving it untouched would have meant either obstruction to the democratic process or submerging criminal justice into deep chaos and ineffectiveness. However, it must be remembered that - if one excludes the Stalinist period - the criminal justice system in Poland had never been as completely totalitarian as in other communist countries, so adapting it to the demands of the new situation was certainly easier than elsewhere. Nonetheless, if one wants to understand problems that face the criminal justice system in a post-communist country, some facts from the past have to be recalled.

As has already been noted, the criminal justice system in communist countries played an essential role in controlling and intimidating the population. But it also played an important role in the economy and ideology of the society.

From an economic point of view, the criminal justice system provided a cheap source of forced labour, which was particularly useful in unpopular branches of production and construction. When one of the communist prime ministers of Poland was urged by a group of academics to limit the prison population, he became quite concerned and answered seriously: 'Gentlemen, I would like to grant your request, but then who would actually be doing any work in Poland'.

From an ideological point of view, the communist system was expected not to have any social and economic bases for social pathology, so phenomena such as crime should either not exist at all or, at least, should gradually die away in time. This 'relic theory', which Soviet criminologists were obliged to adopt until the 1970s, and which remained in favour until much later, claimed that the only cause of crime was class struggle. In classless socialist and communist societies, therefore, it had no causal basis and should vanish with the dying out of class enemies and those whose morals had been corrupted by the former capitalist system. This view, of the perpetrators of crimes as class enemies, was the origin of the severe punitiveness of the communist justice system, later bolstered by the demand for forced labour.

The combined effects of the intimidating function of the criminal justice system, its punitiveness, and the demand for forced labour tremendously inflated the prison population. Overpopulated prisons were always one of the major problems of the communist criminal justice system. The most popular method of solving this problem was through regular amnesties which allowed considerable numbers of prisoners to be released and the prison population to be reduced for some time. For example in Poland, from the implementation of the Criminal Code in 1970, which is still in effect today, amnesties were granted in 1974, 1977, 1981, 1983, 1984, 1986 and 1989. Amnesty was the principal method of controlling the size of the prison population in the communist system. For example, as a result of the 1974 amnesty, the number of prisoners diminished temporarily from about 124,000 to about 81,000. The most recent amnesty, in 1989, reduced the prison population from 67,800 to about 40,000.

In Poland, as in other post communist countries, an excessive prison population, and its consequences, are central problems for current penal policy. They cannot finally be resolved until a new Criminal Code, compatible with European standards in its level of punitiveness, is implemented. A new Criminal Code was approved by the parliament in the middle of 1997 and will be probably implemented in 1998. This should lead to improvements in the future but the present situation remains difficult.

The post-war peak in the prison population was reached in 1973, when 124,685 people were in custody, a rate of 390 prisoners per 100,000 population. On average, up to the late eighties, the number of prisoners oscillated between 90,000 - 110,000, a rate of about 300 prisoners per 100,000 population. On average, up to the late eighties, the number of prisoners oscillated between 90,000 - 110,000, a rate of about 300 prisoners per 100,000 population. This was one of the highest in the world and unparalleled in Europe, except of course, in other Soviet bloc countries. At that time prison overcrowding, often exceeding human endurance, was a permanent problem and varied only in its scale and in the extent of the resulting hardships. Since the late eighties, there has been some reduction of the prison population, as illustrated in table 6.1.

Table 6.1 Polish Prison Population (1987-1995) Numbers and Rates per 100,000 population

	Number	Rate
1987	91140	255.1
1988	67824	212.4
1989	40321	106.2
1990	50165	131.6
1991	58619	153
1992	61409	159.2
1993	61562	160
1994	62719	158.3
1995	61136	158.3

According to the above data some reduction of the prison population (about 30 per cent) has taken place in the few last years, but the numbers still remain high. The rate of imprisonment per 100,000 population, which continues to be over 150, is almost twice the average for the whole of Europe. In 1988, this was calculated at 78.2 per 100,000 population. The 1990 rates for some major European countries are shown in Table 6.2.

In recent years remands in custody have accounted for between 23 and 27 per cent of the total prison population. About 80 per cent of this group spend less than three months on remand during preparatory proceedings and it rarely takes more than six months for a case to come to trial. Before 1990 both processes were much slower.

Table 6.2 Prison Populations as Rates per 100,000 Population Selected European Countries (1990)

	Rate
Hungary	110
Northern Ireland	109.5
England	93.3
France	82.2
Turkey	82.1
West Germany	77.8
Norway	56.5
Greece	48.7
Netherlands	44.4
Iceland	40.6

About 30 per cent of sentenced offenders are serving terms of 1 to 2 years, with another 20 per cent serving 2 to 3 years, 19 per cent serving 3 to 5 years and 10 per cent serving 5 to 10 years. There were 45,725 sentenced offenders in prisons on 31 December 1993, of whom 1,293 (3 per cent) had been sentenced to a term between 10 and 15 years and 643 were serving a term of 25 years - there is no current provision for life imprisonment, although this will be introduced when the new 1997 Criminal Code comes into effect in 1998. About 60 per cent of sentenced prisoners are repeat offenders, who have served previous prison terms. Women make up 2 per cent of prisoners, a small minority (altogether 1,200-1,400 prisoners). They serve their terms in separate prisons, with a specially mitigated regime.

As the above data indicate, despite the considerable reduction in the number of prisoners in Poland in recent years, there are still too many. The

Polish criminal justice system undoubtedly continues to be unreasonably punitive. It does not mean that efforts have not been made to change the situation. Until the old 1969 Criminal Code is replaced, however, these efforts cannot be entirely successful. The 1969 Criminal Code does not contain enough alternatives to prison, sets minimum punishments at too high a level (three months although in practice the courts usually impose six) and requires extended or maximum sentences in too many cases. The implementation of this code in 1970 brought a very sharp rise in the average length of prison sentences, from 13.2 months in 1965 to 25.9 months in 1985 and later, after the implementation of some new bills passed under martial law, to 27.3 months. Unfortunately, that punitive penal policy established itself not only in legislative practice but also in the consciousness of the general public and of public prosecutors and judges. It has not been easy to shift without a base in the form of a new and much more liberal legal code. It is not surprising, then, that the length of an average sentence has only declined slowly. In 1990 it was 26 months and in 1996 still 25.3 months.

The continuation of punitive penal policies by criminal courts can be partly explained by the way that democratization has been accompanied by an upsurge in the level of criminality. If we take, for statistical reasons, 1990 as the turning point from one economic-political system to the other in Poland, we see a steep rise in total numbers of crimes. In 1989 the police recorded 547,589 offences: in 1990, this rose to 883,346, an increase of 61 per cent. Comparing the 5-year periods 1985-89 and 1990-94, recorded crime has increased by 70 per cent. Moreover, since 1990, both the numbers and rates of recorded crime have reached the highest levels ever seen in the history of Polish criminal statistics. Serious crimes have shown the greatest increase. For example, the number of homicides more than doubled, from 556 in 1989 to 1,134 in 1996. Robberies with the use of fire-arms increased eleven-fold, from 140 to 1,519. In these circumstances it is difficult to expect that, without essential changes in criminal law, the average length of prison sentences could significantly diminish. As has already been mentioned, a new and more liberal Criminal Code, which is closer to international standards has already passed in the parliament. When it comes into effect in 1998, the number of prisoners will probably go down. The new criminal code rationalizes the penalty of deprivation of liberty by reducing the minimum penalty to one month and increases possibilities of employing alternative means of punishment which do not involve a loss of liberty.

Some changes in this direction have already started in advance of the new Code. For example, in 1995, some changes were enacted in relation to the regulation of detention awaiting trial. The main change was the elimination of the broadly used principle that detention awaiting trial may be applied when a suspect was charged with an act of 'considerable social dangerousness' - a very vague formulation. The same act took away from public prosecutors the power to detain a person awaiting trial and placed it in the hands of the courts, who were also empowered to restrict the length of time that detention could be used. The introduction of these regulations reduced the numbers of people detained awaiting trail by over 2,000 (about 13 per cent).

The same act also introduced three other regulations that attacked the problem of overcrowded prisons. They allowed:

- The use of suspended sentences and its extension to penalties imposed as a result of non-compliance with others: for example an unpaid fine need not lead directly to a loss of liberty but the more severe sentence may be suspended to give the offender a further opportunity to comply with the original sentence.
- Conditional release in cases of where imprisonment has been substituted for some other penalty.
- The use of community work projects as an alternative to fines.
- More court discretion in deciding on the level and use of fines as a penalty.

As a result of this act, the number of conditional releases has risen considerably, and the number of sentenced prisoners has been reduced by about 13 per cent, from 47,200 to 41,100.

The new Criminal Code rationalizes the use of imprisonment by, on the one hand, making shorter sentences possible and, on the other, by expanding the possibilities for using alternative punishments. It is generally believed that it will markedly reduce the prison population in Poland.

In the new Criminal Code of 1997, the most general penal sanction will be imprisonment for a term of 1 month to 3 years (a term unavailable under the 1969 code). The other categories available, in diminishing order of frequency, are terms from 3 months to 5 years, from 6 months to 8 years, from 1 to 10 years, and from 3 to 15 years. Capital punishment has been abolished and replaced by a life sentence.

The new Criminal Code restores the principle that penalties not involving the loss of liberty should be preferred to those involving imprisonment. In any case where the maximum penalty does not exceed five years imprisonment, the court may impose a fine or a period of restricted liberty rather than a jail sentence. The courts may also substitute a community work sanction as an alternative where the maximum penalty for an offence is a prison term of less than three years. They have also been given greater discretion to impose sentences below the minimum levels specified in the Code where they consider that this would be appropriate.

These legislative changes will make it possible to use alternatives to prison on a large scale. The Code also provides regulations which will reduce the length of stays in prison. It is expected that implementation will reduce the prison population to less than 40,000.

Communist penal doctrine did not treat the deprivation of liberty as the sole dimension of imprisonment as a punishment. The conditions of the prison regime were also part of the sanction, particularly, its demonstration that the prisoner was living under poorer conditions than those outside. Remands in custody were used in anticipation of future penalties, for purely repressive purposes. This philosophy of imprisonment led to the overcrowding of prisons and the neglect of hygienic and sanitary conditions leading to the violation of basic human and civil rights. Before 1989 the minimum area per prisoner was counted in cubic, not square, metres and amounted to 6-8 m^3. As most of the prisons were located in old buildings constructed before the First World War with high ceilings, of 5 metres and more, it meant that the floor space per prisoner was often less than 2 m^2. As a rule, inmates served their sentences or remained in temporary custody in multi-occupancy cells with, in some cases about 50 prisoners in a cell. Many prisoners had to sleep on the floor and multi-storey beds were common. It was impossible for all inmates to have access to a table or stools, although they had their meals in their cells. Sanitary conditions were appalling. It was common that inmates had to relieve themselves in buckets placed in overcrowded cells. It was only in the nineties that space norms were established on reasonable principles. Currently the minimum areas per prisoner are 3 m^2 for men and 4 m^2 for women, and they are, on the whole, being achieved.

Conditions like those described, coupled with the fact that a large number of prisoners were guarded by a relatively small number of Prison Service officers (statistically one officer per 6 prisoners) resulted in a permanent state of tension in prisons. Relationships between staff members and prisoners were of an extremely confrontational and aggressive character. The use of force was the dominant way in which each group dealt with the other. It was not surprising that bloody prison riots broke out with some frequency, especially at times of political crises in the country, such as in the years 1955-56, 1971-72, 1980-81, 1984, and 1989. Those riots were brutally suppressed and then came periods of superficial peace in prisons, called 'normalization' by the authorities. They were accompanied, however, by an increasing number of acts of defiance against prison staff, mainly in the form of hunger strikes and self-inflicted injuries. Informal prison culture became extremely strong among inmates, dominated by hostility and opposition not only to the prison staff, but to the communist system in general. The bucket for excrement found in every prison cell was inevitably called by the family name of the current first secretary of the communist party.

Radical reform of the prison system began in 1989, after the suppression of a wave of protest. Obviously, the most important among the circumstances conducive to the reform was the collapse of the totalitarian state with its obsessive control of the conduct of citizens, especially its opponents. But, paradoxically, one of the most important impulses for reform was the catastrophic financial situation of the prison system. Despite the substantial reduction in the number of prisoners, it remains large enough to make it difficult for the prison authorities to manage its costs without attacking the living conditions of the inmate population and generating internal hostilities. Costs can only be contained by a more liberal and less punitive system. However, the economic problems do not mean that there has been no improvement in the material living conditions of prisoners. For example, a programme to install sanitary cubicles in cells has begun and has now reached over one third of the cells. Hot water is also being laid on and is now provided in almost 20 per cent of the cells. There has also been progress in the supply of food and clothing. However, the necessity of maintaining the prison system at a reasonable level of welfare despite budgetary constraints, and counteracting the effects of overcrowding, has compelled the authorities to look for economies and organizational changes through modifications in the sanction of imprisonment itself.

The main obstacle to reform was the general situation of the prison system, its old buildings, its old administration and its exploitative, unfriendly or even hostile personnel, reflecting attitudes to prisoners learned over many years of previous practice. The problem of Prison Service personnel was probably the key element in the reform. Unless the staff could be brought to support the changes, their implementation would have been impossible. Predictably, the attitude of prison personnel towards the reform was rather hostile because it disturbed traditional relations and was contrary to the material interests of the corrupt part of the staff. The practice of biding one's time until the impetus of a reform had been lost was also common. It was obvious to reformers that a substantial part of the personnel would have to be removed to create a service that was professional, law abiding and had a constructive approach to prisoners. By the end of 1992 nearly half of the former personnel had been dismissed. They left on early retirement, as result of disciplinary proceedings, or at their own request. At the same time appropriate steps were undertaken to gain the remaining staff's approval of the reform, and to recruit new personnel.

According to the declarations of the reformers, its general objectives were to reduce existing tensions and the atmosphere of hostility, and to maintain, 'at all costs', peace and discipline without recourse to violence. The success of the reform also depended on its acceptance by the prisoners. This might be gained by respect for their rights and the renunciation of traditional coercive pressures. This was accomplished mainly through a decisive attack on arbitrary proceedings against prisoners and the development of procedures for lodging complaints and requests. Most important, however, was to gain the confidence of the prisoners that the prison staff would support and assist them in their aspirations to prepare for freedom.

The reform demanded radical changes in prison conditions which were facilitated by the decentralization of the system. Individual prisons were made independent in organizing, within generally formulated guidelines, their own daily routine and in choosing the type of activity suitable for them. This created new opportunities for activity that posed a challenge for the rejuvenated and promoted staff. It also attracted a lot of prisoners who saw opportunities for their own initiatives, such as sports events, concerts, theatrical performances, literary competitions, meetings with representatives of local communities on the prison premises, etc. Prison chaplaincy was restored and many social and civic organizations, like Alcoholics Anonymous and other self-help groups, brought prisons into the range of their work.

The most important factor in gaining prisoners' acceptance for the reform was the practice of granting leave on a wide scale. Approximately 60 per cent of prisoners currently receive leave, although before 1989 this was granted only occasionally. For the prisoners leave constitute a goal which is worth struggling for. The difficult financial situation of the prisons encouraged schemes for prisoners to apply for leave and other means of getting them off the premises, at least temporarily. The budgetary constraints of the prison system also helped to remove many other barriers and burdensome restrictions on prisoners, for example, in receiving food and clothes parcels from families, friends and charities, wearing their own clothes, possessing radio and TV equipment in cells, etc. All these transformed the situation in prisons and made them much more tolerable institutions. In addition, there was a much more liberal policy on granting parole. Although this remained a matter for the courts, the prison administration contributed by submitting their own motions for conditional releases and by supporting applications submitted by prisoners.

The effects of the prison reform are visible simply in the fact that prisons became significantly safer institutions. This is corroborated by a substantial decrease in the number of collective (involving at least 3 prisoners) active protests (riot, dangerous violation of order and safety in prisons), as well as passive ones (hunger strikes, refusal to obey orders), and self-inflicted injuries.

Despite the reform of the prison system and this generally positive evaluation, there are some elements where there has been little progress, or even some regression, relative to the former situation. This is particularly noticeable in the area of prison work. It is true that, in many cases, this was used by the communist regime as a source of cheap forced labour (in the eighties prisoners worked for monthly payment equivalent to the price of a few packs of cigarettes). Nevertheless, opportunities for work, and its financial rewards, deliver substantial support for prisoners' morale and create possibilities of material assistance to families outside. Under the communists, the employment rate among prisoners reached over 90 per cent. Prisoners worked in enterprises outside prisons and in factories inside prisons, the latter being continuously developed. After 1989 unemployment in the whole country, quickly rising in the early nineties, drastically limited the demand for prisoners' labour outside prisons. The demand for products manufactured in the factories and workshops inside prisons has also declined. As a result, in 1994, only 27 per cent of prisoners were employed.

Regression was also noted in the field of prison education. In 1986 there were 8,633 prisoners receiving education in prison. In 1989 this number dropped to 4,127, and in 1990 to 2,701. In later years the number of inmates receiving education has been rising slowly, reaching 4,025 persons in 1994, but this is still less than half the number under the old system. It means that only about 6 per cent of prisoners have studied in prison, mostly at elementary and vocational level, with a small fraction at secondary level. Opportunities for higher education in prison are almost nonexistent although this may happen in individual cases. The system of prison education in Poland is still waiting to be brought up to European standards.

However, the major problem of the Polish prison system, both under communist rule and at present, is its virtual lack of preparation of inmates for release and of follow-up support. There are not enough mid-way institutions to prepare for release prisoners who are completing long-term sentences. Prisoners often have no prospects of housing or employment, especially if they are recidivists. There are no probation officers to offer assistance to discharged prisoners who have no other source of support. The prison system gives only symbolic assistance on release, a railway ticket to the prisoner's formal place of residence and a small amount of money for food in the first days of liberty. For any substantial assistance ex-convicts must apply to charity organizations or public social services alongside other poor and homeless people.

The prison reform in Poland has created some legislative, organizational and humanitarian bases for bringing penal policy nearer to European standards, but has been confronted with financial-economic barriers which cannot be removed until there is a general improvement in the economic situation of the country as a whole.

References

Jasiński, J. (1995), 'Prison System and Prisoners', in Jasiński, J. and Siemaszko, A., (eds.), *Crime Control in Poland*, Oficyna Naukowa: Warsaw, pp.63-7.
Markiewicz, W. (1996), *Sposoby regulowania populacji więziennej w Polsce* [Methods of regulation of prison population in Poland], Mimeograph: Warsaw.
Szymanowski, T. (1996), *Przemiany systemu penitencjarnego w Polsce* [Transformations in the Penitentiary System in Poland], Oficyna Naukowa: Warsaw.

7 Recent Trends in English Penal Policy
Paul Roberts

Introduction

This chapter reviews recent trends in English penal theory and practice,[1] with reference to the political, legal, philosophical and cultural context of developments over the last two decades. The objective is to provide a framework for understanding particular penal policies and their effects. As a contribution to the emerging discipline of comparative criminal justice (see Nelken 1996; 1997), this investigation of penality's consequences and conditions of existence is not confined by the horizons of a single national jurisdiction. Indeed, European regulation has begun to make the notion of 'national' penal policy anachronistic. To date the impact of European standards on English penal policy has been muted (for general introductions, see Swart and Young, 1995; Guldenmund *et al*, 1995; Douglas and Moerings, 1995), but there is considerable scope for future, and potentially radical, development, particularly under the social policy 'third pillar' of European Union integration and the European Convention on Human Rights, soon to be incorporated into domestic English law.

The discussion of recent English penal trends begins with some general remarks on the conceptual and practical nature of 'penal policy'. The next two, more substantive, sections identify the principal ideas, ideals, values and objectives animating late twentieth century English penality, and connect them with the more salient and emblematic features of contemporary penal practice. The chapter concludes with some brief reflections on what the immediate future may hold for penal policy and practice in England and Wales.

Penal Policy-Making in Perspective

The formulation and implementation of penal policy is a complex process, involving many hands and minds. Policy is formulated not only in Acts of Parliament and the executive action of Government Ministers, but also at the 'point of delivery' by judges, magistrates, prison officers and the Probation Service, who are, in England and Wales, the principal officials and agencies comprising the penal system. It is, therefore, inappropriate to draw rigid distinctions between policy formation and implementation, or between penal policy and penal practice. Penal policy is the outcome of a continuous process in which political initiatives are developed and modified, in some cases quite radically, throughout their implementation. Policies voted into law by Parliament, or sanctioned by the Home Secretary through his executive powers, cannot take effect until they have passed through various bureaucratic, institutional and ideological filters which may resist, distort or even subvert their original objectives and values. An account of penal policy which looked only at paper laws and Ministers' speeches would be blind to the distinction between rhetoric and action. It would fail to capture the sense in which penal policy is the result of compromise, not just between sectional political interests but also between the aspirations of government and the abilities, priorities and values of the organizations and individuals who contribute to policy-making in their daily practice. Moreover, the inevitability of *discretion* (professional judgement) in the penal system opens penality to competition and conflict within and between the principal agencies and officials, and exposes government to the tyranny of unintended consequences.

There is yet another important sense in which penal policy-making is more complex and problematic than may readily be apparent. It is useful to think of the 'penal system' (or 'process') as the collection of agencies, institutions, organizations and their practices which governs the treatment of a convicted offender: the penal system, in other words, is that part of the criminal process constituted by 'sentencing and everything after'. To sub-divide the field of criminal justice in this way is helpful in making writing, teaching and thinking about penality more manageable, bounded and focussed. Like any artificial boundary, however, it can also create barriers to insight. Whenever we talk about the penal system we must remember how offenders arrive at the sentencing stage of criminal proceedings. Crimes which result in convictions are a highly selected sub-group of all offences. In a typical case, a judge or magistrate will only have an opportunity to pass sentence if: (1) a person

Recent Trends in English Penal Policy 99

perceives him- or herself to have been the victim of crime *and* (2) decides to report the matter to the police *and* (3) is prepared to co-operate in the investigation and testify at trial if necessary *and* (4) the police treat the incident as a potential crime *and* (5) are able to secure, by investigation or otherwise, enough evidence to charge a suspect *and* (6) decide to commence formal criminal proceedings by passing the case file onto the Crown Prosecution Service (CPS), rather than giving the offender a caution or informal warning *and* (7) the CPS decides that there is enough evidence to prosecute the case in the public interest *and* (8) the court rules that there is a *prima facie* case for the accused to answer *and*, finally, (9) the accused is convicted, either on his plea of guilty or after a contested trial. At any one of these key stages the prosecution could come off the rails, if it ever got started at all. Best estimates suggest that the police successfully clear up no more than 5 per cent of the crime committed in England and Wales, and only about 2 per cent of all offences result in conviction by a criminal court (Home Office, 1995a, p.25). Packer's (1964, p.11) striking image of the criminal justice conveyor belt inexorably processing offenders through to conviction has become part of the conceptual furniture of Anglo-American criminal justice (*e.g.*, Sanders and Young, 1994). However, in the light of these statistics, it is arguably more illuminating to think of modern criminal proceedings as a sequence of key decision-points at which cases are *diverted away from* formal process. Juries, judges, magistrates, prosecutors, police officers and ordinary members of the public in effect all hold, individually and severally, a power of veto over the progression of criminal cases. They are all 'gatekeepers' at the doors to the penal system.

It is important to understand how the exercise of these 'powers of veto' both shapes and is shaped by penal policy. Consider, for example, England's new Crime (Sentences) Act 1997, which introduces mandatory life sentences for certain repeat violent and sexual offenders. This new policy will naturally make an impact on the penal system: its most obvious, intended consequences will be to reduce judges' sentencing discretion, to increase the severity of punishment for some offenders and to exert a degree of upward pressure on the total number of people in prison. But the impact of the policy will probably also be felt 'retrospectively' in earlier stages of criminal proceedings, whether or not its sponsors intended or even foresaw such effects. The 1997 Act could well influence the behaviour of potential witnesses and complainants of serious sexual and violent crimes. Will victims or witnesses be less willing to report an offender to the police if they know that he faces life imprisonment if convicted? Will battered spouses or people with incriminating information about a friend or family member be less willing to come forward? Some offenders, for their part, will probably respond to the new sentencing law by intimidating witnesses to remain silent or committing more serious offences - murder rather than grievous bodily harm or rape - because, if caught and convicted, they will receive the maximum sentence of life imprisonment in any event. Criminal justice professionals can also be expected to adjust their practices to accommodate the new policy. The police might decide to treat some rapes as less serious indecency offences; prosecutors may be tempted to 'down-charge' grievous bodily harm to a more minor assault. Finally, jurors might be unwilling to convict those offenders for whom they think an automatic life sentence would be too harsh. These predictions are not fanciful. An offence of causing death by dangerous driving had to be created in English law because juries refused to return manslaughter verdicts on people who caused death on the roads (Clarkson and Keating, 1994, pp.638-40). Many more examples could be cited, from this and other jurisdictions. The US Federal sentencing guidelines, for instance, replaced judges' wide sentencing discretion with a table of fixed penalties which has, in practice, encouraged prosecutors to alter their charging decisions in order to secure the sentences they consider appropriate. Rigid sentencing guidelines tie judges' hands but empower prosecutors. In the USA the sentencing policies enacted by Congress have been neutralized by prosecutorial discretion (Nagel and Schulhofer, 1992). Discretion in the criminal process has been likened to toothpaste in a sealed plastic tube (Braithwaite and Pettit, 1990, pp.20-4): the paste can be squeezed from one end to the other, but it always remains in the tube.

It is not necessarily regrettable that discretionary decision-making permeates penal policy. Although discretion is always open to abuse, and must therefore be monitored and checked, it also allows professional judgment, common sense approaches to problem-solving and the values of humanity and compassion to enter into the criminal process. Discretion, then, is neither 'good' nor 'bad' in itself: it is a formal attribute of criminal proceedings which may be used or abused, for good or ill, by particular people in particular contexts. Herein lies the opportunity for police officers, prosecutors, lawyers, judges, magistrates, prison administrators and probation officers to fashion penal policy through their everyday practice. Conversely, a government's capacity to formulate and direct penal policy is limited by (amongst other things) its ability to persuade, exhort, cajole, threaten or demand that criminal justice professionals work towards realizing its penological ambitions (also see Mościskier, in this volume).

Ideas, Ideals, Values and Objectives

Ideas, ideals, values and objectives are the intellectual resources of penality, on which penal actors draw for their vocabularies of motive, explanation and justification. English penological developments of the last two decades are marked by three recurrent ideological strands (cf. Bottoms, 1995): (1) the ideal of just punishment; (2) the idea of 'community'; and (3) a managerialist pursuit of economy, efficiency and effectiveness in public services, coupled with a belief that privatization and free market competition are invariably the most reliable means to these ends. Sometimes two or more of these strands have been woven together successfully in a particular penal policy or practice. Just as often, however, they appear to pull in opposite directions, leaving policies riddled with internal contradictions and generating conflict between, on one hand, the designated values and aims of the penal process, and the roles, aspirations and self-perceptions of criminal justice professionals on the other. For most of this century penal policy in England and Wales has been characterized by a catholic mix of objectives and values: punishment, deterrence, rehabilitation, reformation, incapacitation and (until 1965) elimination. This eclecticism was more accident than design, as successive governments displayed little enthusiasm for devising a comprehensive, coherent or integrated programme of penal action. The post-war decades witnessed low-key, 'largely backstage policy-making' (Bottoms and Stevenson, 1992, p.6), informed by positivistic explanations of offending and a welfarist consensus endorsing 'treatment and training' as the penal system's main objectives. Piecemeal legislative and administrative interventions became more frequent from the late 1960s, but these were largely reactions to the twin evils of rising levels of recorded crime and an escalating prison population, both of which, though small by late twentieth century standards, were seriously troubling to the governments of the day. Until quite recently individual judges, magistrates, prison governors and probation officers retained a remarkably free hand, within broad parameters laid down by law and the Home Office, to develop their own idiosyncratic policies at the local level. The sentencing and treatment of offenders was thought to pose essentially technical questions best answered by criminal justice professionals and other penal experts. But all that has since changed. Although the politicization of criminal justice can be traced back as far as 1970 (Downes and Morgan, 1997), the election of Margaret Thatcher and the start of 17 years of continuous Tory government in 1979 marked a decisive penal moment.

Throughout the 1980s the Thatcher administration, as the self-proclaimed party of law and order, took a close interest in criminal justice and penality. In retrospect this interest was to prove problematic, but neither the privilege of hindsight nor suspicions about the motives of particular governments should lead us to underestimate the principled argument for strong political leadership and direction in penal affairs. Once it is accepted that offenders are dealt with for, and in the name of, every member of a political community and that their treatment involves moral choices as well as technical-professional judgement, it is difficult to resist the contention that overriding penal objectives and priorities should be settled by democratically accountable politicians in government, rather than by unelected officials like judges and prison administrators. There are also important fiscal considerations. Public spending on offenders inevitably leaves less money for education, the health service, old age pensions, and social security benefits. The appropriate allocation of tax revenue between these, and other, forms of social welfare provision reflects political priorities. That is why judges properly decide whether, for instance, this or that offender will go to gaol, but not which offence categories should attract custodial sentences or how many prisons should be built. Respect for judicial independence means that judges must be free from political bias, pressure or interference to apply the law fairly and impartially to the cases before them. But it does not follow that there is 'judicial ownership' (Tonry, 1995, p.271) of the sentencing decision, much less that judges should be the sole arbiters, or even the principal architects, of penal policy (see Ashworth, 1983, Chapter 11; Ashworth, 1990-91; Munro, 1992).

In 1991 the British government appeared to grasp the penal nettle by, for the first time, enshrining in legislation an official sentencing philosophy for England and Wales. This new philosophy of punishment was in fact a variation on an ancient penal theme: that law-breakers should suffer just punishment in proportion to the seriousness of their crime - that offenders, in the modern idiom, should get their 'just deserts' (Home Office, 1990, para.2.1). The Criminal Justice Act (CJA) 1991 incorporated imprisonment *and* non-custodial penalties into a comprehensive sentencing framework based on this principle. By making crime seriousness the overriding measure of punishment, the 1991 Act made a decisive ideological break with individualized sentencing based on offender-related criteria, such as criminal history, responses to previous disposals, capacity for rehabilitation or reform, career prospects and the like. That is not to say that English penal policy embraced the ideal of just punishment to the exclusion of all else. A plurality of penal values and objectives is compatible with the 1991 Act, *provided that desert sets the limits of the penal content* - the 'hard treatment' (Feinberg, 1970) - in a sentence. Even in its original form, the CJA 1991 sanctioned longer prison terms on the non-desert ground of public protection and left significant areas of discretion to judges and magistrates (Ashworth, 1992); and further departures from the principle of proportionality were introduced by the Criminal Justice Act 1993 very soon after the 1991 Act came into effect (see below). But having allowed for these imperfections in the transition from principle to practice, it remains true to say that just punishment has been adopted as the principal official ideal and objective of the English penal system (even if, in practice, some judges, magistrates and probation officers refuse to toe the official line).

The idea of community is a second prominent feature of recent penal discourse and practice in England and Wales. Although 'communitarianism' has enjoyed a general resurgence in Anglo-American political and social philosophy since the early 1980s (*e.g.*, Sandel, 1982; Etzioni, 1995; Kymlicka, 1990, Chapter 6), England would appear to be distinctive amongst Western democracies in the extent to which the idea of community has captured the penal imagination (Lacey and Zedner, 1995). There has been talk of 'community prisons' (Woolf and Tumin, 1991, paras.11.49-11.68), a new emphasis on 'community penalties' and 'punishment in the community' (Home Office, 1990, Chapter 4; Home Office, 1995b), policies of decarceration for certain offenders formerly detained in institutions and, in the wider criminal process, community policing, community crime prevention, neighbourhood watch schemes and 'walking with a purpose' (Crawford, 1995). As Nelken and others have observed, the key to the popularity of this idea could be its ability to invoke a collection of somewhat contradictory images of penality *in*, *by* or *for* communities (Nelken, 1985; also see Cohen, 1985, Chapter 4). A consensus may emerge around the rallying cry of community precisely because its meaning and implications lie significantly in the eye of the beholder. Communitarianism appeals to the essentially social nature of humanity. It is bound up with the notion that life's meaning and value is to be found in co-operation and communion with one's fellow creatures, each individual life lived as a collective social project. This ideal is an important corrective to excessively individualistic accounts of personal autonomy and is attractive, if only at some affective level, to us all. But practice may be less edifying than theory. Appeals to community in English penal policy may serve only to divert attention from the reality of damaged individuals being turned out of institutions to fend for themselves, of the power to punish carelessly ceded to private individuals and commercial organizations, and of citizens left to make arrangements for their own policing and security. 'Community' in this sense functions to (re)distribute responsibility for penal affairs between state and civil society, and the modern trend towards 'responsibilization' (Garland, 1996, pp.452-55) may take on more or less sinister connotations. A Foucauldian analysis might identify the extension of surveillance and the dispersal of discipline: Foucault himself spoke of the expanding 'carceral archipelago' (Foucault, 1991, p.298; and see Garland, 1990, Chapter 6) and his expositors of the 'punitive city' busily constructing its 'wider, stronger, different nets' of social control (Cohen, 1979; 1985). Exchanging one metaphor for another, 'punishment in the community' may be seen from this perspective as permeable prison walls allowing a corrosive penalty to seep out and contaminate the social fabric.

Managerialism and its concomitants constitute a third distinctive theme of contemporary English penal policy. Economic approaches to penality are nothing new in themselves (cf. Posner, 1985, p.1193), and, in the trivial sense that public money should not be frittered away needlessly, efficiency is an uncontroversial goal of responsible government. In Britain in the 1980s, however, economic thinking became a new orthodoxy in public life, sponsored by a Conservative administration with a strong ideological preference for the free market and a mission to eliminate what it perceived as avoidable waste in the public sector. Privately run prisons and the reconstitution of the Prison Service as (at least notionally) an independent executive agency of the Home Office are some of the most visible parts of the institutional legacy of these Conservative policies. Yet these are only the most visible effects. The impact on the penal system of managerial, instrumental and market approaches to public service delivery can be described, without exaggeration, as all-pervasive. Government has reconstituted itself as manager and its citizens as consumers (Lacey, 1994). Where once there were grand penal objectives such as rehabilitation, education and punishment, managerialism has substituted systems analysis, audit, and narrowly-focussed organizational performance indicators (Feeley and Simon, 1994; Jones, 1993). This type of thinking chimes well with notions of 'the risk society' and the limited competence of government to manage enduring social problems (Garland, 1996), but it jars against the quintessentially public ideal of just punishment. It is also a source of concern, and not a little soul-searching, for prison and probation officers who have seen their role reinterpreted in accordance with managerialist dogma, often at the expense of their professional standing and occupational aspirations. Men and women who came to their work with a mission to serve have been redeployed as turn-keys, supervisors and accountants. In this way, the influence of managerialism pervades English penal policy from the selection of organizational aims and objectives by senior administrators to the prosaic, mundane details of front-line professionals' working lives.

English Penal Practice in the Last Two Decades

Having surveyed these various trends in twentieth century English penality, it is perhaps no surprise to find that, for most of the 1980s, the British government simultaneously pursued what might be thought incompatible objectives, more incarceration *and* more extensive diversion from custody. In an influential article Tony Bottoms dubbed this a 'bifurcated' policy (Bottoms, 1977, pp.88-91).

Penal bifurcation describes a policy in balance, or in tension, between two objectives: (1) serious crimes must attract condign punishment, almost invariably equated with long sentences of imprisonment; but (2) less serious offences should be dealt with by non-custodial measures, reserving prison places for the truly serious or dangerous offender. The power of this policy lay in its capacity to accommodate the bulk of contemporary penological thinking and thus to engage the sympathy and support of diverse and otherwise divided constituencies. To begin with, a single sliding scale (or 'tariff') of custodial and non-custodial penalties satisfied the retributive principle of proportionality, allowing the punishment to fit the crime however heinous at one end of the scale, or venial at the other. Next must be mentioned a collection of more pragmatic penological, fiscal and political considerations which combined to support the logic of limiting prison use. Enthusiasm for diverting offenders away from custody reflected a loss of faith in the rehabilitative potential of punishment in general, and of prisons in particular, which became Anglo-American penal orthodoxy from the mid 1970s onwards. It came to be realized that, far from reforming offenders, prison could become a kind of informal 'university of crime' where old lags schooled young initiates in the craft skills and knowledge of the professional criminal. Prison, moreover, is expensive. The cost of keeping one person under lock and key for a year (about £24,000) is greater than the annual salary of many university lecturers. By 1990 a governmental policy document could casually observe, as though reporting only what everybody already knew, that imprisonment 'can be an expensive way of making bad people worse' (Home Office, 1990, para.2.7). Non-custodial sanctions, on the other hand, are much cheaper than incarceration and arguably no less effective in reducing recidivism, qualities which would recommend them to the penal system's actuaries and accountants, no less than to a government committed to lowering the burden of taxation. What is more, in addition to benefiting from these flattering comparisons with imprisonment, 'alternatives to custody' derived positive ideological support from the powerful idea of community, which has already been identified as a *leitmotif* of modern English penality. The emerging penal discourse of 'community penalties' and 'punishment in the community' invoked a collection of potent ideas and symbols of communities as places of punishment, agents of penality and repositories of criminal justice ideals. Finally, the first strand of penal bifurcation served programmatic political ends, allowing a law and order government to present itself as 'tough on crime' by pointing to longer prison sentences for rapists, robbers and drug dealers.

The success or failure of penal bifurcation rested crucially on its ability to manage the enduring tensions, conflicts and discontents of the penal system, which the policy seemed to conciliate without resolving. Perhaps bifurcation was doomed from the start. A systematic drive to increase the length of prison sentences for certain classes of offender was storing up trouble for the future, creating an irresistibly expansionist dynamic in the aggregate use of custody over time (fewer offenders go to gaol, but those who do, stay there for much longer). Two decades' experience with 'alternatives to custody' has also taught us some salutary lessons: that new non-custodial penalties tend to be used as alternatives, not to custody, but to each other (Bottoms, 1987); that sentencers are tempted to combine individual measures together in a composite order, if the law allows it; and that more and more offenders end up in gaol because they have breached the terms of their increasingly demanding, composite community penalties. These were the forces (also to be seen at work in other jurisdictions, such as the United States (Blomberg and Lucken, 1994) which might well have derailed bifurcation even if policy-makers had not pre-empted its demise. But, in the short term, the prison population continued to fall after the 1991 Act's implementation and, as it turned out, the reactions of certain criminal justice professionals were of more immediate concern to the government.

The Probation Service, which was inevitably handed the task of administering the newly integrated tariff of community penalties, had been afflicted by a deepening crisis of identity throughout the 1980s, aggravated by financial constraint. Probation work had developed from a religious mission to reform (McWilliams, 1983; 1985) into a social work tradition which, despite the pessimism of recent decades, many rank-and-file officers continued to hold dear. Now they were told that their primary function was to deliver a just measure of pain by supervising offenders in the community and reporting back to court on the progress of their charges. Pressures to conform with centrally designated priorities and reproduce uniformity in probation practice were exerted through *National Standards for the Supervision of Offenders in the Community* (1992). Together with the abandonment of university-based training and graduate entry to probation work, these developments dramatically reduced officers' autonomy and challenged their status as professionals. Senior officers, meanwhile, themselves under pressure to shore up the Service's fragile political credibility, became converted to the managerialist credo which prioritizes organizational performance targets over the helping and human features of probation casework (Rumgay, 1988; Nellis, 1995). Punishment in the community was, and is, unlikely to be delivered effectively by demoralized probation officers who feel betrayed by their leaders, undervalued by government and society at large, and disillusioned or confused about the ideals and objectives guiding their practice. Yet this seems to be the plight of many probation officers in the late 1990s (see generally, Worrall, 1997, Part II; Newburn, 1995, Chapter 4).

The bifurcated policy preserved by the 1991 Act also came under attack from a vocal group of magistrates and judges who complained that intolerable fetters had been placed on their sentencing discretion. Populist sections of the media quickly followed up allegations that repeat offenders were getting off lightly because the CJA 1991 prevented previous convictions being taken into account as aggravating factors, increasing sentence or pushing an offender up-tariff and across the custody threshold. The new system of 'unit fines', which had been designed to promote equality of impact (Ashworth, 1995, pp.79-80) in financial penalties, was also criticized for 'unfairly' demanding vastly different levels of fine from people who had committed essentially similar offences. Yet graduated penalties linked to offenders' disposable incomes are the very essence of a unit fine system! These objections were a direct assault on the Act's fundamental commitment to proportionality. But, instead of defending its carefully formulated and newly enacted penal philosophy against sometimes mistaken or exaggerated claims, the government treated criticisms as though they exposed unforeseen and embarrassing flaws in its policy, and immediately sounded the retreat. New sections were hastily inserted into the Criminal Justice Act 1993 which abandoned unit fines and relaxed the constraints on using an offender's criminal history to increase his sentence (Ashworth and Gibson, 1994). These were significant departures from the just deserts philosophy of the 1991 Act. The episode demonstrates that even the most principled, planned and carefully constructed penal policies remain hostages to political fortune, liable to be thrown off course in an instant by a calamitous turn of events. Penal policy, that is to say, is subject to what the journalist Andrew Marr calls 'the first law of politics' - 'Stuff Happens' (Marr 1997). In the field of criminal justice there is always more than enough stuff happening - horrific assaults on the elderly, tragic child murders, prison escapes, recidivist offending by those released from custody or psychiatric institutions, media-fanned moral panic about dangerous dogs, or knives, or sex and violence on T.V. - to keep policy-making shortsighted and reactive.

Barely one year after the implementation of England's landmark sentencing legislation, changes in personnel at the Home Office confirmed the demise of penal bifurcation. In a *volte face* even more striking than the government's sentencing law amendments, a new Home Secretary, Michael Howard, proclaimed to the 1993 Conservative Party Conference that 'prison works', by which he meant that the public is protected from further criminal victimization for the period in which an offender is in gaol.[2] (Crimes committed by prisoners, such as drugs offences and assaults against prison staff and other inmates, were conveniently forgotten.) Mr. Howard said that his government would build enough new prisons to make sure that those who insisted on committing crimes could be sent to one. This was a new and markedly different approach to penality, much influenced by contemporary penal fashions in America where incapacitation - 'human warehousing' - and 'three strikes and you're out' sentencing policies were now in vogue (for critical discussion see Zimring and Hawkins, 1995; Dubber, 1995). Tough talk about crime played well with certain sections of the media and with Conservative Party activists at their annual Conference. It was a natural move for a 'law and order' government in serious difficulties with other aspects of its programme. And the intellectual resources for a leap from bifurcation to incapacitation were at hand.

With law and order issues, and more particularly the burgeoning crime rate,[3] at the centre of party political debate in the long run up to a general election, both Government and Opposition were keen to advocate 'tough' criminal justice policies. Neither party was under any illusion that to be seen as 'soft on crime' would deal a grievous, and quite possibly fatal, blow to their electoral ambitions. In this climate of opinion a sentencing policy based on just punishment would be vulnerable to penal inflation as policy-makers reacted to popular demands for harsher punishments, sentiments rooted not in justice, but in vengeance, hatred and fear (von Hirsch, 1993, Chapter 10). The explicit logic of the argument for incapacitation may have been buttressed by a diffuse 'populist punitiveness' (Bottoms, 1995), itself fuelled by a perversion of just deserts rhetoric, which wills unbounded violence on criminals and other enemies of society. This hate-inspired 'will to punish', buried deep in the collective psyche, has been a perennial check on the ambitions of penal policy (Pratt, 1993). Authoritarian elements in recent British governments have been willing to pander to these sentiments when it suited their political ends. There is no better example than the Criminal Justice and Public Order Act 1994, which contained provisions restricting suspects' right to remain silent under police interrogation and defendants' privilege against self-incrimination at trial, and offered up a veritable rogues' gallery of scapegoats and folk devils - hunt saboteurs, road and environmental protestors, New Age Travellers, ravers, squatters, ticket touts, unlicensed mini-cab operators - on which to project the blame for society's ills (for overviews, see Allen and Cooper, 1995; Smith, 1995). This censorious, exclusionary, disintegrative 'criminology of the Other' (cf. Garland, 1996, pp.461-63) became a feature of the cultural and political backdrop to English penal policy-making in the 1990s, and provides part of the explanation for the directions in which it developed. Finally, brief mention should be made of victims' rights movements, which have achieved considerable prominence in Britain and the USA over the last decade. Victims of crime have traditionally suffered unforgivably shabby and unnecessarily distressing treatment in English criminal proceedings. The argument in justice and humanity for improving their lot has been unanswerable; and, gradually, reforms are being won (Fenwick, 1997). But, unfortunately, the substance and tenor of the debate in England and Wales too frequently and simplistically promotes the interests of victims in ways which threaten the fundamental rights of suspects, defendants and offenders (cf. Ashworth, 1993). To promote victims' rights in this political climate is to risk stoking the fires of populist punitiveness.

In the final analysis the conditions of existence for Howard's 'prison works' policy must remain conjectural, but its consequences were predictable,[4] unmistakable and alarming: the prison population soared, from a low point of 42,000 in January 1993 (Home Office, 1997c, Figure 1) to a record figure of 63,000 at the time of writing (October 1997: see Bennetto, 1997b), quickening the pace of 'the coming penal crisis' (Bottoms, 1980). It is no mere trope or rhetorical flourish to speak of a 'crisis' in this context (also see Cavadino and Dignan, 1997, Chapter 1). Over the last two decades the Prison Service has endured high profile escapes and breaches of security, widespread rioting and destruction of prison estate, an increasing number of assaults on prison staff, industrial unrest, strikes and low morale amongst the officer grades, censure for unacceptably poor physical conditions from the Council of Europe's Torture Committee and in numerous reports of Her Majesty's Inspector of Prisons, and, in 1993, the unsettling experience of being reconstituted as an independent Agency of the Home Office (see, generally, Morgan, 1997; Cavadino and Dignan, 1997, Chapters 5 and 6). Plans for a smooth transition to Agency status were severely disrupted, first by more escapes, and then by an acrimonious dispute over managerial responsibility and accountability between the new model Prison Services first Director General, Derek Lewis, and Home Secretary Michael Howard, which resulted in Lewis being dismissed in breach of his contract and Howard being accused by a former ministerial colleague of deliberately misleading Parliament over the affair (Travis, 1997; and see Marriott, 1997; Lewis, 1997).

Custodial institutions were by now beset, at the level of ideas, by a serious legitimacy deficit (cf. Sparks, 1994), but in operational terms the crisis in the Prison Service is a crisis of numbers. Overcrowding, especially in the local gaols where the short term prisoners and remand populations are held, has been a catalyst for, and sometimes the main precipitating cause of, the Prison Service's other difficulties. Overcrowding leads to deteriorating living conditions for inmates, and demoralizing working conditions for staff; constructive programmes of work, education and recreation cannot be maintained; prisoners with nothing to do and time on their hands become restive and resentful. These are the conditions which breed rioting and escapes, as well as breaches of prisoners' fundamental rights and a denial of their basic dignity as human beings. Prisoners and their guards become locked into a grim downward spiral of despair. During the brief ascendancy of bifurcation in the late 1980s and early 1990s the number of prisoners fell to a yearly average of below 45,000, but this trend has been spectacularly reversed since 1993. By 1995 the average daily prison population exceeded 51,000, whilst the seasonally adjusted figure at December 1996 was 59,000, a staggering annual increase of some 13 per cent (Home Office, 1997a, p.1). The most recent figure of 63,000 inmates shows no sign of abatement in the rapid growth of prison population. With an incarceration rate of around 120 per 100,000 inhabitants, England and Wales is now amongst western Europe's prison population 'league leaders'. The traditional east/west divide in prison use no longer gapes so wide and, if present trends continue, looks set to close.[5] In 1995 the Home Office was planning for 59,900 prisoners by the year 2004 (Home Office, 1996a), but even at the time this projection seemed to be underestimating the likely impact of changes to the sentencing framework and early release mechanisms (see, e.g., Hood and Shute, 1996). Quickly falsified by experience, the projection was soon revised upwards. The latest official estimate puts the figure at 74,500 by 2005 (Home Office, 1997b).

In its final years John Major's Conservative administration set about the largest prison building programme in Britain since the 1939-45 War. This was good news for construction companies and the financial interests comprising the 'crime control industry' (Christie, 1994), since the government naturally intended to put the building of its new prisons, and in some cases their administration, out to private tender (not, however, such good news for potential prisoners, given that some of the most unstable and violent conditions in English prisons have been found to exist in privately-run institutions: see Cavadino and Dignan, 1997, pp.169-71; Campbell, 1994). Yet it was always doubtful that the building programme would keep pace with the burgeoning prison population. New places could not come on stream quickly enough to meet immediate demand, prompting the government to adopt a number of interim measures, including holding remand prisoners in magistrates' courts cells and buying a de-commissioned 'floating prison' ship from America. But these temporary expedients generated their own problems (Burrell, 1996; 1997) and only seemed to deepen the crisis. Looking to the future, the drive to incarcerate, rationalized by a policy of incapacitation and underwritten by an attitude of populist punitiveness (which finds expression in the decisions of juries, lay magistrates and judges, as well as influencing policy-making and general voting patterns: see Ashworth and Hough, 1996), has set the English prison system on course for virtually unlimited expansion. As Rutherford (1986), Christie (1994) and others have shown, prison population size is only tenuously related to the crime rate: a conscious and determined policy of diversion from custody will be required to halt, let alone reverse, the current prison numbers explosion. This gloomy prognosis might be checked by the expectation that policy-makers' hands will be forced by financial imperatives, and sooner rather than later. Surely no government will be prepared to write a blank cheque to fund indefinite expansion? But this argument assumes that rational economic planning can gain some purchase on the climate of populist punitiveness, an assumption that Nils Christie, amongst others, rejects: 'Who considers money in the midst of war? The war on drugs, the war on violence, the war on pornography, - the urgent need for safe streets and property, these are archetypical situations where money is not allowed to reign' (1994, p.199).

New Labour, New Penality?

The election last May of the first Labour government for 17 years holds out the prospect of new directions in English penal policy. The architect of New Labour's approach to criminal justice, encapsulated in the slogan 'tough on crime, tough on the causes of crime', was Prime Minister Tony Blair himself, who, in Opposition, had held the shadow home affairs portfolio. It is too early to say whether being tough on crime *and* its causes will translate into more socially responsible and progressive penal policies (though it might be observed that early indications, including new powers to incarcerate 12 year olds (Bennetto, 1997c), are hardly encouraging: see Rutherford, 1997a; 1997b). Whatever the present government's plans may be, however, the expansionist dynamic bequeathed to the Prison Service by the last government will dominate the immediate future of English penal policy. Intervention is urgently required to reverse the alarming rate at which the prison population continues to grow, if further disturbances and injustice are to be avoided (cf. Bennetto, 1997a). Yet two decades' experience of community penalties and 'alternatives to custody' supplies no easy answers and limited reason for optimism (Worrall, 1997, Chapters 2-4; Rutherford, 1997c). At this time, criminal justice policy in England and Wales appears to have fallen victim to a set of political and cultural circumstances which are working their pernicious effects right across the Western penal landscape (Radzinowicz, 1991). As Andrew Rutherford observes, in a sombre conclusion to his recently published retrospective on 1980s criminal policy in the USA, the Netherlands, and England and Wales:

> The combination of a populist agenda and the pressures of managerialism have combined to dilute, if not dismantle, those limits which protect society from the pursuit of ever more simplistic and authoritarian solutions. These contemporary tendencies pose complex challenges to people within liberal democracies who are determined to do something about crime without making matters worse (Rutherford, 1996, p.134).

Recent Trends in English Penal Policy 113

Acknowledgements

Grateful thanks are due to Rob Canton for his shrewd and insightful comments on an earlier draft of this chapter, and to my Law Department colleague Stephen Livingstone for providing me with materials on the Derek Lewis affair.

Notes

1. References to England include Wales. The other two components of the United Kingdom, Scotland and Northern Ireland, are separate legal jurisdictions for which the Westminster Parliament tailors specific criminal justice and penal policies.
2. Although other sentencing objectives such as general deterrence and rehabilitation were sometimes invoked in a supporting role, incapacitation was the predominant justificatory theme of Mr. Howard's prisons policy. Unveiling his 27-point plan to tackle crime at Party Conference, Howard told delegates: 'Let us be clear. Prison works. It ensures that we are protected from murderers, muggers and rapists - and it will make many who are tempted to commit crimes think twice' (quoted in Rutherford, 1996, p.128). Later, in defence of the mandatory sentencing provisions of what became the Crime (Sentences) Act 1997, he wrote: 'I accept that this is likely to mean an increase in the prison population. But prison works. Research has found that imprisoning a recidivist burglar, for example, may prevent between three and 11 burglaries for every year he spends in prison. Prison also protects the public from dangerous criminals and acts as a deterrent to would-be criminals. Time in prison can be used to rehabilitate offenders' (Howard, 1996).
3. Recorded crime in England and Wales has grown exponentially since the War. There were 500,000 notifiable offences recorded in 1950, 1.6 million in 1970, 2.5 million in 1980, and 5 million in 1994 (Home Office, 1995a, pp.2-3). Since then the numbers have fallen off somewhat, with 4.8 million offences recorded for the 12 month period to June 1997 (Home Office, 1997d). Of course, statistical records of crime are notoriously incomplete, largely for the reasons touched on in the first section of this chapter. Victim surveys provide a clearer picture of 'the dark figure' of unreported and unrecorded crime. The 1996 British Crime Survey (BCS), presenting data for 1995, arrived at a headline figure of 19.1 million offences in England and Wales, a 4% increase since the previous Survey of crimes committed in 1993. Since it was first conducted in 1981, the BCS has recorded a 73% rise in crime (Home Office, 1996b).
4. Policies which are thoroughly mediated and developed through practice can still have predictable outcomes. The Conservative government's 'prison works' policy was implemented by modifications in sentencing structure and executive early release mechanisms (see Cavadino and Dignan, 1997, Chapter 7) which were bound to increase prison numbers. Moreover, these effects were accentuated by more diffuse, yet still perfectly predictable, influences on the attitudes and behaviour of sentencers in a climate of populist punitiveness. The broad direction of change is usually easier to predict than its magnitude or detail, however. In this case, government policy produced far more prisoners

than were bargained for.
5. For example, at 1 September 1995 incarceration rates per 100,000 inhabitants stood at 120 in Hungary, 145 in Slovakia, 170 in Poland and 190 in the Czech Republic. However, other eastern European countries still register much higher rates, especially Russia (695), Belarus (505) and the Ukraine (390). (These figures are taken from Home Office (1997a, Table 1.14), and are rounded to the nearest 5.)

References

Allen, M.J. and Cooper, S. (1995), 'Howard's Way - A Farewell to Freedom?' *Modern Law Review*, 58, pp.364-88.
Ashworth, A. (1983), *Sentencing and Penal Policy*, London: Weidenfeld and Nicolson.
Ashworth, A. (1990-91), 'Sentencing and the Constitution', *Kings College Law Journal*, 1, pp.29-40.
Ashworth, A. (1992), 'The Criminal Justice Act 1991', in Munro, C. and Wasik, M. (eds.), *Sentencing, Judicial Discretion and Training*, London: Sweet & Maxwell.
Ashworth, A. (1993), 'Victim Impact Statements and Sentencing', *Criminal Law Review*, pp.498-509.
Ashworth, A. (1995), *Sentencing and Criminal Justice*, 2nd edn. London: Butterworths.
Ashworth, A. and Gibson, B. (1994), 'The Criminal Justice Act 1993: (2) Altering the Sentencing Framework', *Criminal Law Review*, pp.101-109.
Ashworth, A. and Hough, M. (1996), 'Sentencing and the Climate of Opinion', *Criminal Law Review*, pp.776-87.
Bennetto, J. (1997a), 'Crowded Jails "Ready to Blow"', *The Independent*, 26 February.
Bennetto, J. (1997b), 'Jail Conditions Dreadful, Says Chief Inspector', *The Independent*, 16 October.
Bennetto, J. (1997c), 'New Powers to Lock Up Young Offenders', *The Independent*, 16 October.
Blomberg, T. and Lucken, K. (1994), 'Stacking the Deck by Piling up Sanctions: Is Intermediate Punishment Destined to Fail?', *Howard Journal of Criminal Justice*, 33, pp.62-80.
Bottoms, A.E. (1977), 'Reflections on the Renaissance of Dangerousness', *Howard Journal of Criminal Justice*, 16, pp.70-96.
Bottoms, A.E. (1980), 'An Introduction to "The Coming Crisis"', in Bottoms, A.E. and Preston, R.H. (eds.), *The Coming Penal Crisis*, Edinburgh: Scottish Academic Press.
Bottoms, A.E. (1987), 'Limiting Prison Use: Experience in England and Wales', *Howard Journal of Criminal Justice*, 26, pp.177-202.
Bottoms, A.E. (1995), 'The Philosophy and Politics of Punishment and Sentencing', in Clarkson, C. and Morgan R. (eds.), *The Politics of Sentencing Reform*, Oxford: Oxford University Press.
Bottoms, A.E. and Stevenson, S. (1992), '"What Went Wrong?": Criminal Justice Policy in England and Wales, 1945-70', in Downes, D. (ed.), *Unravelling Criminal Justice*, London: Macmillan.
Braithwaite, J. and Pettit, P. (1990), *Not Just Deserts: A Republican Theory of Criminal Justice*, Oxford: Oxford University Press.
Burrell, I. (1996), 'Prisons to Overflow to Court Cells: Secret Home Office Plan to Deal with

Surge in Jail Population', *The Independent* 18 October.
Burrell, I. (1997) 'Fire-Risk Prison Ship Abandoned: Inmates Moved Ashore from £15m Vessel', *The Independent*, 27 June.
Campbell, D. (1994), 'Inmate Hangs Himself at "Out of Control" Privatised Prison', *The Guardian* 17 August.
Cavadino, M. and Dignan, J. (1997), *The Penal System: An Introduction*, 2nd edn. London: Sage.
Christie, N. (1994), *Crime Control as Industry: Towards GULAGS, Western Style*, 2nd enlarged edition. London: Routledge.
Clarkson, C.M.V. and Keating, H.M. (1994), *Criminal Law: Text and Materials*, 3rd edn. London: Sweet & Maxwell.
Cohen, S. (1979), 'The Punitive City: Notes on the Dispersal of Social Control', *Contemporary Crises*, 3, pp.83-93.
Cohen, S. (1985), *Visions of Social Control: Crime, Punishment and Classification*, Cambridge: Polity Press.
Crawford, A. (1995), 'Appeals to Community and Crime Prevention', *Crime, Law & Social Change*, 22, pp.97-126.
Douglas, G. and Moerings, M. (1995), 'Prisoners' Rights in the Netherlands and England and Wales', in Fennell, P., Harding, C., Jörg, N., and Swart, B. (eds.), *Criminal Justice in Europe: A Comparative Study*, Oxford: Oxford University Press.
Downes, D. and Morgan, R. (1997), 'Dumping the "Hostages to Fortune"? The Politics of Law and Order in Post-War Britain', in Maguire, M., Morgan, R. and Reiner, R. (eds.), *The Oxford Handbook of Criminology*, 2nd edn. Oxford: Oxford University Press.
Dubber, M.D. (1995), 'Recidivist Statutes as Arational Punishment', *Buffalo Law Review*, 43, pp.689-724.
Etzioni, A. (1995), *The Spirit of Community: Rights, Responsibilities and the Communitarian Agenda*, London: Fontana.
Feeley, M. and Simon, J. (1994), 'Actuarial Justice: The Emerging New Criminal Law', in Nelken, D. (ed.), *The Futures of Criminology*, London: Sage.
Feinberg, J. (1970), 'The Expressive Function of Punishment', reprinted in Duff, A. and Garland, D. (eds.) (1994), *A Reader on Punishment*, Oxford: Oxford University Press.
Fenwick, H. (1997), 'Procedural "Rights" of Victims of Crime: Public or Private Ordering of the Criminal Justice Process?' *Modern Law Review*, 60, pp.317-33.
Foucault, M. (1991) [1977], *Discipline and Punish: The Birth of the Prison*, Trans. Alan Sheridan, London: Penguin.
Garland, D. (1990), *Punishment and Modern Society: A Study in Social Theory*, Oxford: Clarendon Press.
Garland, D. (1996), 'The Limits of the Sovereign State: Strategies of Crime Control in Contemporary Society', *British Journal of Criminology*, 36, pp.445-71.
Guldenmund, R., Harding, C. and Sherlock, A. (1995), 'The European Community and Criminal Law', in Fennell, P., Harding, C., Jörg, N. and Swart, B. (eds.), *Criminal Justice in Europe: A Comparative Study*, Oxford: Oxford University Press.
Home Office (1990), *Crime, Justice and Protecting the Public*, Cm.965. London: HMSO.
Home Office (1995a), *Digest 3: Information on the Criminal Justice System in England and Wales*, London: HMSO.
Home Office (1995b), *Strengthening Punishment in the Community: A Consultation Document*, Cm.2780. London: HMSO.

Home Office (1996a), *Projections of Long Term Trends in the Prison Population to 2004*, Home Office Statistical Bulletin 4/96. London: Home Office Research and Statistics Department.

Home Office (1996b), *The 1996 British Crime Survey England and Wales*, Home Office Statistical Bulletin 19/96. London: Home Office Research and Statistics Department.

Home Office (1997a), *Prison Statistics England and Wales 1996*, Cm.3732. London: HMSO.

Home Office (1997b), *Projections of Long Term Trends in the Prison Population to 2005*, Home Office Statistical Bulletin 7/97. London: Home Office Research and Statistics Directorate.

Home Office (1997c), *The Prison Population in 1996*, Home Office Statistical Bulletin 18/97. London: Home Office Research and Statistics Directorate.

Home Office (1997d), *Notifiable Offences England and Wales, July 1996 to June 1997*, Home Office Statistical Bulletin 23/97. London: Home Office Research and Statistics Directorate.

Hood, R. and Shute, S. (1996), 'Protecting the Public: Automatic Life Sentences, Parole and High Risk Offenders', *Criminal Law Review*, pp.788-800.

Howard, M. (1996), 'The Key to Our Protection', *The Independent* 4 April.

Jones, C. (1993), 'Auditing Criminal Justice', *British Journal of Criminology*, 33, pp.187-202.

Kymlicka, W. (1990), *Contemporary Political Philosophy: An Introduction* Oxford: Oxford University Press.

Lacey, N. (1994), 'Government as Manager, Citizen as Consumer: The Case of the Criminal Justice Act 1991', *Modern Law Review*, 57, pp.534-54.

Lacey, N. and Zedner, L. (1995), 'Discourses of Community in Criminal Justice', *Journal of Law and Society*, 22, pp.301-25.

Lewis, D. (1997), *Hidden Agendas: Politics, Law and Disorder*, London: Hamish Hamilton.

Marr, A. (1997), 'For Tony Blair, the Real Enemy is within the Walls of Cabinet',*The Independent*, 23 December.

Marriott, J. (1997), 'Would you Buy a Used Car from this Man?', *The Guardian*, 16 May.

McWilliams, W. (1983), 'The Mission to the English Police Courts 1876-1936', *Howard Journal of Criminal Justice*, 22, pp.129-47.

McWilliams, W. (1985), 'The Mission Transformed: Professionalisation of Probation between the Wars', *Howard Journal of Criminal Justice*, 24, pp.257-74.

Munro, C. (1992), 'Judicial Independence and Judicial Functions', in Munro, C. and Wasik, M. (eds.), *Sentencing, Judicial Discretion and Training*, London: Sweet & Maxwell.

Morgan, R. (1997), 'Imprisonment: Current Concerns and a Brief History Since 1945', in Maguire, M., Morgan, R. and Reiner, R. (eds.), *The Oxford Handbook of Criminology*, 2nd edn. Oxford: Oxford University Press.

Nagel, I.H. and Schulhofer, S.J. (1992), 'A Tale of Three Cities: An Empirical Study of Charging and Bargaining Practices Under the Federal Sentencing Guidelines', *Southern California Law Review*, 66, pp.501-66.

Nelken, D. (1985), 'Community Involvement in Crime Control', *Current Legal Problems*, pp.239-67.

Nelken, D. (1996), 'Whom Can You Trust? The Future of Comparative Criminology', in Nelken, D. (ed.), *The Futures of Criminology*, London: Sage.

Nelken, D. (1997), 'Understanding Criminal Justice Comparatively', in Maguire, M., Morgan R. and Reiner, R. (eds.), *The Oxford Handbook of Criminology*, 2nd edn. Oxford: Oxford University Press.

Nellis, M. (1995), 'Probation Values for the 1990s', *Howard Journal of Criminal Justice*, 34,

pp.19-44.
Newburn, T. (1995), *Crime and Criminal Justice Policy*, London: Longman.
Packer, H.L. (1964), 'Two Models of the Criminal Process', *University of Pennsylvania Law Review*, 113, pp.1-68.
Posner, R.A. (1985), 'An Economic Theory of the Criminal Law', *Columbia Law Review*, 85, pp.1193-1231.
Pratt, J. (1993), '"This is Not a Prison": Foucault, the Panopticon and Pentonville', *Social and Legal Studies*, 2, pp.373-95.
Radzinowicz, L. (1991), 'Penal Regressions', *Cambridge Law Journal*, 50, pp.422-44.
Rumgay, J. (1988), '"Probation - The Next Five Years": A Comment', *Howard Journal of Criminal Justice*, 27, pp.198-201.
Rutherford, A. (1986), *Prisons and the Process of Justice*, Oxford: Oxford University Press.
Rutherford, A. (1996), *Transforming Criminal Policy: Spheres of Influence in the United States, the Netherlands and England and Wales During the 1980s*, Winchester: Waterside Press.
Rutherford, A. (1997a), 'The Government, Crime and Public Order', *New Law Journal* (20 June), 147, pp.932-33.
Rutherford, A. (1997b), 'Labour and the Prison Numbers Crisis', *New Law Journal* (4 July), 147, pp.1004-5.
Rutherford, A. (1997c), 'Community Penalties Under New Review', *New Law Journal* (1 August), 147, pp.1159-60.
Sandel, M. (1982), *Liberalism and the Limits of Justice*, Cambridge: Cambridge University Press.
Smith, A.T.H. (1995), 'The Criminal Justice and Public Order Act 1994: The Public Order Elements', *Criminal Law Review*, pp.19-27.
Sparks, R. (1994), 'Can Prisons be Legitimate? Penal Politics, Privatization and the Timeliness of an Old Idea', *British Journal of Criminology*, 34, pp.14-28.
Sanders, A. and Young, R. (1994), *Criminal Justice*, London: Butterworths.
Swart, B. and Young, J. (1995), 'The European Convention on Human Rights and Criminal Justice in the Netherlands and the UK', in Fennell, P., Harding, C., Jörg, N. and Swart, B. (eds.), *Criminal Justice in Europe: A Comparative Study*, Oxford: Oxford University Press.
Tonry, M. (1995), 'Sentencing Reform Across National Boundaries', in Clarkson, C. and Morgan, R. (eds.), *The Politics of Sentencing Reform*, Oxford: Oxford University Press.
Travis, A. (1997), 'Howard Used Break-out Report "as Excuse to Sack Jails Chief"', *The Guardian*, 20 May.
von Hirsch, A. (1993), *Censure and Sanctions*, Oxford: Oxford University Press.
Woolf, Lord Justice and Tumin, His Honour Judge (1991), *Prison Disturbances April 1990*, Cm.1456. London: HMSO.
Worrall, A. (1997), *Punishment in the Community: The Future of Criminal Justice*, London: Longman.
Zimring, F.E. and Hawkins, G. (1995), *Incapacitation: Penal Confinement and the Restraint of Crime*, New York: Oxford University Press.

PART II
SOCIAL POLICY
AND
ECONOMIC CHANGE

8 Higher Education and the Labour Market in Britain
Daniel Lawrence

The collapse of communism in Poland has been associated with a rise in unemployment and significant changes in the labour market. But Britain too, without a comparable communist past, has had a not dissimilar experience in recent years. The reforms introduced by successive Conservative governments, to move Britain away from the mixed economy and welfare state established during the period of relative political consensus which followed World War II, have brought in their wake high unemployment, greater job insecurity amongst those in work and corresponding changes in the nature of the labour market.

Before the collapse of communism in Poland, jobs which required higher education, though not necessarily better paid than jobs that could be entered immediately on completing school, did usually attract higher status. However, this is no longer necessarily the case given the glamour that attaches to private sector employment. Whilst higher education can give graduates the combination of qualifications which makes them attractive to Western-based private companies, and still gives them exclusive access to some positions in the public sector (e.g. medicine and education), Roberts and Perzyna (1994) emphasize that the benefits of higher education are now uncertain, especially given the fact that many students have to finance their own studies. Indeed they note that some of the young people interviewed had chosen higher education simply as an alternative to unemployment or as a means of avoiding military service.

Given the temptation to assume that Poland's employment problems relate to the legacy of, or transition from, communism, the concluding section of Roberts and Perzyna's paper, dealing with higher education and the labour market, is very important. After noting that there was no guarantee that their Polish respondents would be able to fulfil their occupational ambitions, they considered it important to emphasize that this was equally true of Britain.

As happens in other countries, including Britain, it was likely that, on graduating, many would be willing to take virtually any jobs into which employers were willing to recruit them (Roberts and Perzyna, 1994, p.34).

The problem of graduate unemployment and under-employment in Britain has not received the attention it deserves. Nor is it something which the universities have been anxious to bring to the attention of those who, at often considerable personal cost, enter higher education, in increasingly large numbers, with an expectation that it will lead to jobs not available to those who enter employment on leaving school.

Before Robbins

In his 1960 essay, 'The Changing Functions of Universities', Halsey emphasized that the by then obvious 'linkage of the university to the economy' was relatively new. His point was not only that the universities were, in their medieval origins, 'an organic part of religion rather than economic life' (Halsey, 1962a, p.457) but that 'vocationalism' had been resisted 'long after the religious domination of curricula had been overcome and long after secular universities had been founded on the basis of state and industrial patronage' (Halsey, 1962a, p.458). Even in 'the age of coal and steam' the universities were dominated by their function as preserves of the aristocracy and gentry. Their record was one of successful resistance to 'the pressures set up by economic change': a form of resistance exemplified in Huxley's famous assertion that 'the primary business of the universities is with pure knowledge and pure art - independent of all application to practice; with progress in culture not with increase in wealth' (Halsey, 1962a, pp.458 and 464).

The aristocratic domination of universities continued, despite all the changes ushered in with the industrial revolution, well into the 19th century. Higher education which, since the 14th century had been monopolized by Oxford and Cambridge, began to expand when some of Britain's largest industrial cities established their own universities. What emerged in the early 20th century was a two tier structure. Oxford and Cambridge remained national institutions and educated the elite for subsequent employment in the fields of politics, the civil service, business and the professions. The new universities, even London, were provincial. They recruited the bulk of their students from their own region. They were also distinctive, in that their courses trained students predominantly for the newer technological and professional occupations. Moreover, whereas Oxford and Cambridge had long been associated with an aristocratic-gentry culture, the cultural roots of the newer universities were those of the non-conformist provincial business classes.

Only in the 1950s did these provincial universities emerge as fully-fledged national institutions, and the gap between Oxford and Cambridge and the newer universities begin to close in terms of intellectual activity (though not status) as the former expanded their provision for scientific and technological elites, and the latter increased their provision for those wishing to study the arts. Nevertheless, university education remained very selective. Students were overwhelmingly upper and middle class and, though in relative terms there was a significant increase in the number of undergraduates, absolute numbers remained small.

In the first decade of the 20th century, there were only about 20,000 university students. By the inter-war years, the figure had grown to 35,000. In 1950, after the election of Britain's first Labour government with a large majority, it rose to 68,000. However, by the final decade of the century, as a result of increases in the number of places in traditional universities, the creation of new universities and redefinitions - both of what kinds of institutions may be called 'universities' and what kinds of courses warrant the award of degrees - the number of students had risen to 1.5 million.

After Robbins

In 1961, the then Conservative Prime Minister, Harold Macmillan, appointed Lord Robbins to chair a committee on the future of higher education. It reported in 1963 and the adoption of its key recommendations created the framework within which higher education developed in the following two decades (Robbins, 1963).

Robbins recommended not only an expansion of higher education but also the adoption of the principle that 'all young persons qualified by ability and attainment to pursue a full-time course in higher education should have the opportunity to do so' (Robbins, 1963, p.49). His report was published just before the re-election of a Labour government which was happy to endorse its recommendations for both ideological and economic reasons. The new government wanted to expand educational opportunities for working class young people previously markedly under-represented in selective grammar schools and largely excluded from higher education. It did so by replacing grammar schools with comprehensives and adopting Robbins' recommendations on higher education. However, the government was also in favour of this opening up of the educational system because it was widely believed that it would, at the same time, improve Britain's economic competitiveness.

There was nothing new about such an idea. The economist Alfred Marshall had argued as early as 1890 that:

> There is no greater extravagance more prejudicial to the growth of the national wealth than the wasteful negligence which allows genius that happens to be born of lowly parentage to expend itself in lowly work (Marshall, 1890, p.176).

What was different by the time of the Robbins Report was that this notion had become part of the conventional wisdom.

> The essential new fact is that a developed society and economy are less than fully effective if anyone is educated to less than the limits of his/her potential (Drucker, 1962, p.15).

Within a relatively short time of the publication of the Robbins Report, several entirely new universities were established and other institutions elevated to university or polytechnic status. The number of those leaving higher education as graduates was boosted further by the introduction of a specific degree in education for those training to be teachers. Within seven years, the adoption of the Robbins' recommendations led to a doubling of the numbers in higher education, from 216,000 to 435,000 (Halsey, 1972, p.194).

The successful adoption of Keynesian economic policies during the period of relative political consensus which followed World War II meant that the Robbins expansion of higher education coincided with a period of full employment. This, in turn, led to improved market conditions for employees, particularly those who had been to university. Growing numbers of young people from working class backgrounds, like their middle class counterparts in earlier generations, could now expect to have a choice between jobs with much better terms and conditions of employment than those of their parents. To help them take advantage of these new labour market conditions, improved careers education and guidance was made available for both school-leavers

Higher Education and the Labour Market in Britain 125

and undergraduates. By the time prospective students had applied for university they had already received general careers education from designated teachers in secondary schools and more specialist advice from professional careers officers (Lawrence, 1993; 1994). In addition, at university, students had access to a careers advisory service which helped them identify which employment fields were suited to their interests and provided them with information both on what was involved in particular jobs and the relative merits of potential employers. So eager were major employers to recruit the best undergraduates that, instead of merely advertising their vacancies and waiting for students to come to them, they established an annual tour around universities and polytechnics to 'sell' their companies to the undergraduates about to come on to the labour market. As Peston noted in 1981:

> Without begging the question of whether there is a positive net return (social or private) in investment in higher education, graduates certainly earn higher salaries than the national average and work in superior conditions (Peston, 1981, p.134).

Peston's statement about the relationship between higher education and the labour market may have been correct in general terms, but the market for graduates did vary significantly between subject areas (Sanderson, 1987, 15). The variations became particularly marked in the early years of Thatcherism when there was a marked rise in unemployment, particularly amongst young people. As would be expected, those taking vocational courses were more likely to be in work in the 6 months following their graduation than those taking purely academic courses. However, those reading science did not necessarily have better employment prospects than those taking courses in the arts and social sciences. Indeed, in 1983, the highest level of unemployment was amongst graduate zoologists (48 per cent). The corresponding figures for physicists, chemists and geologists were 23 per cent, 29 per cent and 47 per cent respectively, not markedly out of line with those for sociologists (36 per cent) and students of English (40 per cent).

Growing Doubts

The period of optimism about the economic benefits of investment in education proved short-lived. As early as the 1970s, academics, politicians and businessmen began to argue that, despite the opening up and expansion of education, it was failing to meet the needs of industry and commerce. This growing disillusionment was given a new legitimacy with the Ruskin College speech made by James Callaghan, the then Labour Prime Minister, in 1976. It is important to note his role in challenging the conventional wisdom on investment in education because there is a marked similarity between his thinking and that of Mrs Thatcher who replaced him as Prime Minister in 1979. Her explicit rejection of political consensus has encouraged many to believe that the recent fundamental questioning of the nature of education can be attributed to her period in office. In fact, whilst Mrs Thatcher may have transformed rhetoric into reality, it was Mr Callaghan who was the first prime minister to challenge the then conventional wisdom.

One of the main criticisms of the expansion of higher education was that most of it had been allowed to develop on the basis of free market principles. Whilst there had been 'manpower' planning in some professional fields (e.g. medicine and teacher training) and flirtations with it in other subjects (e.g. chemistry), universities and polytechnics had, to a considerable extent, provided places on courses on the basis of the demand for them by students. Ironically, doubts about this reliance on supply and demand were voiced most stridently by those who claimed, in more general terms, to be in favour of the operation of the market. Despite the fact that, by the 1970s, about 40 per cent of students in higher education were on vocational courses (Hunter, 1981, pp.8 and 41), particular concern was expressed at the alleged 'swing away from science' evident in the pattern of student choices; the failure of the polytechnics to offer a sufficiently distinctive form of vocational education; and the allegedly unduly academic nature of many of the degree courses in science and technology provided by both universities and polytechnics. Reviewing the education of engineers, for example, the Finniston Report noted that:

> Complaints continuously voiced, especially by employers, are that the education of engineers is unduly scientific and theoretical; that newly-graduated engineers lack awareness of 'real-life' constraints to text book solutions; that they are oriented too much towards research and development work and are not interested in working in production or marketing functions; and that they lack understanding of the factors in the commercial success of the employing organization (Finniston, 1980, p.83).

Thatcherism and its Legacy

The election of Conservative governments in 1979, 1983, 1987 and 1992 had a profound impact on Britain's system of higher education. Mrs Thatcher claims that her radical political programme was based on a passionate belief that only a major reduction in both public spending and state control, and a return to free market principles, could restore Britain's economic success and national pride (Thatcher, 1993). In practice, her policies departed markedly from such principles.

Cuts in University Spending

In the case of higher education, Thatcherism certainly meant major cutbacks in public spending. In 1981, the universities suffered an 11 per cent cut in funding and an open-ended scheme was introduced to induce staff to take early retirement. What followed was markedly different from what the government had envisaged (Sanderson, 1987, p.17). There were over 6,000 early retirers, twice as many as had been anticipated and, contrary to government hopes, they came disproportionately from science and technology. Since the early retirers joined a comparable number leaving through natural wastage, a severe shortage of university teachers developed and it proved necessary to establish a 'new blood' scheme to fill vacancies. Comparable reductions in funding levels, and further early retirement schemes followed in the 1980s and 1990s, as successive Conservative governments drove down the cost of delivering higher education still further. By 1996, the unit of resource (the amount given by government to fund each student place) had fallen by over 50 per cent compared to 1971 (Shattock, 1996).

Loss of University Autonomy

What Thatcherism promised at the start of the 1980s was not just a reduction in public spending but also a reduction in state control. Whilst the universities have certainly experienced a reduction in the former, they have not enjoyed a reduction in the latter. On the contrary, the financial cuts have been accompanied by a massive increase in direct and indirect control by central government. Via a combination of ministerial fiat and the imposition of state rather than market-determined performance indicators, more characteristic of a communist regime than a liberal democracy, increasing competition between institutions of higher education has been achieved - but neither in a form nor via the kind of mechanisms that would normally be associated with a free market.

Whilst universities continue to enjoy formal autonomy, they no longer have anything resembling the same degree of real freedom as their 1960s counterparts. By instituting a progressive reduction in state funding to a level where many institutions now operate on the verge of bankruptcy, their managements have little option other than to follow the directions indicated by government ministers and those acting on their behalf. For example, the government now exercises considerable control over student recruitment, through a combination of direct and indirect measures, and has effectively abandoned the Robbins principle that access should be limited only by ability and attainment. The total number of home students is fixed by an agency appointed by the government and financial penalties follow any significant departure from the quotas set. In addition, by determining, and manipulating, sometimes at very short notice, the 'unit of resource' provided for students in particular subject areas, it is possible for the government to implement a crude form of 'manpower' planning in an effort to encourage movement away from courses in the arts and social sciences towards those in science and engineering where places remain unfilled. It is worth noting that whilst successive governments have taken such measures to shift the balance of recruitment in favour of science and technology, in the belief that this will make Britain more competitive internationally, they have done so despite the fact that Britain already has a higher proportion of students studying science and technology than many of its major European competitors (Sanderson, 1987, p.134). Moreover, as a recent consultation paper noted, many employers are less concerned by the absolute numbers graduating from science and engineering than with the quality of those graduates (Allen and Higgins, 1994, p.164)

The Growth in Student Numbers

The 1980s and 1990s, like the 1960s, have been associated with a marked increase in student numbers (albeit without a corresponding increase in funding). Perhaps the most crucial point to be made about this latter period of expansion is that, unlike the changes following the Robbins Report which occurred in a period of low unemployment, the recent changes in higher education have taken place against a background of high unemployment. So, whilst the stated political objective of the expansion has been to increase the quality of Britain's work force to help it compete more effectively in international markets, one obvious political advantage of the expansion has been that each additional student in higher education is one fewer potential member of an already embarrassingly large unemployment register.

By the mid-1990s, the student population had grown from less than 0.5 million in 1971 to over 1.5 million. Although this is the equivalent of 1 in 3 of the 18-21 age group, the participation rate of this particular age group is still only about 1 in 4, less than the government's official target of 1 in 3. (Association of Graduate Recruiters, 1993. i). Most of the recent expansion in higher education has not come from this traditional university age group or those with traditional entry qualifications. Nor has the expansion taken place primarily in the universities which existed when Mrs Thatcher was first elected. Indeed over the 1980s there has only been an 8 per cent increase in the 18-21 age group in such institutions. It is in the less-well funded polytechnics (which were re-named universities in 1992) and colleges of higher education where most of the expansion has taken place. Even though many of them still find it difficult to fill their places, and struggle to remain financially viable, there was a 91 per cent increase in the number of students in such institutions between the sessions 1988/9 and 1993/4 (Young, 1996). What has brought about the bulk of the expansion of higher education is the increased participation rate of those in older age groups, and the relaxation of traditional university entry requirements (Roberts, 1995, pp.19, 67, 119).

Reduced State Support for Students

British students entering higher education in the 1990s receive much less state support than in the past. Following the Robbins expansion, university students were entitled to appropriate welfare benefits in addition to a small but mandatory maintenance grant adjusted to take account of parental income. During the 1980s, these benefit entitlements (other than health care) were withdrawn from students and tax arrangements changed so that parents were no longer able to claim an allowance for their dependent children in higher education. Then, in 1989, the level of maintenance grants was frozen. They have since been cut still further (by 10 per cent in each of the academic years 1994-97) whilst the costs of travel, books and accommodation have risen faster than the general level of inflation. The political defence offered for this series of cost-cutting exercises, that Britain previously 'had the most generous system of student support in the western world' is without foundation (Lawrence, 1991).

As a consequence of the cuts, students have had to take out increasingly large loans and leave university in considerable debt (Judd, 1995; Ward, 1995; Berliner, 1995). The fifth annual Barclays Student Debt Survey published in 1996 revealed that, on average, the amount students owed had doubled since 1992 and that, on average, they anticipated being about £3,000 in debt on graduation (Abrams, 1996). That figure, as the final section in the chapter will show, is soon to increase around four fold.

These financial circumstances have inevitably led to an increasing 'drop out' rate. In the early 1990s, about 13 per cent of students did not complete their courses. By 1996, the proportion who started but did not graduate was close to 20 per cent. More specific research, conducted by the Committee of Vice Chancellors and Principals, showed that the annual drop-out rate, i.e. the proportion of students leaving in each academic year, had risen from 5 per cent in 1993 to 6.5 per cent in 1995 (Kirkman, 1996). Despite the fact that the proportion dropping out of higher education had become so large that it actually threatens to eclipse the expansion, governments continue to boast about the record numbers starting courses but ignore the uncomfortable fact that only 80 per cent of them graduate.

An equally crucial point about the current numbers of university drop-outs is that only a small minority leave because they fail their examinations. The large majority leave for financial reasons. Moreover, what is not known is how many of those who do leave for academic reasons may have failed their examinations because they were obliged to work during term time. As a spokesperson for the Committee of Vice Chancellors and Principals has admitted:

> Financial hardship and academic failure are often connected. Students fail their courses for economic reasons. They may be working their way through university and spending too much time doing a part-time job and not enough in the library (Judd, 1996a).

This is a particularly significant consideration given that, in recognition of the hardship faced by many students, one in three universities now runs a job bureau for them.

Graduate Unemployment

As well as having to invest more of their own resources in their higher education, students now get less in return, both in terms of teaching (because staff numbers have been falling whilst student numbers have been increasing) and in terms of employment prospects. The experience of those graduating in the recession years of the early 1990s amply demonstrates that a degree alone does not provide immunity from unemployment. For example, in December 1992, as many as 13 per cent of those who had graduated 6 months earlier were known to be still unemployed and a further 6 per cent were in temporary work. Since then the employment situation has improved but, even in 1993 and 1994, the corresponding figures for the unemployed were 12 per cent and 10 per cent and for those in temporary work 7 per cent and 7 per cent. Moreover, the modest economic recovery does not mean that those unemployed in previous years have been able to find work commensurate with their graduate status. Many who graduated during a period of high unemployment have subsequently found that their degrees appear to have a 'sell-by-date' in that employers tend to favour those applicants who are most recently graduated. As a report by the Association of Graduate Recruiters (AGR) has noted:

> There is a serious risk that the years of recession may produce a lost generation of graduates; capable people whose choice of career was squeezed out by the severe crunch on jobs. This certainly applies to people who are forced to turn casual, low-skilled jobs into permanent employment. It also applies to graduates who simply could not get into the field of their choice because employers were making few - or no - offers and instead went for their second or third or fourth choice (AGR, 1993, p.17).

Add to this number those who had similar experiences in the recessions of the 1980s, and it is clear that there are now a great many graduates who will have suffered, not just in the short term but also in the long run, from the bouts of high unemployment Britain has experienced over the past two decades.

The Devaluation of Degrees and Under-Employment of Graduates

Two additional problems have compounded the difficulties faced by those who have graduated during this latest period of educational expansion and high unemployment. The first is that because there are now many more people with degrees, the currency represented by a degree has been devalued: graduates are no longer the tiny educational elite they represented in the days before the Robbins expansion. This important point, about the declining labour market exchange value of a degree, was highlighted in a recent survey by the National Institute of Economic and Social Research (Mason, 1995).

It found a very variable pattern of employment opportunities for graduates. The position in manufacturing did lend support to the view that investment in education can be beneficial to employees and employers. Pay and job satisfaction were high. The skills of the graduates appeared to being put to good use and seemed likely to improve the productivity and competitiveness of their employers. However, the massive shift from manufacturing to service industries, actively encouraged by Thatcherite economic policies in the 1980s, means that manufacturing now absorbs only 15 per cent of graduates and the terms and conditions of employment of those entering the service sector are shown by the study to be markedly different. Growing numbers are found in jobs that require only a low level of skill and are paid a commensurately low salary - with no significant prospect of promotion; jobs, in other words, which in the past would have been undertaken by school-leavers. Banks and building societies, for example, are increasingly recruiting graduates as clerks, on the same pay as inexperienced non-graduate cashiers. Overall, about half of all employed graduates interviewed had gone into jobs for which no degree was needed. Others, as indicated above, have been even less fortunate and have experienced both prolonged as well as short spells of unemployment despite being graduates.

Such findings are in line with a series of explicit statements in a recent AGR report which emphasises that the traditional 'graduate job' is now a career 'route for only a tiny share of graduates coming into the workforce each year'. The report also acknowledges that whilst the employment prospects of graduates may fluctuate with the general state of the economy, their prospects are also affected by more fundamental processes which relate to 'the changing requirements of employers' and 'the ways we do business and run our organisations' (AGR, 1993, pp.18 and 16).

> It can be hard for them [students] to realise that they are not on Easy Street, that a degree is not a guarantee of anything.... There will be many more graduates entering jobs which are not even remotely 'jobs for graduates' and which amount to sometimes quite serious under-employment (AGR, 1993, p.16).

A more recent survey, conducted by recruitment specialists Reed Graduates, has shown that even with an improvement in the overall employment situation, about two out of three 1996 graduates 'failed to find a job in their chosen field' (Clement, 1997).

The second problem confronting those graduating during the current period of expansion in higher education arises from the fact that they are graduating from a much larger and more diverse range of institutions than in the past. The 1992 Further and Higher Education Act abolished the 'binary divide' i.e. the distinction between universities and polytechnics. As a result, there are now around 100 autonomous universities with the authority to award their own degrees and a further 70 colleges which have been authorized to award the degrees of a university with which they are associated. One important consequence of this growth in the number of institutions awarding degrees is that employers are increasingly distinguishing between the exchange value of university degrees in terms of the institutions which confer them. The competition between institutions, which has been fostered by the government to try to drive down overall unit costs and provide higher funding levels for those with the best research records, has encouraged newspapers and other bodies to draw up league tables of universities. The results of these inevitably arbitrary comparisons, coupled with the traditional prejudices which tend to favour the more established universities over the new, is that those graduating from less fashionable universities are more likely to find themselves in a disadvantageous position in the labour market.

This is manifesting itself in two ways. As formally autonomous institutions, universities set their own examinations and award their own degrees and this has led to doubts about the comparability of degree standards between institutions, especially given the very marked differences in entry standards and the major discrepancies between the performance of students in nationally moderated public examination and the class of degree they are subsequently awarded at university. The huge increase in the proportion being awarded higher grade degrees is, like the number acquiring graduate status, having the effect of devaluing the currency and driving down the exchange value of those degrees in the labour market. Whilst many students, because of this 'grade inflation', now regard anything less than an upper second class honours degree (the second highest level awarded) as tantamount to failure, outside the universities this difficult to explain upward drift in degree classifications has served only to raise doubts about what those degrees mean and whether universities should continue to enjoy autonomy in conferring them (Young, 1994). Following a survey of 250,000 graduates which confirmed suspicions of a 'grade inflation' in degrees, and the conclusion of the director of the 3- year Graduate Standards project set up by the Higher Education Quality Council, 'that there are now very few people who believe that a degree is a degree is a degree', it appears that the Higher Education Quality Council would prefer universities to abandon traditional degree qualifications altogether and replace them with a simple threshold system. However, even that change cannot be introduced until 'moves have been made to ensure more comparability between degrees' (Haughton and Hodges, 1996; Judd, 1996b; Ward, 1997a).

The second, more direct, way in which the expansion is affecting students in the labour market is that employers are now casting their net much more selectively when recruiting students, in ways consistent with the doubts indicated above. For example, in the annual tour of universities by major employers, many institutions no longer receive a visit. In an independent survey of 257 large companies, asked which universities they considered produced the strongest applicants in ten, widely varying, subject areas, the established universities came out very clearly on top. The new (i.e. former polytechnic) universities did not appear in the top ten in any of the subject areas. A similar survey, conducted amongst 105 leading companies revealed that almost half of them had definite preferences when recruiting graduates and now work on the assumption that there is a small 'premier league' of universities (PIP, 1996 and Passmore, 1996).

Differentiation and competition between universities has now become an extremely contentious issue. Yet, despite the appearance of a free market, it is not easy for would-be undergraduates to make fully informed choices when making applications. Ironically, at a time when the government is publishing more information on the performance of schools than ever before, to help parents make informed choices for their children and facilitate the operation of market forces, comparable information is becoming less available for those applying to universities. As Professor Alan Smithers, Director of the Centre for Education and Employment Research, has pointed out, during the days of the binary divide between universities and polytechnics, it was possible to obtain information on the entry qualification of students on individual university courses, but not for those on comparable courses in polytechnics. Since the abolition of the binary divide that information is now no longer available for either the old universities or the former polytechnics. The editor of the *Push* guide to universities has also complained that he can no longer obtain drop-out statistics for individual universities (Young, 1996).

The difficulty in obtaining such information relates to the increasingly fierce in-fighting between universities during a period of major cutbacks in state funding and the need to recruit sufficient students to remain financially viable. Whilst the former polytechnics complain that they do not receive a fair share of existing resources, a small group of established universities has entered into an informal grouping to argue that excellence can only be assured if a much more selective funding policy is adopted.

Dearing

In response to widespread criticism that the cumulative impact of their policies had been to create a state of crisis, the Conservative government of 1996 commissioned Sir Ron Dearing to conduct the most searching inquiry into higher education since the Robbins investigation of the early 1960s. Waiting for Dearing to report had the advantage of allowing politicians to contest the 1997 general election without confronting one another on what had become very controversial issues. However, for the Conservatives, it had the disadvantage of preventing them from going ahead with their own ideas for higher education for the remainder of their term in office. What seems clear from their submission to the Dearing Inquiry is that, had they not been obliged to put their plans on hold, they would have tried to move higher education still further away from the traditional conception of a university. Indeed the vision of the university contained in their submission to Dearing was the very antithesis of Huxley's assertion that 'the primary business of the universities is with pure knowledge and pure art - independent of all application to practice'.

The Conservative vision offered to Dearing was ultimately a commercial one. There was even an explicit acknowledgement that the real consumer of higher education was the employer rather than the student. In a process analogous to the production of factory-farmed chickens for supermarket shelves, students would be processed by universities to ensure that, on coming off the higher education conveyor belt, they would be in a form suitable for consumption by employers. To ensure that the products of higher education would meet the demands of employers, a national committee of business people should be established with a remit 'to monitor and advise on how the sector might take more account of employment considerations'. Consistent with this commercial emphasis, the traditional academic degree would cease to be the norm. Universities would provide a large number of 'employer-friendly' sub-degree level courses, specifically designed to prepare people for work. State funding would be tied to job-related benchmarks to ensure that universities complied with these targets and forged much stronger links with employers (Targett, 1996).

The very first and many other Dearing recommendations explicitly endorse this proposed shift towards a more vocational and employer-orientated approach to higher education. He considers that priority should be given to sub-degree level courses. So, whilst Dearing argues that the existing 'cap on full-time undergraduate places should be lifted over the next two to three years', he insists that 'the cap on full-time sub-degree places should be lifted immediately' (Dearing, p.6, Recommendation 1). Several of Dearing's recommendations are specifically designed to ensure higher education is more closely geared to meet the needs of employers and that students acquire the kind of skills which employers deem useful. Irrespective of the subject being studied, institutions should 'increase the extent to which programmes help students to become familiar with work' and encourage 'entrepreneurship through innovative approaches to programme design' (Dearing, p.9, R18; p.6, R11). In a similar vein, the government is urged to work with representative employer and professional organizations to 'ensure that students are offered more opportunities for work experience' (Dearing p.9, R19) and 'provide equity funding to help members of staff or students take forward business ideas' (Dearing, p.12, R39). Higher education institutions, in turn, are urged to 'establish more technology incubator units...within which start-up companies can be fostered' (Dearing, p.12, R40).

Dearing recommended not only the expansion of sub-degree, more vocationally-orientated courses, but also that this expansion should be concentrated in colleges of further education (Dearing, p.16, R67). In addition, he urged that priority be given to the recruitment of entrants from non-traditional groups. Institutions able to demonstrate an ability to recruit from such groups should, in turn, be rewarded in the allocation of public funds (Dearing, p.7, R2, R3, R4). If adopted, Dearing's proposals will give a further impetus to growth in the new universities and colleges of higher and further education at the expense of the older universities, especially when linked to his recommendation that, increasingly, public funding should follow the student rather than be based on a block grant system (Dearing p.18, R72). These Dearing proposals appear to have caused consternation amongst university vice-chancellors, particularly those from 'older', 'research-led' universities. Whilst they insist, despite their currently advantageous position, that they need significantly higher funding in order to maintain existing standards of teaching, it is readily apparent that, even without central direction, it is their 'newer', 'upstart' competitors who already provide most sub-degree, vocational courses and recruit most effectively from amongst non-traditional entrants to higher education.

Dearing's recommended pattern of funding is particularly controversial because it was above all the problem of the level and distribution of funding which led to his Inquiry. Despite widespread agreement that there was a case for a higher level of funding, there was no agreement on either the most appropriate way of raising or distributing it. Throughout the Inquiry it was envisaged that Dearing would be the arbiter in this prolonged dispute. Yet, at the very instant that the Dearing Report was published, the newly elected Labour government rejected its key proposals on finance. Dearing recommended that mean-tested maintenance grants be retained but that students should contribute to the cost of higher education through a system of loans to cover not only maintenance but 25 per cent of tuition fees. The new government, instead, announced the abolition of maintenance grants *and* the introduction of tuition fees. From 1998, students from even low-income families will have to rely on loans to meet all of their maintenance costs, a decision widely seen as a betrayal of the Labour Party's traditional working class supporters. The fact that the least well-off will be spared the payment of tuition fees will not compensate for the loss they incur through the abolition of the maintenance grant. For the remainder, the tuition fee will be just another regressive indirect tax. As one newspaper correspondent asked, 'Is it fair that tomorrow's £25,000 a year teacher should pay the same as tomorrow's £250,000 a year lawyer?' Equally significant, and perhaps a further testament to the social gulf between the leadership of the Labour Party and its traditional supporters, is the apparent failure to appreciate that for many working class families being substantially 'in debt' is of great symbolic significance and is not the cultural equivalent of a member of the middle class calculating that a state subsidized loan is a sensible way of 'investing in one's future'.

It also seems that this decision has been made without serious attention being given to how the greatly increased cost of higher education to students will impact on the existing problem of graduate unemployment and under-employment, or on the fact that the exchange value of higher education qualifications will be still further diluted if, as Dearing recommends, the proportion of the age group in higher education is to be raised from 32 per cent to 45 per cent. It seems inconceivable that primarily financial considerations will not weigh heavily with many students when choosing courses, something difficult to reconcile with Dearing's claim that the pursuit of knowledge for its own sake should remain one of the principles of higher education. As a 1997 survey (conducted before Dearing reported) revealed, 88 per cent of sixth-formers already gave 'improving career prospects' as a main reason for going to university (compared to 78 per cent in 1994) - twice as many as those who gave 'interest in the subject' as a main reason). The respondents answered in these terms despite their widespread ignorance of how much attending university was likely to cost them and how much debt they would accumulate (Eaglesham, 1997). Since next year's intake is likely to be more realistic about costs, given the publicity given to the introduction of tuition fees and the abolition of the maintenance grant, even fewer are likely to choose their course on the basis of their interest in the subject matter.

Students are not the only group unhappy with the way in which the government has introduced tuition fees. University vice-chancellors are also unhappy, despite the fact that many of them have long pressed for top-up tuition fees. The problem is that the government (contrary to what Dearing recommended) has refused to give an assurance that all the income from students' tuition fees will be allocated to the institutions from whose students it will be raised (Ward, 1997b). So, with no guarantee that they will receive the same additional income from tuition fees that they would receive from their own institution-specific top-up fees, some universities continued to threaten to introduce them. In response, the Labour Government is seeking to legislate to prevent this and taking the opportunity to give itself an unprecedentedly wide range of powers to micro-manage the universities.

Conclusion

This review of change in higher education and the graduate labour market was originally prepared (for publication in Polish) before Dearing reported. Despite the range of questions he addressed, there is no need to change the conclusion of the earlier paper. Indeed, if anything, it can now be stated more emphatically. Given Dearing's failure to find solutions to the major problems raised above (e.g. the devaluation of degrees and the lack of comparability between them), all that can be stated with certainty is that the universities at the start of the 21st century will bear only a passing resemblance to those that existed in the first years of the 20th.

References

Abrams, F. (1996), 'Students count cost of study: £3,000 debt', *The Independent*, 6 July.
Allen, A. and Higgins, T. (1994), *The Careers Adviser/Higher Education Interface*, Heist Research in association with UCAS: Leeds.

Association of Graduate Recruiters (1993), *Roles for Graduates in the Twenty-first Century*, The Association of Graduate Recruiters: Cambridge.
Berliner, W. (1995), '£142 million owed to loans firm may not be repaid', *The Independent*, 24 November.
Clement, B. (1997), 'Going gets tough for graduates', *The Independent*, 19 June.
Crequer, N. (1997), 'Universities dig in over fees', *The Independent*, 12 September.
Crequer, N. and Nash, I. (1997), 'College degree growth resisted', *Times Educational Supplement*, 19 September.
Dearing, R. (1997), *Higher Education in the Learning Society*, HMSO: London.
Drucker, P. (1962), 'The Educational Revolution', in Halsey, A.H., Floud, J. and Anderson, C.A. (eds.) *Education, Economy and Society*, Free Press: New York, pp. 13-22.
Eaglesham, J. (1997), 'Career goals main reason for going to university', *Financial Times*, 12 August.
Finniston, M. (1980), *Engineering Our Future. Report of the Committee of Inquiry into the Engineering Profession* (Cmnd 7794), HMSO: London.
Gerard, L. (1995), 'Debt drives third more students to drop out', *The Independent*, 28 June.
Halsey, A.H. (1962a), 'The Changing Functions of Universities', in Halsey, A.H., Floud, J. and Anderson, C.A. (eds.) *Education, Economy and Society*, Free Press: New York, pp. 456-66.
Halsey, A.H. (1962b), 'British Universities and Intellectual Life' in Halsey, A.H., Floud, J. and Anderson, C.A. (eds.) *Education, Economy and Society*, Free Press: New York, pp. 502-13.
Halsey, A.H. (1972), 'Higher Education' in Halsey, A.H., *Trends in British Society since 1900. A Guide to the Changing Social Structure of Britain*, Macmillan: London, pp. 192-228.
Halsey, A.H., Floud, J. and Anderson, C.A. (eds.) (1962), *Education, Economy and Society. A Reader in the Sociology of Education*, Free Press: New York.
Haughton, E. and Hodges, L. (1996), 'Action sought on degree standards', *The Independent*, 24 October.
Hunter, L.C. (1981), 'Employers' Perceptions of Demand' in Lindley, R. (ed.) *Higher Education and the Labour Market*, Society for Research into Higher Education: Guildford, pp. 4-49.
Judd, J. (1995), 'Students relying on parental hand-outs', *The Independent*, 8 July.
Judd, J. (1996a), 'Student drop-out rate up by 10 per cent', *The Independent*, 17 January.
Judd, J. (1996b), 'Too many students pass with honours', *The Independent*, 4 December.
Kirkman, S. (1996), 'Debts of ingratitude', *Times Educational Supplement*, 20 September.
Lawrence, D. (1991), 'Students on the Cheap', *Education*, 178.24, p.475.
Lawrence, D. (1993), 'The Rise and Fall of the Local Government Careers Service', *Local Government Studies*, 19, pp.92-107.
Lawrence, D. (1994), 'The English Careers Officer. An Honest Broker?' in Holstein J.A. and Miller, G. (eds.), *Perspectives on Social Problems Vol 6*, JAI Press: Greenwich, CT, pp. 257-80.
Lindley, R. (ed.) (1981), *Higher Education and the Labour Market*, Society for Research into Higher Education: Guildford.
Marshall, A. (1890), *Principles of Economics*, Macmillan: London.
Mason, G. (1995), *The New Graduate Supply-Shock: Recruitment in British Industry*, NIESR: London.
Passmore, B. (1996), 'Firms favour older universities', *Times Educational Supplement*, 20 September.
Performance Indicator Project (1996), *Signposts to Employability. PIP Graduate Recruiters'*

Survey, PIP: Harlaxton, Grantham.
Peston, M. (1981), 'Higher Education Policy' in Lindley, R. (ed.), *Higher Education and the Labour Market*, Society for Research into Higher Education: Guildford, pp. 120-48.
Robbins, Lord (1963), *Higher Education* (The Robbins Report) (Cmnd 2154), HMSO: London.
Roberts, K. (1995), *Youth Employment in Modern Britain*, Oxford University Press: Oxford.
Roberts, K. and Perzya, A. (1994), *Old and New Routes into Post-Communist Poland's Youth Labour Markets*, University of Liverpool, Issues in Sociology and Social Policy: Occasional Paper no.2: Liverpool.
Roizen, J. and Jepson, M. (1985), *Degree for Jobs. Employer expectations of higher education*, SHRE & NFER-Nelson: London.
Sanderson, M. (1987), *Educational Opportunity and Social Change in Britain*, Faber and Faber: London.
Shattock, M. (1996), 'Adding an annexe to ivory towers', *The Times Higher Education Supplement*, 18 October.
Society for Research into Higher Education (1985), 'The Future of Higher Education' in Jaques, D. and Richardson, J.T.E. (eds), *Proceedings of 19th Annual Conference of the Society for Research into Higher Education 1983*, SHRE & NFER-Nelson: Guildford.
Targett, S. (1996), 'Bosses to call the shots', *The Times Higher Education Supplement*, 18 October.
Thatcher, M. (1993), *Margaret Thatcher. The Downing Street Years*, Harper Collins: London.
Ward, L. (1997a), 'Universities should scrap degree classifications', *The Independent*, 4 July.
Ward, L (1997b), 'University chiefs want cash from fees', *The Independent*, 10 September.
Ward, L. and Judd, J. (1997), 'Universities stand firm over fees threat to students fees', *The Independent*, 13 September.
Ward, V. (1995), 'Students march against cash cuts', *The Independent*, 24 November.
Young, S. (1996), 'Comparisons need to become much less odious', *Times Educational Supplement* 2 August.
Young, S. (1994), 'Degree standards to be investigated', *Times Educational Supplement* 8 July.

9 Trends of the 1990s in Swedish Welfare Policy - Implications for Social Work Education

Lennart Nygren

Background

The aim of this chapter is briefly to describe recent trends in the development of the Swedish welfare system, particularly as these affect social services, and to discuss the impact these trends are having on social work education.

The conditions for social work education in Sweden were quite stable until the end of the 1980s. Education programmes had grown quickly in response to the rapidly growing labour market for skilled social workers as the municipalities expanded their social services. While the 1960s had been an age of optimism and growth, the 1970s were a period when social work became politicized. That decade also saw a growing consciousness of the existence of unsolved social problems. In the 1970s the important work towards a radically new social service act was finished. Although there was still some development in the 1980s, more and more signs of ideological reconsideration emerged, both in the form of a more aggressive neo-liberalism in political debate and in the so-called 'war of the roses' between traditionalists and modernizers within the Social Democratic party, which had dominated Swedish governments since the 1930s (Nygren, 1994).

Around 1990, Sweden began to experience growing fiscal problems and high unemployment. The economy slowed down and, as the century draws to a close, the Swedes have had to abandon their self-image of being one of the four or five richest countries in the world. The serious problems of the Swedish economy were closely reflected in the conditions for social work, both in terms of resources for provision and transfers by means of taxes and benefits, and in terms of the pressure from a growing number of people with financial and social problems. These problems were further complicated by the internationalization of Swedish society and economy with EU membership and an increasing openness to the immigration of refugees.

Financial Pressures, Ideological Influences and New Social Problems

The Swedish model of social policy is well-recognized and has often been used as a particular type in comparative research. One reason for this particular attention seems to be that Sweden represents a unique combination of a market economy and a large public sector. Sweden often stands for a 'Scandinavian model', which also includes Norway, Denmark and, sometimes, Finland (Sipilä, 1997). However, this model is more a reflection of history than the actual experience of the mid 1990s. There has been an intense political debate in Sweden which has questioned the large public role in the welfare state. Interestingly, though, public opinion about the welfare system has remained surprisingly stable (Svallfors, 1996), and the changes have mainly been legitimated through the need for budget control perceived by the political class.

During the 1990s, Sweden has changed her various policy programmes in a way that makes it more and more difficult to talk about a 'unique' model. Quite a few other West European countries are now more generous in their levels of some types of social security benefit and family allowances. Even so, as a whole, the Swedish system would still today be considered as 'one of the most comprehensive and generous systems of welfare provision in Europe and the world' (Gould, 1996, p.91).

The reasons for the cuts in the social security system during the early 1990s were both economic and ideological. From 1989 onwards, the Swedish state budget went into a dramatic deficit, partly due to a tax reform that reduced revenue. The obvious solution was to cut expenditures. The alternative strategy - increasing taxes - was also used, but had political (and economic) limits. At the same time as these internal financial problems, the growing internationalisation of the economy made Sweden very vulnerable to fluctuations on the global financial markets. The currency was exposed to speculation and interest rates remained high. In such a situation, there was a strong political imperative to present an appearance of fiscal stability towards the international financial markets. Mr Persson, the Minister of Finance and, later, the Prime Minister, embodied this strategy through his uncompromising defence of tight budgetary control.

Ideological developments interacted with these economic issues. Since

1980, neo-liberal influences have had a visible impact both outside and inside the dominating Social Democratic Party. Concepts like cost-efficiency, privatization, marketization and customer-orientation have been introduced and disseminated as ways of changing the production of welfare (Nygren, 1994).

At the same time, new social problems have emerged. These are due to demographic changes, to the recognition of new issues and to a dramatically worsened labour market situation. Poverty has emerged as a particular problem among the growing elderly population and posed new challenges to social service agencies. The unemployed often experience financial difficulties. Many new immigrants are unemployed and, among them, middle-aged women from southern Europe (Greece and Yugoslavia) are often effectively early retired (Ekberg and Gustafsson, 1995, p.125).

In summary, the Swedish social security system remains as a system and the main changes are in the level of benefits paid when someone is ill, unemployed or on parental leave. However, there is a spill-over effect from the cuts in government spending at local government level and the consequent reduction in social care services. This is more directly relevant for social workers, as they are faced with the indirect effects of the reductions in social security benefits on the living conditions of socially vulnerable people.

Recent Trends in Swedish Social Services

Economic Retrenchment and New Problems

When the Social Service Act came into effect in 1982, Swedish social services were organized in three different areas: care of the elderly (and the disabled); child care; and individual and family care (IFC) . The cuts of the 1990s are most visible in children's day care. The number of children per staff member, for example, has gone up (Hanssen, 1997, p.186). The IFC sector is quite different since it is more selective. It includes treatment for drug and alcohol abuse, foster care and social assistance (financial aid to families and individuals). As a very preliminary analysis of the changes, one could say that it has been easier for local politicians to make reductions in their looser responsibilities for care of the elderly and day care for children than in the IFC sector. This could reflect a believe that there are alternatives - at least in theory - for elderly and child care: families have been expected to assume more and more responsibilities for taking care of old relatives and of children (and elderly relatives are frequently used as a replacement for public child care).

The IFC sector is more complex and there are no obvious alternatives, as in elderly and child care. The demand for foster care, for example, arises because of a need to remove children from their families and the absence of alternative carers. Family members cannot be expected to provide financial support in place of public assistance since the system already rules out such aid if the person in need has relatives who could help.

Sweden has gone through two distinct phases in its treatment of drug and alcohol abuse. There was a rapid growth in private institutions during the 1980s. Most of these were small with 4-20 patients. Since this was not really an intended result of a policy, but the result of an oversight by the political system, it was labelled as the 'privatization of the century' (Socialstyrelsen, 1991). The municipalities paid high daily fees for the care in these institutions but poor accounting control systems led to a delay in discovering how expensive they were. One reaction was to partly return the responsibility for the institutions to the national (state) level and while another was to develop new forms of open care in the abuser's own neighbourhood. In this phase we can see a differentiation of clients: one group which is too problematic to treat without institutional control, and another that is expected to be successfully, and of course more cheaply, treated within their already existing networks and communities. A critical question for social work, of course, is that of discriminating accurately between these groups, especially where the cost of treating one is so much greater than the cost of treating the other and there are pressures to minimize public expenditure.

At the same time as cuts are hitting the IFC sector, it is also facing heavy demands from new client groups. One is being created by the rapid growth in unemployment, especially of a long-term nature. Another group consists of refugees and other immigrants. A large number of the refugees that have come to Sweden in the last decade have found it difficult to integrate into the labour market. This group is experiencing a kind of poverty that is new to Sweden. A third group arises from changes in the practice of psychiatry. As in most other Western countries, the old institutions are being closed down and group homes are being developed. This is falling as an extra cost on the municipalities, since the responsibility has been shifted down from county level, where health care is funded, to form part of the local social care system without a matching transfer of resources. The numbers involved are quite substantial: one third of the 3,000 homeless in Stockholm are currently reported to have serious psychiatric problems (Unpublished report from the

Stockholm Bureau for Research and Development - FoU-byrån - cited in *Svenska Dagbladet*, 4 September 1997). At the same time, the municipalities are seeing a growth in the numbers of elderly and disabled people needing care.

The strongest impact on IFC budgets, however, comes from the fall-out of cuts in the national social insurance schemes. The number of people receiving social assistance has increased dramatically during the 1990s as more and more people find it impossible to live on the money they get as unemployed, long-term sick, on parental leave etc (Salonen, 1996). The reduction in child allowances and the abolition of extra allowances for families with more than two children have forced many families with three or more children onto social assistance. Instead of being supported by a general and relatively effective national insurance system, these cuts have generated new clients for the staff-intensive, and consequently expensive, social welfare agencies.

The nationalisation of institutional care for drug and alcohol abusers is an exception to the overall tendency to decentralise responsibility for social services in Sweden. More and more has been passed down from the national and county levels to the municipalities. Beside the burden of providing for the financial needs of citizens, one of the clearest examples is the change in the responsibility for medical care of the elderly (the so called ÄDEL reform), where the municipalities became the new authority instead of the counties. This has affected the social work by putting pressure on the municipalities to develop their health services by, for example, employing nurses. In turn, this has created conflicts between more socially oriented municipal home carers and the medically oriented nurses. However, there has also been a genuine demographic increase in the numbers of 'old old' people needing more labour-intensive types of care (Nygren, 1994, p.164).

Marketization

In Sweden privatization has not been as important as it has been in, for example, the United Kingdom (Olsson, 1993). However the concept of privatization needs further analysis. Some activities have been lifted out - 'contracted out' - from the public sector, like, for example, cleaning of care institutions, food production and distribution and some of the drug abuse treatment as described above. We have also seen a growing number of private consultants remunerated by the municipalities. There are several examples of social workers who have developed expertise in rehabilitation, evaluation methods or various kinds of special therapies, who have gone private, but this still is not a big market.

The orientation towards marketization has been observable in almost all public organizations over the last ten years, including social services, and has forced administrators and politicians to think in market terms (Nygren, 1994, p.100-101). They have to plan budgets more carefully, and be more considered about the economic consequences of their activity. This has caused much frustration for social workers who did not previously have to think in these terms. There is an obvious risk that 'expensive' clients will be either ignored or referred to other authorities so that the budget unit can show better results. There are many examples of Swedish municipalities trying to develop what could be called quasi-markets. They really are 'quasi' because there is neither competition among the producers, nor a real market since the 'customers' do not have any money to buy the services (cf. LeGrand, 1993, Bartlett et al, 1994). Instead there is a market-like communication between one side of the municipal organization (the buyer) and another side (the producer) and the real instrument to measure success is not the 'profit' but a careful evaluation. As a response to this, many social service organizations have created departments of field research and development, employing research educated social workers from the universities.

An issue related to the marketization process is the relative priority of problem prevention and problem solving. The issue for a quasi-market organization is that preventive efforts will often give a result at an unspecifiable time in the future and for some other sector. This is the case, for example, with social work in schools, children's day care and youth recreation centres. The outcome measures are very uncertain, the activities are quite costly and it is quite impossible to know specifically when a certain activity has reduced social problems in the future. In other words - who really wants to buy and pay for the prevention of social problems?

A New Social Service Act

The Social Service Committee has been working on a revision of Swedish social service legislation since 1991. Two of their reports (SOU, 1994, p.39; 1995, p.58) envisage a number of trends relevant for social work. These include the following:-

- The proposed new social service act includes a more explicit perspective on children's interests and rights. This means that social

workers have to be more aware of children's perceptions of their conditions and to listen more carefully than before to abused children. This will demand some changes in social work education and new research to establish how social workers can improve their skills in communicating with children.
- The voluntary sector of social services is more on the agenda in Sweden than before. Working within, or in partnership with, voluntary organizations demands a different kind of competence for social workers than in an era when almost all of them were employed in the public sector.
- The importance of community work is expected to grow. Today's social service workers are mainly working with a psychological and individualised view of social problems. The community work traditions demand a somewhat different approach, which has been very weak in Swedish social work. It is however surprising to see this formulated by the Committee - it almost seems like a renaissance of the idea of social engineering and social planning that was strong during the 1970s but almost disappeared during the 1980s.
- Evaluation and quality assurance in social services is another area where the Committee has identified a need to develop social work education. This has to do with the trend towards marketization. The costs of services have to be related to their effects, and this demands new instruments to specify and measure outcomes.

Education

The Swedish educational system relating to social service work operates at different levels. In this chapter, only the university or college (*högskola*) level will be considered, but there are also programmes for students in the *gymnasium* (age 16-18). The IFC sector mainly recruits from academic social work education (*socionom* - BScSW) which is available in seven Swedish universities. This course lasts three and a half years and will be the focus of the following discussion.

The institutions for drug and alcohol abusers also employ a relatively small group of 'social pedagogues', who work with clients in a more directive way to develop self-reliance. They are educated at colleges and are sometimes in competition with the socionoms. There are also college-level programmes for people working in the care of the elderly and the disabled. The colleges do not have post-graduate studies in any substantial way, and their education is vocational rather than theoretical, as in the more academic socionom courses. However, there is a current (1997) move to align the education of social pedagogues and home carers with that of the socionoms, partly as a response to the perceived need for more administrative and planning skills among all social workers.

In children's day care there are two groups of professionals: child carers (educated at colleges) and pre school teachers (with university education). Emphasis here is put on the pedagogical aspects more than the caring aspects, which also reflects a policy trend to move day care of children from social services to the public school system.

Conclusions

The picture of change in the Swedish social welfare system is a complicated one, even if the general trend towards harder financial times and more difficult social problems is clear. Decentralization and the growing pressure of need are putting new and strong demands on the social work education system. The demands are two-sided. One is that employers are asking for students to be prepared in the detailed skills needed for better planning, research and administration. The changing burden of social problems also leads to demands for a greater competence in dealing with difficult psychiatric clients, more advanced work with children and new forms of open care and treatment of drug and alcohol abusers. The other side is a need for general knowledge, theory
and values in order to become more reflexive and more flexible in a time of rapid change.

As a result, new conflicts are appearing and old conflicts are reappearing. One conflict is between specialists and generalists. It has been suggested that there should be a general basic education in social work at university level and that specialization would develop through practice. An alternative approach would be to create a more differentiated exit from the education system, with students choosing to specialize in, for example, drug and alcohol abuse treatment, community work or youth work towards the end of their university course.

Another conflict is between more theoretical/academic and more vocational/practical programmes. This conflict is visible within all current courses in social work where 'theories', 'skills' and 'values' struggle for available curriculum space. A similar conflict exists between the allocation of time to teaching general social theory and teaching more specific areas of knowledge, often with a more integrated 'tool-like' theory-and-practice approach. Examples of this might be the various kinds of therapies for families or abusers, for work with abused and neglected children, for work with refugees and for budget advising to people living on social assistance. In each of these, there are free-standing, goal-oriented techniques which purport to draw on theories unique to work with the client group receiving the intervention rather than being specific applications of more general theories of behaviour and of the associated generic means of achieving personal change.

How can social work educators respond to these trends in the welfare state and in educational thought? The answer very much depends on what we regard as general knowledge in social work. It is obvious that a social work student should be able to be critical about both educational and political trends and also be prepared to work under various and changing conditions. This demands a general approach in social work education. Within this, it seems to be important to put strong emphasis on values and theory rather than skills, or, at least, to focus on those skills defined as generic, that is to say skills that are not merely temporary fashions in the field.

The kind of knowledge to be acquired by the student can be described in the following general terms (cf. Nygren and Soydan, 1997):-

a. General and critical knowledge about the construction of social problems and oppression: Which social activities are labelled as social problems? For what reasons? What are the consequences for people affected by these labels? How can we explain these consequences? Who has the power to impose these labels? What are the sources of that power? How can we evaluate its use for good or ill?

b. Knowledge about conditions for human change: What is 'change'? How does the relationship between the individual and the community affect the process of change? How can we analyse the values involved in seeking to change people?

c. Knowledge of the political, individual, legal and other conditions which require or justify intervention from social workers in different types of situations?

d. An understanding of the skills, responsibilities, talents and preferences available to individual practitioners to carry out such interventions?

If less emphasis is put on levels a and b there is a risk of producing uncritical and instrumental practitioners.

What is the role, then, of the practical skills that are so often emphasised as a core area in social work education? These skills are certainly important but represent a kind of knowledge that is more or less tacit. Practical skills are mainly developed in the field of practice and not in the field of education, even if education can be a forum for reflection and deeper understanding. Attempts to incorporate skill training within education programmes often end up with problems about the reality of the experience offered and risk being outdated by the time the student graduates. The flexibility to deal with change in professional life is an important argument for stressing the importance of a theoretical and generalist approach. A final argument is the importance in all kinds of social work education of developing a firm ethical foundation for practice. People who are involved in a profession whose task is to bring about or impose changes on others must constantly reflect on the rightness of their actions. They can only do this if their education has given them a good understanding of the theoretical basis of moral arguments and challenged them to use this in critical analysis.

In the end, we find a strange paradox: While the pressure of new social problems and the restrictions on public expenditure are leading to a more selective and complex task for Swedish social workers, it appears as if the abandonment of universality in the welfare system will demand a stronger emphasis on generalist and critical knowledge in social work education.

References

Bartlett, W. *et al.* (1994), *Quasi-markets in the Welfare State. The Emergent Findings*, SAUS: Bristol.
Ekberg, J. and Gustafsson, B. (1995), *Invandrare på arbetsmarknaden*. [Immigrants in the labour market], SNS förlag: Stockholm.
Gould, A. (1996), 'Sweden: The Last Bastion of Social Democracy', in George, V. and Taylor-Gooby, P. (eds.) *European Welfare Policy*, Macmillan: London.
Hanssen, J-I. and Elvehøi, O-M. (1997), 'A Statistical Summary of the Development of Social Services for Children, Elderly and Disabled in the Scandinavian Countries', in Sipilä, J. (ed.), *Social Care Services - The Key to the Scandinavian Model*, Ashgate: Aldershot.
LeGrand, J. (1993), *Quasi-markets and Community Care*, SAUS: Bristol.
Nygren, L. (1994), *Trygghet under omprövning. Välfärdsstaten och 90-talets utmaningar*. [Social Security Reconsidered. The Welfare State and the Challenges of the 90s],. Publica:

Stockholm.

Nygren, L. and Soydan, H. (1997), 'Social work research and its dependence on practice', *Scandinavian Journal of Social Welfare*, 7, pp.217-24.

Olsson, S. E. (1990/1993), *Social Policy and Welfare State in Sweden*, Arkiv: Lund.

Salonen, T. (1996), *Övervältringar inom socialsektorn - effekter av statliga nedskärningar på socialbidragshushåll* [Spill over within the social sector - the effects of cuts in national schemes on the social assistance households],Komentus: Stockholm.

Sipilä, J. (ed.) (1997), *Social Care Services - The Key to the Scandinavian Model*, Ashgate: Aldershot.

Socialstyrelsen [The National Board for Health and Social Affairs] (1991), *Privat och offentligt i vården - en analys av utvecklingen under 1980-talet inom barn- och ungdoms- och missbrukarvården* [Private and Public Care - an Analysis of Developments during the 1980s in the Care of Children, Youth and Drug and Alcohol Abusers], Socialstyrelsen: Stockholm.

SOU (1994), *139: Ny socialtjänstlag* [New Social Service Act], Fritzes: Stockholm.

SOU (1995), *58: Kompetens och kunskapsutveckling - Om yrkesroller och arbetsfält inom socialtjänsten* [Competence and Knowledge development - On professional Roles and Fields Within Social Services], Fritzes: Stockholm.

Svallfors, S. (1996) *Välfärdsstatens moraliska ekonomi. Välfärdsopinionen i 90-talets Sverige.* [The Moral Economics of the Welfare State. The Welfare Opinion of Sweden in the 90s], Boréa: Umeå.

10 The Prevention and Relief of Unemployment in Britain
Paul Ransome

Drawing on the post-war experiences of the United Kingdom, this paper poses a number of general questions about the causes and consequences of unemployment. The most important are: first, 'who is responsible for unemployment'; and, second, 'who is responsible for providing relief for people who have become unemployed'?

The essence of these questions, is whether, and to what extent, the state should assume responsibility for maintaining high levels of, or even 'full', employment, and whether, once unemployment has occurred, the state is responsible for providing financial and other forms of relief for the unemployed. At the outset it should be acknowledged that unemployment relief or 'unemployment benefit' is only one of a number of demands which individuals make of the state. In West European welfare systems, the 'welfare state' is called upon to deliver physical and mental health care, help for the young, elderly and disabled, help with housing and remedial education, together with a wide range of other personal services aimed at securing and maintaining a minimal level of 'social security' amongst the population.

The point of departure for this paper, however, is that opportunities for stable employment provide the most secure foundation for both individual and social stability. Although unemployment may not be the only factor, it is very often the case that many of the security demands which people make on the state can be associated either directly or indirectly with the consequences of becoming unemployed. Unemployment, in other words, is not a discrete form of social insecurity, but is intimately connected with, and may lead to an escalation in, people's other welfare needs. In the context of our present discussion of the development of social policy, we can therefore say that governmental decisions about accepting responsibility for the welfare of the unemployed are central to decisions about the state's responsibility for social security more generally.

Looking at the experiences of the United Kingdom over the course of this century, perceptions of the state's role in maintaining high levels of employment, and, consequently, of taking responsibility for the welfare of the unemployed, have passed through a number of more or less distinct phases. It will be useful to examine these in terms of two interconnected dimensions of change, namely political ideology and economic and social change. From the turn of the century until the period of the second world war, the prevailing political view was that levels of employment and unemployment were simply determined by the operation of the 'free market'. In the context of *laissez faire* capitalism, the responsibility of the state was to keep external regulation of the economy to a minimum. As long as the market was allowed to operate without state interference, it was believed that competition between producers would give rise to increasing levels of prosperity for all. If unemployment did occur, it was a regrettable but none the less 'natural' consequence of free market capitalism. Under some circumstances, it could even be claimed that unemployment was beneficial to the economy since it provided employers with a pool of labour from which they could draw during periods of economic growth. Similarly, there was no logical reason why the principle of competition should not include competition between workers in seeking employment. If competition for jobs intensified, this would have the advantages of improving the quality of work and productivity among those who were still employed and of putting downward pressure on the cost of wages.

From the point of view of the unemployed however, loss of employment almost inevitably resulted in acute poverty. The plight of the unemployed became particularly intense during the economic depression and slump of the 1930s, and it was during this period that the government began to accept that the state should accept at least some responsibility for their welfare. Although history records that measures aimed at 'the relief of poverty' were initially brought about through the efforts of a relatively small number of liberal philanthropists, these measures were also a response to the more general recognition that high levels of unemployment and poverty could pose a significant threat to the basic structure of society. At a time in British history when radical socialist ideas were still current among the working class, and especially among their leadership, there is no doubt that government and employers feared that the unemployed could represent a revolutionary force in society. While accepting, then, that the efficient operation of the free market economy should not be constrained by state intervention, it was also acknowledged that, even if unemployment was a natural effect of the economy, the state must accept some responsibility for providing financial relief for the unemployed. Both for humanitarian and for political reasons, it was expedient and legitimate for the state to intervene in this way.

With the election of the first majority Labour government in 1945, political and popular attitudes towards state intervention changed. Rather than accepting that the state should continue with the non-interventionist strategy of the pre-war years, a general feeling emerged that the operation of the free market was imperfect, and that economic stability and prosperity could not therefore be achieved without direct intervention by the state. There are a number of reasons for this change of perspective, which affected not only the day-to-day operations of the economy, but also highlighted the need for improvements in the social security and welfare of the population more generally. In the case of the former, the ideas of the economist John Maynard Keynes were adopted as the most effective means of restructuring the post-war economy. The key feature of this strategy was that the state, because of the large financial and organizational resources at its disposal, resources which had developed during the war, could and should play a leading role in the economy. It was argued that a massive expansion of public employment, together with the financing of large-scale public projects which were necessary literally to rebuild the social infrastructure after the destruction and disruption of the war years, would stimulate demand within the economy. The demand by employers (including the state-as-employer) for employees to work on these projects would increase the prosperity of the workforce, which would in turn generate consumer demand for new products. This demand would accelerate growth throughout the economy. The revenues generated through public taxation on corporate and individual incomes would provide the necessary funding for this action by the state.

Regarding political attitudes towards social security and welfare, this acceptance of the legitimate role and responsibility of the state in economic affairs was also reflected in a forthright acknowledgement that the state should accept responsibility for providing the population with the means of satisfying their growing expectations for housing, for education, for health care and for a range of other personal services. Although these responsibilities were accepted for ideological and political reasons, including popular socialist expectations amongst the working class, it was quite logical that discharging these new responsibilities was entirely compatible with the new interventionist economic strategy. Building new houses, schools and hospitals for example, would meet the objectives both of stimulating demand within the economy and of providing the infrastructure for social and welfare security.

Central to these developments was an acknowledgement that high levels of employment were a necessary precursor to both economic and individual security. There was almost universal acceptance that under no circumstances should British society return to the levels of unemployment and poverty it had experienced before the war. While accepting that a minimal level of unemployment (perhaps 2 per cent of the total population of working age) was necessary for mobility within the workforce, the objective of full employment rose to the top of the political agenda. If high levels of employment could be maintained, the security of the economy and of the working population could also be maintained. In line with the general principle of the social responsibility of the state, it was also accepted that if unemployment did occur, then the unemployed were entitled to expect financial and other support from the state. The introduction of a National Insurance Scheme, through which individuals made direct contributions from their earnings, together with contributions made on their behalf by employers, provided a pool of resources from which the unemployed would receive their benefits. High levels of employment would ensure that this insurance fund would be considerably in excess of the demands made upon it.

Throughout the 1950s and 1960s, and in line with other West European economies, the British economy prospered. Full employment was maintained as economic efficiency and productivity increased. Although the British economy became more and more interconnected with the global economy, and therefore had to accept both the negative and positive impact of changes in world markets, prolonged economic stability had been achieved. In the context of employment security and an increasingly consumer-oriented mentality, the quality of life of the majority of the population continued to improve. These high levels of economic well-being and security not only generated a sense of optimism about the prospects for the future, but also tended to consolidate general expectations about what the individual was entitled to in terms of state provision. Aspirations for universal welfare benefits which had emerged in the post-war period, had, by the 1960s, become a reality. To all intents and purposes, it seemed that the theory of state intervention in the economy was working, and both Labour and Conservative governments continued to accept that this was the most appropriate economic and political strategy.

As already noted above however, personal prosperity and social welfare are conditional upon economic prosperity. In turn, economic prosperity is dependent upon a reasonably high level of predictability and stability in the mechanisms of the economy. During the 1970s a number of significant developments took place which tended to undermine this stability. In the global context, massive increases in the price of oil resulted in a very large escalation in the costs of economic production. At the same time, other economies, particularly in the Pacific Rim, were beginning to mount a significant economic challenge to the established industries of Western Europe and the USA. In the domestic context, the process of technological innovation greatly accelerated with the introduction of microelectronic technologies. Perhaps ironically, the mature industrial economies started to lose their competitive advantage as younger industrial economies were much more willing to accommodate technological innovation. In Britain, these circumstances combined to produce a deceleration, and subsequently a fall, in economic growth and prosperity. Established 'traditional' industries, particularly in raw materials, manufacturing and engineering became inefficient compared with those of other economies.

Partly as a consequence of falling global demand for their products, and partly in an attempt to improve productivity, many employers started to reduce the size of their workforces. For the first time since the war, unemployment began to rise. As the cost of living began to rise with inflation, the trade unions became more and more aggressive in attempting to maintain the incomes of the workers they represented. Unfortunately, however, increasing wage costs resulted in higher prices for the products they produced, so adding to, rather than relieving the problem of inflation. Because many industries were publicly owned, the state-as-employer could not detach itself either from the need to prevent further economic decline, or from accepting responsibility for the consequences of falling prosperity. Throughout the 1970s, economic instability resulted in increasing political instability as the principle of state intervention in the economy was reassessed. This question became more and more urgent as the costs to the state of providing welfare and social services increased with rising unemployment.

The election of the Conservatives under the leadership of Margaret Thatcher in 1979 signalled the beginning of a reversal of many of the policies which had been sustained throughout the post-war period. Central to the new policy was a forthright rejection of the belief that the state had a legitimate interventionist role to play in the economic sphere. It was argued that, although the market was imperfect, regulation by the state hindered its free operation to such an extent that economic recovery would never be achieved. This hindrance was particularly acute in the realm of innovation and increased efficiency, where, it was argued, the free play of market forces was essential. At the same time it was suggested that the burden of responsibility placed on the state for the provision of welfare services had grown too large. From this perspective, the welfare state no longer simply provided an insurance against the effects of economic and other forms of hardship, which had been its original purpose, but had come to be seen as a guarantor of prosperity.

In response to this revival of free market economics, legislation was introduced to bring about the withdrawal of the state from regulatory intervention in the market and from direct involvement in economic planning. At the same time, the size of the state, both as employer and as corporate participant, was reduced through the privatization of many industries which had been in public ownership. Rather than being 'responsible' for regulating the market through demand management, the state was now 'responsible' for allowing the market as much freedom as possible. In terms of maintaining levels of employment, the withdrawal of the state, together with an extensive restructuring of the economy, resulted in a rise in unemployment from 1.5 million (5.8 per cent of the workforce) in 1979 to 3.2 million (11.5 per cent) in 1985. Although unemployment started to fall during the late 1980s, it began to rise again during the early 1990s, reaching 3 million in February 1993.

In terms of state responsibilities towards individual welfare, a right-wing philosophy emerged in which 'responsibility' was much more directly attributed to the individual rather than to society. It was argued that while the state could still accept responsibility for providing for basic welfare needs, individuals had to accept that they too bore a share of this responsibility. It was in other words, a question of restoring a balance between individual self-reliance and reliance on the state. Although successive Conservative governments proceeded with progressive reductions in the levels of unemployment benefit and other forms of welfare provision, and therefore achieved a considerable reduction in the amount of money being spent on these welfare services, they were far less successful in attracting popular support for their policies.

The election of a Labour Government in 1997 - the first for eighteen years - was partly a reflection of the fact that a majority of the population had decided that it was no longer prepared to accept any further reduction in both the extent and depth of welfare services. Although the unemployed do not have, and do not seem likely to develop, a 'political voice' of their own, an increasing proportion of the population now have personal experience of some form of social and welfare insecurity. Interestingly though, rather than returning to the political and social philosophy of the post-war years, the new administration's policy towards welfare benefits for the unemployed includes many of the principles which had emerged under the Conservatives. Among the most important is the idea that the unemployed are not simply 'victims' of economic restructuring, but have a responsibility for improving their own circumstances. This shift reflects important changes which have taken place in the economic environment during the 1990s. First, whereas 'employment' was previously seen in terms of more or less permanent full-time jobs in 'traditional' industries, increasing fluidity in employers' demand for workers has placed much greater emphasis on the general rather than the particular skills of potential employees. To match the flexibility of the labour market (both in terms of the number of people required, and in the kinds of skills they have), people now have to reassess their 'employability' in a more proactive way. Having a particular skill, or a particular kind of experience is not sufficient under circumstances where employers are as least as interested in a person's potential to be adaptable, to learn new skills, and to work in a team- and group-oriented environment. Second, and closely related to these shifts, the notion of unemployment has also become more fluid. Whereas 'unemployment' used to be seen as a 'discrete' or 'total' situation, it is now seen as lying along a continuum of various degrees of job insecurity. Under current circumstances, everyone has to face the prospect of changes in the circumstances of their employment, including for example, movement between full- and part-time working, more frequent shifts from one employer to another, and shorter spells of contract rather than payroll working.

Politically, this fluidity and almost universal insecurity has resulted in the attitude that, as a condition of receiving benefit, individuals are obliged to take whatever steps are necessary for them to improve the 'portfolio' of skills and experiences upon which their employability is based. Rather than being 'passive' recipients of a welfare entitlement, the unemployed are now seen as being in an 'active' contractual relationship with the benefits system. Claimants have a right to be provided with a minimal amount of income, but society also has a right to expect that claimants will repay this 'debt' by accepting that any kind of work-related training or experience will improve their prospects of becoming self-providers.

Although therefore, successive British governments have accepted that the state is an economic institution and, as such, is inevitably implicated in maintaining employment, the form in which this responsibility makes itself manifest has changed from one of direct intervention through large-scale state-funding of public projects, through more indirect forms of intervention, and most recently towards one of mutual obligation between the state and the individual. In terms of the provision of welfare more generally, the principle of personal responsibility has, at least for the more prosperous portion of the population, been translated into a growth in the number and variety of private insurance schemes. Although there is clear evidence that a centralized and publicly owned health service is much more efficient that a host of independent providers, an increasing number of people no longer seem willing to rely on the public health services. Perhaps ironically, doubts about the future reliability of the welfare state are beginning to generate new feelings of insecurity. This tendency can in part be interpreted as a consequence of the historically very high levels of security which emerged during the prosperous years of the 1950s and 1960s. It could reasonably be argued that a significant proportion of the population had come to take state provision of welfare security more or less for granted. For these people, experiences of the economic depression of the late 1980s and early 1990s, and their negative impact upon levels of welfare provision, have come as something of a shock. This sense of disillusionment may be felt even more clearly by a younger age group of people who have spent much, if not all, of their lives living along the margins of state benefits and insecure employment. For these people, participation in private health and welfare schemes is simply not a realistic possibility. It may be that the recent change of government is partly attributable to a general rejection of the 'competitive individualist' philosophy of the 1980s and a revival of 'communitarian' social democratic political ideology, but it remains to be seen what form the revived idea of 'social responsibility' will take against the background of an inherently unstable economic environment. Whatever the final extent of these trends, it remains the case that social and welfare security are closely connected with, if not directly dependent upon, the security of the economy. In the context of an increasingly volatile global market, and under conditions of rapid and continuous technological innovation and change, it seems likely that economic stability may become almost impossible to achieve. Rather, modern market economies may have to adopt much more flexible strategies in which 'stability' is a relative rather than an absolute phenomena. What we already know, is that in Britain, and elsewhere in Western Europe, the proportion of the total population who are dependent on those who are economically active is increasing, and that the expectations of this dependent proportion regarding health care and other essential welfare needs are higher than they have ever been. While many would accept that high levels of welfare benefits, and particularly cash benefits paid to the unemployed, might tend to undermine the motivation of welfare recipients to take positive steps themselves towards improving their circumstances, it remains the case that both economically, and especially politically, the state cannot simply relinquish all responsibility for the unemployed, the sick, the poorly educated and the physically and mentally disabled. In purely financial, let alone in humanitarian terms, this strongly suggests that the costs of welfare will continue to rise at a time when economic prosperity is becoming less and less certain.

11 Changes in the Polish Labour Market During the Period of Transformation

Ewa Giermanowska
Józefina Hrynkiewicz

Changes in the Economic System and their Implications for the Nature and Structure of Employment

The changes in the nature and structure of employment since 1989 do not simply reflect the changing labour market but the whole socio-economic process of the transformation in Poland. From 1945 until 1989, employment policy was directed towards one of the most 'utopian social goals of socialism' - full employment (or concealed unemployment, as some used to call it). The whole social system was closely based on the provision of employment and wages by the state. From the beginning of the transformation in 1989, the most important qualitative change in the system of social policy was the state's abandonment of an obligation to guarantee work, wages and social benefits to all citizens. This has influenced all aspects of the provision of employment and benefits to workers and has also initiated a process of rationalization, including:

- the creation of a labour market regulated by the laws of supply and demand. A permanent shortage of labour, typical of centrally planned economies, has been converted into a permanent surplus;
- the attempt to eliminate employment in excess of the actual needs of enterprises through the replacement of central planning by market mechanisms.

The development of the labour market has taken place during a deep economic recession. This resulted in mass unemployment which made it difficult to rationalize the use of labour. Many employees were dismissed without any offer of new employment, although the government did enhance early retirement provisions. Changes in the economic system have not been the only cause of unemployment. Its scale and structural nature were aggravated by radical liberal concepts of economic reform. According to the authors of these proposals, all social and economic problems would be solved by 'the invisible hand' of *laissez faire*. Their thinking did not acknowledge the possibility of social costs and, as a result, made no attempt to resolve these problems or to prepare the population for any difficulties. The policy of dismissals and the introduction of early retirement has led only to an illusory economic success, as the need to guarantee subsistence for those lacking any gainful employment has led to increased taxes, both direct and indirect, and growing public debt.

Unemployment, initially perceived as evidence of the functioning of an effective labour market in Poland, proved to be a complex phenomenon. After 50 years absence, the lack of employment was a new and unexpected experience for most Poles. At first, neither public authorities nor families were ready to cope with the problem. It grew rapidly. At the end of 1989, there were 10,000 people looking for work and 620,000 vacancies available (Bujak and Górniak, 1992). In January 1990, the number of registered unemployed had increased to 55,800 and exceeded one million by December. At the end of 1992, registered unemployment was over 2.5 million and continued rising to 2.9 million in December 1993. At the end of July 1994, registered unemployment reached its highest ever level at almost 3 million, representing 16.9 per cent of the economically active population.[1] There were neither appropriate laws nor policies to combat this trend.

The State's Responsibility for Unemployment

Many Poles were surprised by the sudden appearance of unemployment and its growth to such a high level. The majority have not accepted mass unemployment, although a minority do see it in positive terms. Asked in a 1993 survey whether unemployment had been necessary to the rationalization of the economy, half the respondents gave a negative answer, while a quarter agreed (Reszke, 1995). Disapproval of unemployment was most often expressed by older people, residents of small towns, women, the unemployed, women heading households, employees and retired people. Those accepting the necessity of unemployment included people under 25, students, owners of firms, employees feeling no personal threat of unemployment, specialists, managers and those with higher levels of education. Half the respondents thought that unemployment had no positive impact, but 38 per cent found both positive and negative effects. Among the negative consequences listed were poverty, crime and the demoralization of young people.

However, disapproval of unemployment has been accompanied by a lack of knowledge about its real causes and an inadequate understanding of the interrelation between the situation in the labour market and the general condition of the Polish economy (Reszke, 1995). Most unemployed people blamed the state for their lack of a job. In August 1993, around three quarters of them thought that unemployment was the result of defects in national economic policy. Over half thought that these defects were the most important cause of unemployment.[2] Other factors blamed for unemployment included: privatization - 44 per cent of respondents; incompetent management - 39 per cent; economic recession - 30 per cent. These reasons were all associated with government economic policy. According to the unemployed, their own lack of the skills required by a market economy was less important. Only about a quarter of them thought that their unemployment was an inevitable element of economic transformation or a permanent feature of a market economy.

Unemployed People's Expectations of the State

No preparation had been given to unemployed people in order to help them to cope with the problems they faced in the labour market. Most of their working lives had been spent under a centrally planned economy where employers competed with each other to recruit new employees. The unemployed have not understood that the power enjoyed by employees, typical of 'real socialism', has been transformed into an employers' power. Initially, the unemployed simply drew their benefit and waited to be offered a position in a state-owned enterprise similar to that which they had enjoyed before they became redundant. They have not, in general, changed their behaviour, expectations, way of thinking and life-style - typical of state industrial workers under 'real socialism' (Marcinkowski and Sobczak, 1993). They are convinced that the state has failed to protect the Polish labour market. In 1993, only around 2 per cent of respondents believed that the problem of unemployment was being taken seriously by the government and acted upon.[3] Of the other respondents, 28 per cent were convinced that assistance for the unemployed was insufficient, 27 per cent believed that the problem had been discussed but no action had been taken, and 16 per cent thought that actions for the unemployed were rare and ineffective. The activities of labour offices in trying to generate job offers and to give individual assistance to job-seekers were regarded as unsatisfactory. In the view of the unemployed, assistance had been limited to registering them and paying benefits. They had expected action to create new jobs (72 per cent of respondents). About one third of the unemployed thought that unemployment should have been reduced by organizing public and seasonal works and ensuring access to training; and about one quarter thought there should have been more protection for existing jobs and the provision of loans for starting one's own business activity.

The unemployed had diverse expectations. About 40 per cent of those under 24 thought that on-the-job training was a desirable method of reducing unemployment, but only 20.5 per cent of those above 45 years shared this view. The willingness to take an initiative to establish a business increased proportionally with educational level. Opinions and employment behaviour varied depending on age, sex, educational attainment, profession, seniority, place of residence, family and health status.

Media Stereotypes of Unemployment and the Unemployed

From the beginning of the period of transformation, the media have not, as a matter of principle, acknowledged its negative consequences and have studiously avoided drawing attention to any defect of a market economy. Politicians have avoided speaking plainly about the inevitability of unemployment as a social cost of transformation (Dybalski, 1993). Unemployment has often been used as an argument in political disputes. Government programmes have focussed on coping with the consequences, rather than the causes, of unemployment. The statistics have been manipulated by changing definitions of unemployment, eliminating some groups of people from the count and taking a more stringent approach to registration. Consequent reductions in unemployment rates have been claimed as government achievements!

The media have often described the unemployed as lazy and workshy individuals, sponging on the hard-working population. Rare individual cases of people refusing to work and living off social assistance benefits have been generalized and attributed to everybody who is out of work (Worach-Kardas, 1993; Kłosiński, 1994). This has led to a worsening of the physical and mental conditions of the unemployed, increasing deprivation, reducing self-esteem and lowering their expectations. There has been a negative impact on their attitude to work and willingness to be flexible in the search for employment. For most unemployed people, their new situation has been a tragic and painful experience, often connected with a feeling of hopelessness. They have felt lonely and lacking help from families, friends and assistance institutions.

The lack of reliable information about unemployment, the tampering with unemployment statistics, and the propagation of negative stereotypes of the unemployed have not contributed to public education. Despite numerous protestations to the contrary, government policy has been largely passive and has not provided adequate support to unemployed people who did not understand the causes of their situation and lacked individual strategies to combat it. Active employment policies have only been implemented to a limited degree because of financial constraints and the lack of qualified personnel, such as labour agents and vocational counsellors. This has contributed to passive attitudes among the unemployed and abuses of the right to benefits by people out of work. Consequently, increasingly restrictive regulations have been introduced, such as the obligation to report regularly to employment offices, even if they have no jobs to offer, as well as more elaborate tests for being officially recognized as unemployed. As the media and politicians have propagated negative stereotypes of the unemployed, employers have shown little enthusiasm for recruiting people sent to them by the 'employment office'.

The Nature and Effects of Legal Responses to Labour Market Problems, 1989-97

'Unemployment' and 'the unemployed' appeared as legal concepts for the first time since 1945 in an Act of 29 December 1989.[4] The Act defined as 'unemployed' any person able and willing to work, not employed, and registered with the employment office. The breadth of this definition made its practical application difficult and it was defined more tightly in an Act on Employment and Unemployment dated 16 October 1991.[5] Under that Act, a person is only legally unemployed if they:

- are over 18 years old (except for those completing school at 18 who are not counted for a period of 12 months);
- are less than 60 years old (women) or 65 years old (men);
- do not attend a stationary school (an educational programme for young people not in employment;
- are not involved in any business activity;
- have not acquired the right to draw a retirement pension;
- are able and willing to work full-time (or half-time, if disabled) and are registered with the employment office.

Unemployment benefit is paid from the Labour Fund, which was established by the state to mitigate the effects of unemployment, to provide work for those directed into particular kinds of employment and to support people in their search for work.[6] The Fund's income is generated by compulsory contributions from employers (in 1997 they represented 3 per cent of gross wages) and subsidies from the national budget. In 1991-96 the majority of the Fund's income was provided by the budget subsidy (around 63 per cent in 1993-94 and 64.2 per cent in 1995). Its work has two aspects:

- *protective*, performed through payment of unemployment benefits, pre-retirement benefits and early retirement benefit;
- *activating*, reducing unemployment by means of training and retraining, subsidized and public works, loans to the unemployed to start new businesses and for job creation by employers.

Assistance for the unemployed has taken different forms. At first, an unemployed person was entitled to benefit if:

- he or she had no job (but had been employed in a job for at least 12 months before losing it, except for school leavers, released prisoners and people discharged from military service); and
- he or she had no disability pension or other monthly income exceeding half the minimum wage; and
- he or she did not live in a common household with a spouse whose income was more than twice the average wage.

If these requirements were met, unemployment benefit would be paid for a period of 12 months. Benefit might be refused, however, if the person was responsible for the loss of their job, for example by leaving voluntarily. Payment of unemployment benefit to people with a long period of employment (25 years - women, and 30 years - men) might go on for an extended period.

On 1 December 1991, these benefits were restricted by regulation. A woman who had given birth could receive benefit for an additional period of 14-26 weeks - equivalent to a maternity leave. The extension of the period of benefit was limited to people with a longer period of continuous employment (30 years - women and 35 years - men).

The right to unemployment benefit is accompanied by rights to certain other benefits, including family allowance, nursing benefit, death allowance, occupational disease or injury benefits and health care benefits. An unemployed person loses their right to benefit if they have failed to visit an employment office, have refused to take a job which has been offered, have gone abroad or have received a loan to start their own business. People who lose their right to unemployment benefit may be granted social assistance (welfare) benefits.

On 14 December 1994, the Sejm adopted a new Act on Employment and Counteracting Unemployment.[7] This Act was intended to encourage special programmes to mitigate the consequences of unemployment. It introduced a new definition of the 'unemployed' and specified their rights and duties. To be registered as unemployed, people had to prove that they met more than a dozen requirements. This Act was further amended, by regulation, on 22 December 1995 and 6 December 1996.[8]

The amendment of 22 December 1995 abandoned the previous link between unemployment benefit and average wages. A rate fixed at 36 per cent of the average wage was replaced by a fixed benefit, adjusted quarterly in line with changes in the consumer prices index. At the same time, the definition of 'appropriate employment' was changed to give the authorities increased discretion in determining 'appropriateness'. The old definition had linked 'appropriate employment' to being 'professionally prepared'. In the new definition, the phrase 'is professionally prepared' were replaced by 'has sufficient qualifications'. This allowed district employment offices to offer unemployed people jobs inconsistent with their previous occupation and level of education.

The amendment of 6 December 1996 made the criteria for achieving the status of unemployed (and the right to benefit) more difficult to meet. From the beginning of 1997, benefit cannot be combined with work. A person who has taken *any* paid work loses the status of unemployed. An unemployed person is someone who is not employed, is able and willing to work, does not take part in regular daily education, and is registered with the employment office. A person who receives pre-retirement allowance or benefit is not recognised as unemployed. This amendment tightened control over the unemployed, making benefits less accessible. The principles of granting benefits were changed as follows:

- the period of prior employment required for eligibility was extended from 180 to 365 days;
- the baseline for entering an individual into the Labour Fund (participation in which is a condition of being eligible for benefit) was increased from 50 per cent to 100 per cent of the minimum wage,

excluding a large number of part-time workers earning less than the minimum;
- the unemployed were not allowed to receive any income from employment;
- people who left their jobs voluntarily were required to wait 6 months before becoming eligible for unemployment benefit.

Differential benefit rules were introduced, reflecting local labour market conditions and the length of time that someone had been employed prior to losing their job. There is considerable geographical variation in the rate of unemployment - from 40 per cent in north-eastern Poland to 3.6 per cent in Warsaw (June 1996). In regions with unemployment rates lower than the national average, the duration of the right to benefit was shortened from 12 to 6 months.

The proposal to vary unemployment benefits depending on the length of prior employment was widely supported. The benefits for unemployed people with shorter periods of work experience (less than 5 years) were reduced to 80 per cent of the regular level, while benefits for those with over 20 years of work were increased to 120 per cent. This was intended to motivate younger unemployed people to intensify their efforts to find a new job. However, unemployment among older workers may increase as a result.[9]

As these regulations have evolved, they have established more stringent criteria for eligibility and the right to benefit. Each new law has been an unthinking response to immediate problems and offered little practical assistance to the unemployed in re-entering the labour market. The notification of vacancies, vocational counselling, job training and retraining, and loans for starting one's own business are possible means of helping the unemployed enter or re-enter economic activity. However, the finances allocated for such purposes are insufficient. Although the Labour Fund has the power to intervene more actively, high unemployment has meant that most of its resources have been committed to the payment of benefits. The proportion of expenditure on active forms of counteracting unemployment is shown in Table 11.1.

Changes in the Polish Labour Market During the Period of Transformation 169

Table 11.1 Percentage of Total Labour Fund Expenditures Committed to Active Programmes to Combat Unemployment 1991-1996

	Proportion of Expenditure as %
1991	7.0
1992	4.7
1993	11.1
1994	9.0
1995	11.9
1996	10.7

Source: Budget Laws

Subsidies for active labour market polices are distributed among voivodships (provinces) in proportion to their unemployment rate and numbers of registered unemployed. Allocations for active policies in the regions particularly threatened by unemployment have been increased.

However, the way in which the money is spent has become increasingly ineffective. The largest share is being allocated to 'emergency' and public works, representing almost 75 per cent of 'active' expenditures from the Fund in 1995 and almost 65 per cent in 1996. The proportion spent on reimbursing employers for the wages of school leavers and graduates increased, to 8 per cent in 1995 and 15 per cent in 1996. At the same time, expenditure on loans to the unemployed and working establishments in order to create or develop new businesses declined. Small sums of money were distributed for training. 'Emergency' and public works are costly and temporary measures usually unable to ensure permanent jobs. Expenditure on training and retraining has been reduced, even though it is the cheapest form of intervention and surveys show a growing willingness of those seeking jobs to take up such opportunities. The quality and practical relevance of training organized by employment offices has also improved.[10] There is no right to such benefits: decisions are made by local employment offices depending on available funds.

Other means of enhancing employment opportunities include tax relief for employers who create new jobs. In communes affected by structural unemployment, tax relief is also given to existing employers who increase employment.

Support for Specific Groups

Employment of the disabled Employers of 50 or more workers are required to ensure that at least 6 per cent of jobs in their firms are taken by disabled people.[11] Employers who do not meet this requirement are obliged to make a payment to the National Fund for the Rehabilitation of the Disabled (PFRON). Money from this centrally-administered Fund is used to finance the employment and rehabilitation of disabled people. However, there is a lack of staff and institutions to carry out the objectives of this legislation and the costs of vocational training for disabled children and young people cannot be met from this source.

Assistance for graduates and school leavers Graduates and school leavers have a special legal status, guaranteeing them many employment rights and facilities. At first, from 1989, this status was confined to graduates from higher schools of regular daily studies and from vocational schools.[12] The scope has since been extended to cover people graduating from secondary schools of general education and special schools, as well as disabled people who have obtained certified qualifications to practice a profession, people trained in the Voluntary Labour Corps or other vocational training (daily) courses lasting at least 24 months and people who have completed postgraduate studies or doctoral courses.

Young people's rights to benefits have, however, gradually been reduced. The 1989 law gave them a preferential position. Benefit for higher school graduates was fixed at 200 per cent of the minimum pay (150 per cent in case of graduates from vocational schools) to be paid for the first three months of unemployment, whereas those who had not worked before registration were entitled to benefit equal to the minimum pay. The level of benefits for other categories of unemployed people depended on their previous earnings and the length of time they had been out of work. About 9 months after its introduction, the provisions of the 1989 law were modified and the level of benefit for graduates was lowered. Despite this, benefits received by graduates and school leavers were sometimes still higher than those received by people who had already been in employment. The 1991 Act on Employment and Unemployment reduced the duration of benefit entitlement to 9 months and levelled the rate down to that received by other unemployed people. The level of benefit for all unemployed was fixed at 33 per cent (from 1992 - 36 per cent) of average wages. The 1994 Act on Employment and Counteracting Unemployment then reduced the level of benefit for graduates relative to that of other unemployed people. The rate was fixed at 28 per cent of the average wage for adult graduates and 12 per cent for adolescent graduates until they came to full age. It also introduced the principle that a graduate could only benefit once from this special payment of benefit not matched by contributions.

Further amendments to the Act on Employment and Counteracting Unemployment, from 1 March 1996, withdrew the right to unemployment benefit from unemployed graduates and school leavers, replacing it by a training grant. Unemployed graduates and school leavers who register with the employment office are entitled to this grant provided that they take up:

- training (job training, retraining and improvement of professional qualifications);
- apprenticeship with an employer, as agreed between a district employment office and the employer;
- education in a further education college.

Graduates may now be sent by the employment office to perform public service work for six months in a half-time job not related to their qualifications - in public utilities or organizations in the field of culture, education, sport and tourism, health care or social welfare. Subsidized employment based on contracts between the employer and the employment office (where the employer receives partial reimbursement of the wage and social insurance costs of employed graduates) continued. Unemployed graduates are also covered by other programmes: 'emergency' work, public works, and loans to start their own business.

The introduction of training grants in place of benefits was aimed at increasing the initiative of young people in seeking jobs. It was intended to reduce pathological behaviour including, among other things, the mass registration of all leavers on the last day of school and waiting until the expiry of the right to benefit before seeking work. The old provisions were found to encourage abuse of the right to benefit by many young people, with the growing cost of unemployment benefits reducing the funds available for promoting employment opportunities. It was also felt that graduates and school leavers became accustomed to idleness, reducing their employability.

There is too little experience of this new regime fully to assess its effectiveness. According to information received in 1996 from the National Labour Office, the most effective form of promoting the employment of young people was the use of temporary subsidies through contracts with employers - after their termination, permanent jobs were offered to 60-70 per cent of the young people involved. Vocational training and loans to start new businesses generated less interest. The proportion of graduates performing 'emergency' and public works also decreased. In 1996, graduates began to refuse to take up apprenticeships with employers because of the low level of grants for the work, and the lack of contracts of employment and guarantees of eligibility for employment or benefit after the termination of an apprenticeship. There was no interest in public works or grants to continue education in the regions affected by structural unemployment.

As a result of the new regulations, there was a certain statistical (and propaganda) success from a reduction in the unemployment rate among graduates and school leavers. Young people who had lost their rights to benefit ceased to be registered with the employment office. Before these changes came into effect, there were more than 200,000 graduates registered with district employment offices. In June 1996, the number was 72,000 in September 1996 - 104,000 in December 1996 - 86,000 and in March 1997 - 62,000. It is difficult to assess the extent to which depriving young people of their right to unemployment benefits has motivated them to seek work more actively. The new programmes have generally not proved to be attractive and are likely to need further amendment.

The Development of the Labour Market 1990-97[13]

The loss of jobs affected all industries and services. The heaviest losses were incurred in 1989-1992, when employment fell from 17.56 million to 14.97 million, and affected most sectors of the economy: manufacturing industry (down by 20.7 per cent), construction (by 19.1 per cent) and agriculture (by 10.8 per cent), with the highest falls in science (by 36.3 per cent) and culture and arts (by 25.2 per cent). In numerical terms, however, 80 per cent of the total loss in this period occurred in three sectors - manufacturing industry, construction and agriculture. As a result of the recession, it was a pure reduction in employment rather than a sign of increased efficiency in the use of labour. Productivity actually fell by around 8.4 per cent. Employment increased only in finance and insurance (by 15.2 per cent), administration (by 13.8 per cent) and trade (by 10 per cent).

Since 1992, total employment has stabilized at around 15 million (15.01 million in 1992 and 14.97 million in 1995 - these figures do not include employment in the army and police, respectively, 339.3 thousand in 1990 and 356.6 thousand in 1995). Actual employment in Poland is greater than this, due to the persistence of the black economy. Various estimates suggest that this might have amounted to 365 - 700,000 workers in 1993 and 805,000 in 1995 and 1996. The scale of the black economy reflects the weakness of labour market institutions and labour inspection, as well as public support for illegal employment, when illicit work is still treated as indicating the personal enterprise of both employee and employer, rather than as illegal behaviour, exploiting workers and the public sector.

The proportion employed in the public sector of the economy decreased from 54.9 per cent in 1989 to 38.1 per cent in 1995, with a simultaneous increase in the private sector from 45.1 per cent in 1989 to 64.0 per cent in 1995. The number of public sector employees decreased from 9.6 million in 1989 to 5.98 million in 1995, a one-third fall. The number of people employed in the private sector increased gradually from 4.24 million in 1989 to 5.62 million in 1995, also by one-third. Rising employment in the private sector resulted mostly from privatization. The individual economic activity of citizens, only led to the creation of about 400,000 jobs in the private sector.

The rationalization of employment is still incomplete. Surplus labour (hidden unemployment) has not disappeared. It still exists, mainly in state-owned industry and individual farming. The latter is a 'shelter' for redundant employees, including farmers losing supplementary jobs in manufacturing and construction and young people in rural areas, although many of these prefer to remain unemployed rather than take over an agricultural holding. The decreasing trend in employment continues because of the failure to restructure the mining industry. The transformation of mining and agriculture will lead to a substantial reduction in employment.

The scale of redundancy cannot be specified in detail. It may appear in the progress of privatization. Thus far, privatization through the creation of employee partnerships has tried to protect workers' interests (including the protection of jobs). Privatization contracts always contain a clause guaranteeing existing employment, usually for the next two years.

Part of the inheritance of central planning (where pay only supplemented social benefits) is a low-wage policy. This is being continued in the market economy, in both public and private sectors. Indeed, according to official statistics, wages in the private sector are actually 15 per cent lower than in the public sector. Employers' approach to labour management has begun to change. However, the practices of the centrally planned economy still persist, including excessive employment in the public sector and the continuation of low-wage policies which do not reflect the true costs of labour. The elimination of hidden unemployment has been carried out at a very slow pace. The inadequacy, ineffectiveness and limited scope of assistance for the unemployed has led to a situation where employees of almost all privatized enterprises have been guaranteed that jobs existing at the time of the transformation will not change for several years. The objective has been to reduce trade unions' resistance to dismissals. Shares have been given to employees of privatized enterprises to encourage their support for the change of ownership. Low wages contribute to the continuation of redundant employment and do not encourage rationalization, the improvement of working conditions and the modernization of enterprises. Labour represents a low per centage of production costs - after the first three years it had reached 30 per cent. There is no incentive to increase low labour productivity.

Further creation of employment in the private sector depends on the capital available for investment. Privatization processes have so far taken place in the traded sector and in modern and efficient enterprises (which have not required capital investments). In future, enterprises less advanced in technology and in need of capital will also be privatized. The transfer of employment opportunities to the private sector has not been accompanied by a simultaneous relocation of fixed assets. The transformation of the labour market has been dominated by the creation of jobs 'for oneself'. There has been a continuous growth in the numbers of employers and in those working on their own account. The average number of employees per firm in the private sector was only 1.6 in 1993, which means that private enterprises are too small for efficient economic development. Their future expansion will depend on their capacity to create new jobs.

An Assessment of the Changes in the Labour Market since 1989

The following general changes in the labour market since 1989 can be identified:

A fall in the economic activity of older groups in the population, resulting from the displacement of older workers onto the social security system (the average age of a retired pensioner decreased by 2 years, and that of a disability pensioner by more than 3 years. The pressure on older employees to retire intensified, especially between 1990 and 1993 when more than 1.8 million retired (i.e. became eligible for old-age or disability pension), twice as many as in the previous and following years. Such opportunities were however limited in subsequent years.

Rising female unemployment as a result of the reduction of employment opportunities in sectors traditionally dominated by women, particularly textile, electromechanical and electronic industries. Female unemployment is four percentage points higher than male unemployment. In 1996, the proportion of women among the unemployed increased by 3.2 per cent and, at the end of that year women represented 58.3 per cent of all registered unemployed. The decline in registered unemployment since 1994 has benefited men rather than women. The number of unemployed men fell in 1996 by 16.6 per cent, compared with 5 per cent for women. The proportion of unemployed women ineligible for benefit is growing. In 1996 they accounted for 62.1 per cent of all unemployed without this right, a 10 per cent increase on the previous year. Women are also the majority of the longer-term unemployed. In 1996, women made up 56.7 per cent of all those unemployed for 3 to 6 months, 59 per cent of those for 6 to 12 months, 62.3 per cent of those for 12 to 24 months and 71.8 per cent of those out of a job for more than two years. Women are more often dismissed and face more problems in getting a new job, although unemployed women tend to be more educated than unemployed men and more often take part in training and retraining activities (they are 60.5 per cent of all the unemployed participating in training). An overwhelming majority (74.5 per cent) of women would like to engage in economic activity.[14] The principal motives are largely financial: husband's income insufficient (36.5 per cent of respondents); desire for financial independence (25.2 per cent); need to ensure subsistence for the family (24.0 per cent) and wish to improve the family's living standard (2.7 per cent). The women who were not seeking employment did so mostly because of poor health, a desire to bring up their own children or to act as a housewife, or because they were receiving old-age or disability pension.

Rising youth unemployment, whose actual picture is obscured (as has been stressed in many surveys of economic activity) by the limitations of the systems of monitoring developments in the labour market. Youth unemployment is lower than presented by official statistics, as a considerable number of young people work in the black economy, allowing their employers to evade taxes. Analyses show that it is easier to maintain an job already held than to get a new one. Even if young people have found employment in the private (non-agricultural) sector twice as often as older applicants, this has not compensated for the reduction of public sector jobs. In November 1995, the unemployment rate of those aged 15-24, reached 30.9 per cent and was more than twice that of the whole economically active population. Despite a decrease in the unemployment rate to 11.5 per cent in November 1996, and to 26.2 per cent in respect of those aged 15-24, this relationship remains intact.

Social policy regards youth unemployment as an important source of social and political destabilization. Special programmes for combatting youth unemployment in Poland have emphasized the economic aspects of the problem, but put less emphasis on its political and social dimensions.

Unemployment mostly affects low skilled and less educated people. 79 per cent of unemployed men had less than a secondary level of education (60.6 per cent for women). Unemployment mostly threatens people with primary and basic vocational education. The employment problems of this group (amounting to almost 2 million people in 1993) will not be solved even by an economic recovery, as there will be little demand for their skills (usually low and narrowly specialized). A special programme to create new job opportunities for them will be needed. There is also a need for reform of Poland's educational system in order radically to reduce the scope of basic vocational education. Almost half the post-primary education in Poland is provided in this track which normally leads to school leaving at about 14 or 15 with no marketable qualifications. Only about ten per cent of these students transfer onto a secondary vocational track which can lead to further or higher education.

Geographical distribution of unemployment in Poland is a consequence of the low mobility of workers (resulting from poor infrastructure, especially the lack of housing) and small regional disparities in wages. There is a big difference between town and country. The urban unemployed have fewer problems in getting work (whether in a new trade or in their previous one) than unemployed people living in rural areas.

The proportion of long term unemployed is growing. The impact of active labour market policies on unemployment reduction has been very small. These policies cover only a small percentage of that population. In December 1992 only 127,700 (or 5 per cent of all registered unemployed) participated in such programmes, increasing to 166,500 (5.8 per cent) in December 1994 and 197,900 (8.3 per cent) in December 1996. In 1995-96, over 40 per cent of the unemployed had been without work for more than 12 months and at the end of 1997 about 17 per cent had been unemployed for more than 2 years.

Long term unemployment reflects the elimination of people with low skills and limited mobility from the labour force. It can only be addressed by specific microeconomic policies. Manual workers represent around 70 per cent of the unemployed, every third unemployed worker has attained only primary education (whether completed or not) or basic vocational education. Their best opportunities are likely to lie in the construction sector with support for repairs and modernization of infrastructure.

The Polish educational system makes an important contribution to the persistence of structural unemployment. Since 1989 the structure of the system has been slowly changing. Nevertheless, most pupils completing primary education choose basic vocational schools, whose curricula have little market value. Structural changes are more evident in higher education. This is mainly due to the spontaneous development of private high schools and colleges. In 1996, almost one student in five attended such an institution.

An increase in the working-age population in Poland, which seems to be very large in comparison to other European countries. The population of working age will rise by around 3.5 million (14.7per cent) over the period 1991-2010. In Europe as a whole, excluding the territory of the former Soviet Union, it will increase by 6.5 million. This means that Poland will account for almost 54 per cent of the total European increase in labour supply. The increase in working age population will be accompanied by a shift in its age structure. The numbers in younger age groups (up to 44) will stabilize, while the numbers in older age groups (over 45 years) rise by 3.2 million.[15]

Forecasts of Employment and its Structure - Challenges and Background to Change

The labour market is shaped by many social, demographic and economic factors. Economic growth, achieved in Poland since mid 1992, has not generated an adequate demand for labour leading to a significant reduction in unemployment. The number unemployed began to decrease slowly in 1994, although there was no increase in the recorded numbers in employment until 1996. There is, however, strong pressure from the demographic increase in labour supply. Poland's population of working age (i.e. 18-64 years for men and 18-59 years for women) will increase up to 2001 as a result of the high birth rates observed in 1977-83. It is estimated that over 2 million new jobs will need to be created by 2010 in order to deal with this (Kałaska and Witkowski 1997).

The private sector will play a key role in the transformation of the Polish economy. Its share of employment increased from 45.1 per cent in 1989 (including individual farming) to around 64 per cent in 1996. However, the structure of Polish employment, dominated by agriculture-forestry, construction and services, is rather different from that in highly industrialized countries. Agricultural occupations still represent around a quarter of the total employment. The reduction of employment in agriculture and mining will be realised through economic restructuring. These processes may be supported by eliminating hidden unemployment in manufacturing and by reducing the size of the black economy. Not only must new jobs be created for dismissed workers, but their skills must be adjusted to future needs.

The prospects for people seeking new jobs, and of those dismissed from work or redundant on farms, will depend on the development of Polish education. The problem of unemployable graduates and school leavers, who can only be prepared for employment by retraining needs to be addressed. Older workers made redundant need new opportunities for updating their skills or acquiring new ones.

In the future, rational labour management in Poland will depend mostly on educational progress, increasing expenditure on education and adjusting its directions and curricula to fit the present and future needs of the economy, as well as strengthening active labour market policies. The dynamic growth of labour supply may create an opportunity to develop Poland's economy, provided that the quality and accessibility of education can be improved. From 1989-1996, the educational aspirations of young Poles have risen and the number of students has doubled. More and more young people are continuing their education. These factors have made it possible to ease the demographic pressure on the labour market and to manage some of its negative implications. In the coming years, further and higher education could absorb some of the excess labour. However, this will depend on allocating more money for education, vocational training, research and development, and regarding them as a key investment in the future position of the Polish economy, its modernization and competitiveness.

Concerted action by the institutions responsible for education and employment will be necessary. Adjustments of the content and structure of vocational education to meet labour market demand are carried out more slowly than the changes in the market. Lack of information about occupations with a surplus (or a deficit) of employees, and forecasts of demand for high-skilled personnel, makes it difficult to influence education and training policies (Kabaj, 1997). Any future reduction of unemployment will also depend on labour market policy. At present the attempts to mitigate the effects of unemployment in Poland differ substantially from public needs and expectations. Increased expenditure and improved effectiveness are needed on active labour market programmes. There must be more encouragement for the economic activity of the unemployed, the development of active labour exchange and vocational counselling and individual consideration of each case of unemployment. The methods applied by the state in the labour market should also be changed by the introduction of unemployment insurance and an extended institutional basis for labour management. Currently, labour market policies are implemented by the Ministry of Labour and Social Policy and its subordinate offices. They need to be integrated with educational, macroeconomic, and regional policies. Local government, in particular, should be brought into partnership with a power to initiate local employment programmes.

Notes

1. Data refer to unemployed registered with employment offices.
2. Data collected in a survey of the economic activity of the population (BAEL) carried out in August 1993. The BAEL research - conducted every quarter since May 1992 - defines someone as unemployed if they are over the age of 15, without a job in a given week for even an hour, actively seeking a job and willing to take up a job.
3. Data from BAEL survey.
4. Act of 29 December 1989 on Employment.
5. Act of 16 October 1991 on Employment and Unemployment.
6. This resulted from the regulation of the Act of 29 December 1989 on Employment.
7. Act of 14 December 1994 on Employment and Counteracting Unemployment.
8. Amendments of 22 December 1995 and 6 December 1996 to the Act on Employment and Counteracting Unemployment.
9. See: Semenowicz A., *Komentarz do ustawy, Biuro Studiów i Analiz Kancelarii Senatu*, (typescript), 1996.
10. Data provided by the National Employment Office. The effectiveness of unemployment training is measured by the unemployment rate following the conclusion of the course (as percentage of total number of trained): in 1993 this was 34.6 per cent, in 1994 it was 44.6 per cent and in 1995 it was 58.6 per cent.
11. Act of 9 May 1991 on Employment and Rehabilitation of the Disabled
12. This covered about two thirds of school leavers who have followed a vocational track in basic, secondary or further education. It excluded about one third of school students, who were following a more academic programme, about two thirds of whom would eventually enter higher education.

13. This analysis of factors determining the level and structure of employment in Poland from 1990-97 has been based on information provided by the Central Statistical Office.
14. *Sytuacja społeczno-zawodowa kobiet in 1994*, GUS: 1994. Survey carried out on a sample of 3409 women of working age (i.e. 18-59 years), belonging to households covered by survey of family budgets.
15. Hrynkiewicz J., *Demograficzne uwarunkowania polityki społecznej*, Warsaw, 1993.

References

Bujak, K. and Górniak, J. (1992), 'Wybrane zagadnienia formowania się rynku pracy w Polsce', *Humanizacja Pracy*, No. 1-2 (special issue), pp.5-20.

Dybalski, W. (1993), 'Bezrobocie - postrzeganie problemu przez środki masowego komunikowania', in Fratczak et al. (eds), *Bezrobocie - wyzwanie dla polskiej gospodarki*, GUS: Warsaw, pp.122-31.

Dzięcielska-Machnikowska, S. (1993), 'Problemy życiowe bezrobotnych',in Fratczak et al. (eds), *Bezrobocie - wyzwanie dla polskiej gospodarki*, GUS: Warsaw, pp.337-46.

Goszczyńska, M. (1995), 'Bezrobotny jako podmiot zagrożenia ekonomicznego. Analiza pamiętników bezrobotnych', in *Bezrobocie. Psychologiczne i społeczne koszty transformacji systemowej*, Uniwersytet Śląski: Katowice, pp.24-32.

Kabaj, M. (1993), *Program przeciwdziałania bezrobociu*, IPiSS: Warsaw.

Kabaj, M. (1995), 'Rozwój i zatrudnienie zasobów pracy, Polska 95', *Raport o rozwoju społecznym*, Warsaw, pp.99-117.

Kabaj, M. (1997), *Strategie i programy przeciwdziałania bezrobociu*, Wydawnictwo Naukowe SCHOLAR: Warsaw.

Kałaska, M. and Witkowski, J. (1997), *Rynek pracy w Polsce w 1996 roku: kontynuacja korzystnych tendencji*, GUS: Warsaw.

Kłosiński, M.(1994), 'Semiotyczna analiza pojęć "bezrobocie" i "bezrobotny" ("bezrobotni") w wypowiedziach prasowych', *Kultura i Społeczeństwo*, No. 3, pp.151-62.

Kowalska, A. (1994), 'Psychospołeczne problemy bezrobotnych', in *Społeczno-ekonomiczne położenie bezrobotnych*, GUS: Warsaw, pp.196-225.

Krencik, W. (1993), 'Procesy zmian dynamiki i struktury zatrudnienia i płac w 1992 roku' (part I and II), *Praca i Zabezpiecznie Społeczne*, 8, pp.20-32 and 9, pp.7-21.

Marcinkowski, A. and Sobczak, J.B. (1993), 'Bezrobotni i instytucje - interpretacje, definicje i strategie działania', in Borowicz, R. et al. (eds), *K.L. Syndrom bezrobocia,*, Warsaw, pp.35-49.

'Pomoc państwa w rejonach zagrożonych wysokim bezrobociem'(1993), *Przegląd Rządowy* No. 8, pp. 82-3.

Program przeciwdziałania bezrobociu i łagodzenia jego negatywnych skutków (1993), MPiPS: Warsaw.

Reszke, I. (1995), *Stereotypy bezrobotnych i opinie o bezrobociu w Polsce*, Fundacja im. F. Eberta: Warsaw.

Strzelecka, J. (1993), 'Bezrobocie długotrwałe w świetle wyników badań aktywności ekonomicznej ludności', *Wiadomości Statystyczne* No. 8, pp. 13-17.

Worach-Kardas H.(1993), 'Indywidualne i grupowe strategie reagowania na bezrobocie - aspekt zdrowotny i demograficzny',in Fratczak, et al. (eds), *Bezrobocie - wyzwanie dla polskiej gospodarki*, GUS: Warsaw, pp.388-98.

PART III
SOCIAL WORK
IN THE
NEW EUROPE

12 The Irish Model of Social Work
Fionnuala Lordan
Izabela Rybka

The Beginnings of Social Work in Ireland

In Ireland, structural poverty has been a severe problem for centuries. Thousands of Irish men and women have been driven to mass migration (mainly to the United States and Great Britain) in search of work and better living conditions. Political independence from British rule, achieved in 1922, 'did not alter the marginal economic position within the United Kingdom which Ireland had filled since the beginning of the previous century. If anything that marginality increased' (Breen et al.,1990). The civil service and government continued to be patterned on British models. Ireland remained largely dependent on its rural economy until the 1960s when the Programme for Economic Expansion, introduced in 1958, began to demonstrate results. Between 90-95 per cent of the population of the new state were Catholic and the Church wielded considerable influence on social policy.

Such is the context within which modern Irish social work originated. As in Britain, there were, of course, earlier developments in the form of the mendicity societies, which mirrored the 'scientific' charity organization movement of the nineteenth century. There were also early twentieth century influences from the settlement movement and university extension programmes, working to improve the social and physical conditions of the poor in urban tenement areas (See Mark Lymbery's Chapter 13 in this volume).

Springing, as they did, from denominational voluntary initiatives reacting to the needs of the poor, the welfare services were fragmented. There was 'little co-operation between the different bodies involved in welfare work' (Kearney, 1987). This led to unplanned and piecemeal service provision, with a large variety of agencies helping specific groups of people. These groups operated quite independently and the state's programme of social policy neither specified their role nor their scope of competence and duties in the field of social welfare. These agencies were the pioneers and the pathfinders. Their personnel first recognized the need for workers with expertise who would devote their working lives to addressing the problems they encountered. From them sprang the first demands for social work training.

Professional Roles of Social Workers

In Ireland, social work education and training takes place in the universities. The first professional courses were introduced in the 1960s. Before this, there were basic social science degree courses and diploma courses in social studies with a practice component to prepare graduates for work in this field. The professional courses were initially accredited by the United Kingdom's Central Council for Education and Training in Social Work (CCETSW). This was a private arrangement between the universities and CCETSW so that standards would be assured and recognized. This link was important for the employment of Irish graduates in the UK, as many emigrated partly due to an initial lack of employment opportunities in Ireland and partly to obtain experience in a country where social services were more developed. CCETSW had no legal jurisdiction over courses in the Republic of Ireland and its role was limited to course accreditation. This arrangement continued until 1990, when CCETSW withdrew its services. The Irish government then appointed an ad hoc Committee on Social Work Qualifications to fill the gap and make recommendations for the future. A National Body has since been established. Its mandate is:

- to accredit Irish professional social work courses;
- to award the national professional social work qualification;
- to accredit non-national qualifications and to advise prospective employers as to the recognition of national and non-national qualifications (Report, May 1995-1997).

This Board was established by statute as The National Social Work Qualification Board in 1997 (S.I.No.97 of 1997).

The influence of the strong link with CCETSW meant that Irish social work education and practice were very closely linked to the British model, although many of the earliest social work academics received their training in the USA. They adopted a rather different orientation. The resulting debates, together with the specific cultural and economic factors in the country, provided an environment where there was sufficient diversity to support the development of a uniquely Irish model of social work. As Lorenz put it 'where the state is openly reluctant to become involved in welfare provision, social work skills must of necessity include imaginative wheeling and dealing for resources, negotiating with the informal sector for institutional places and generally 'keeping the balance' on behalf of society' (Lorenz, 1994).

Social workers are represented by both a professional association and a subgroup of a trade union. These two organizations articulate the interests of social workers in negotiations with government. The specific role of any social worker is largely defined by his or her employing agency's function. There are, however, some general principles of social work which have been drawn up by the Irish Association of Social Workers (IASW). These definitions are based on the knowledge and expertise of IASW members, an analysis of the state of social security in Ireland and knowledge of international developments. In the view of the IASW, the role and task of the social worker in Ireland can be stated in the following terms:

> Social Workers work with individuals, families and groups experiencing social and emotional difficulties. The social worker endeavours to help clients identify options and make decisions for themselves so that they can develop ways of improving their quality of life. The social work role may take the form of individual or group counselling, giving information on social support services, mobilisation of resources, advocacy on the clients behalf, participation in policy formulation, research and teaching (IASW, 1994).

The majority of people who make use of social work live in straitened circumstances. Many experience poverty and are struggling to cope with a variety of problems. A social worker aims to co-operate constructively with the service user. The first stage of social intervention involves a comprehensive assessment of need. The user and the social worker jointly analyse the user's whole life in order to identify all problems which impair the user's functioning. The next step is to prepare several alternative approaches to overcoming the difficulties. The most suitable course of action should be chosen by the person seeking help. As a result of taking an active part in the entire assessment-decision making process, users are more likely to approve of the help being offered and readier to engage consistently with the specially designed programme of ancillary services. A social worker's role is to discover and activate the actual and potential personal resources of every individual seeking help. The assistance offered must never take the form of an arbitrary decision made without consulting the service user. He or she should be actively involved in carrying out the programme which is aimed at improving living standards: relieving people of duties has a destructive and demotivating effect. Those who do not feel responsible for their own lives develop passive and claiming attitudes. Institutions or agencies who do not empower those with whom they work to make their own decisions about their own lives are merely perpetuating problems. This concept of social work has another significant advantage, namely its educational nature. The service user is given a chance to become familiar with various ways of coping with a crisis. They learn how to prevent certain problems and, if they do occur, how to solve them.

In the Irish model of social work, employees of statutory organizations are expected not only to work directly with service users but also to help in preparing social policy programmes, at least at a local level. The basic professional activities of social workers vary. For instance, social workers may be expected to do any of the following:

- To provide individual and group counselling.
- To supply information about available resources, both statutory entitlements, such as grants, benefits and allowances for particular categories of people, and voluntary services which may be responsive in a specific situation.
- To promote the provision of statutory services to meet the needs of service users and to prepare proposals to obtain financial aid for necessary services in the community.
- To act as advocates for the rights and interests of those with whom they work.
- To analyse the causes and effects of existing social problems in order to help in creating long-term projects in the development of social service provision.
- To participate in research carried out by academic centres or by social work agencies both statutory and voluntary.
- To teach social work either by
  a) co-operation with universities where future social workers study. (Fifty per cent of social work training takes place in social work agencies where students work under the supervision of a professionally trained fieldwork teacher);
  b) training other professionals or volunteers to develop their skills and their understanding of the social implications for those with whom they work.

The Irish Model of Social Work 187

Statutory Social Work Services

Social workers employed in the public sector are mostly employed by three separate government departments. These are:

- *Regional Health Boards*, which operate under the auspices of the Department of Health.
- The *probation services*, which are administered by the Department of Justice.
- Local *housing authorities* which are controlled by local government.

The majority of social workers are employed in the field of health protection by the regional health boards. Their focus is on children at risk and their families, and on older people living in neighbourhood communities or in health care institutions, both medical and psychiatric. The Regional Health Boards were created in 1970 under the terms of the Act on Health Protection (Health Act 1970), which divided the country into eight administrative districts, each with a separate institution directly subordinate to the Department of Health. Regional Health Boards are responsible for carrying out the health care and social programmes approved by the government. Their administration is divided into three programmes, each with its own manager. These are Community Care, General Hospitals and Special Hospitals. Most social workers are employed within the community care system. They are, however, just one of the professional groups involved in the realization of this long-term programme of social care which covers three basic spheres:

- preventive health care, embracing comprehensive paediatric care, prevention of the spread of sexually transmitted diseases and addiction, and the promotion of a healthy life style;
- basic health care, comprising general medical services, nursing services for patients at home and the reimbursement of other treatment costs;
- community welfare, which includes some financial payments such as disabled persons maintenance allowance, domiciliary care, allowance for disabled children, home help service, grants to voluntary welfare organizations and child care services.

The concept of team work is fundamental to the operation of the social services in Health Boards. All caring personnel - doctors, public health nurses, social workers, home helps or whatever - plan an integrated approach to their work and liaise constantly on matters of mutual concern.

The Health Boards employ social workers within the community care programme to provide two quite distinct levels of service delivery. Traditionally the delivery models have been defined as casework and community work. In the former, the focus is on direct person to person interventions and the amelioration of existing social problems for a specific service user, whether an individual or a family is seen as the social work goal. The latter, on the other hand, focuses more on prevention, supporting community initiatives for self help, encouraging the development of services at neighbourhood level with voluntary input and the development of community networks and an environment which promotes a healthy life style for all citizens.

The essential objective of social workers is to help people cope with their life tasks, when they are driven by serious, health, financial or housing problems to seek psychological assistance or material support. Social workers are interested first and foremost in working with the individual living in his or her family milieu. They offer a counselling service to enable those in crisis situations to find ways of resolving their problems and to maintain a satisfactory level of functioning in the community. They link people with the resources available to lessen their stress and poverty.

In a society where the demands for service far outpace provision, child care has become the central concern of social workers since the Child Care Act came into force in 1991. Child protection has become a public issue and, as social workers are seen as the relevant experts, it has been established as their major priority. Social workers are mandated by the statutory authorities to be responsible for protection, assessment and intervention when children are at risk of abuse or neglect. The acknowledgement of the problem of child sexual abuse has further propelled social workers into defining the limits of their role and responsibility.

Protection means working with families who are having problems, whether they stem from the breakdown of relationships, alcoholism, drugs, poverty or whatever, in a manner which will support parents in their efforts to provide for their children. Where possible resources are focussed on enabling the natural family to rear their own children. However in cases of abuse or neglect this may not be possible. In such cases, social workers work closely with the courts to represent and defend the child's interest. If abuse or neglect is proven, children may become wards of the court and be placed in the care or under the supervision of the health board.

Social workers provide wide ranging services which help families to function and develop. They not only run family casework clinics and supervise children in their own homes but have also set up day centres for children in multi-problem families. The aim is to offer sufficient support to enable children to remain with their own families even though their parents may be experiencing difficulties in caring for them adequately. Social workers attempt to rebuild relationships and resources in the home environment so that the family is able to fulfil its basic role and to guarantee conditions for a child's healthy development. A child will only be placed in a foster family or educational-guardian institution if it is justified to suppose that his or her health and safety is threatened by remaining at home because the parents are either unwilling or incapable of providing adequate care. In such a situation social workers look for a foster family or a guardian institution suitable for the child. If a child is legally available for adoption they will engage in appropriate proceedings. Social work departments have specialist staff to assess homes and to educate potential substitute parents about working with the traumatized children coming into care. Social workers have a duty to maintain regular contact with all children in care and they work in close partnership with foster parents. They encourage the continuance of links with natural parents when possible and desirable for the welfare of the child and they facilitate and supervise regular meetings between children in care and their natural parents. Social workers also have a mandate to support parents who have difficulties caring for a child with special needs. In these situations their role is to link the family with specialist services and sources of allowances to cover the extra costs of rearing a disabled child, to offer counselling about family relationships and to advice on matters of child rearing practice, rehabilitation and other services when required.

The second focus of intervention is at a more preventative level. Here community workers work with voluntary groups at neighbourhood level stimulating self help initiatives in 'service' provision. They act as animators, facilitators in bringing together groups who have a vested interest in creating voluntary initiatives, support services and neighbourhood resources in a specific area. The community worker facilitates community leadership. Residents are helped to identify their most pressing needs and those aspects of the wider society which are having negatively effects on their lives. These groups develop local management structures which will provide services to meet these needs. Through the intervention of community workers, volunteer initiatives to strengthen bonds between neighbours, and people in general, are linked to the activities of the statutory agencies. This type of social work is naturally directed at stimulating and supporting the development of grassroots mutual aid movements and of social organizations independent of government programmes. Their work involves family services, youth services, and services for older people. These programmes are almost entirely voluntary and receive minimal support from public funds. They include services such as family centres, where there are educational and support activities for parents, and playgroups for children; youth clubs, where there is a wide range of activities and interests; and services for older people, which include meals-on-wheels (a daily delivery service of meals to the homes of older people unable to provide for themselves), home visiting of older people by volunteers and clubs for older people. The ultimate goal of these various initiatives is to build viable social structures, to promote altruistic attitudes and, in the long run, to sustain civil society.

Various other categories of social workers are employed in the field of health care and health protection. Unlike the community care social workers, they generally have a significantly narrower and more specialized range of duties and authority. These social workers are hospital based, both in general hospitals and within the psychiatric services. Their mandate is to offer direct help to patients and their families where illness and medical treatment are complicated by social and emotional factors. Their activities are aimed at eliminating or at least alleviating the negative effect psycho-social factors have on the course of treatment and recuperation. The work of the medical social worker includes carrying out psycho-social assessments to aid diagnosis and treatment, crisis counselling, bereavement counselling, and the mobilization of a large range of resources and welfare services to cushion the impact of illness and to facilitate the discharge of the patient to a supportive environment, conducive to recovery. There are teams of medical social workers at most hospitals. In small towns and in rural areas, they form organizational units of four or five persons, whereas in Dublin they are in groups of up to twenty workers.

Social workers in the psychiatric service tend to be even more specialized. They are based in psychiatric hospitals, psychiatric units located within general hospitals, or outpatient clinics in the community. Psychiatric social workers intervene in the system of relationships in which a mental health problem occurs. They work both at a psychotherapeutic level, facilitating adaptation and change in the coping patterns of patients and their families, and at an environmental level, to reduce stress and pressures which influence mental health problems. 'Many social workers in the psychiatric context have postgraduate training in psychotherapy' (Walker, 1994). There is considerable

The Irish Model of Social Work 191

interest among psychiatric social workers in developing a preventative role, and in building up supportive and educational programmes in the community to avert the development of mental illness. The aim of programmes within the framework of social prevention and civic education is to help to overcome social alienation and the feeling of 'loneliness in the crowd', and to restore informal social structures based on direct interpersonal and intragroup bonds.

The second major statutory employer of social workers is the Department of Justice. There are over 200 probation and welfare officers employed in programmes for people who are in conflict with the law. They work preventatively, to keep people out of prison; rehabilitatively, to prepare criminals serving a prison sentence for their return to society; and supportively, to aid the families of prisoners. Probation officers work closely with the court system. They carry out intensive studies of convicted people and their families, assessing an individual's motivation and potential for change so that a court can make an informed decision about the implications when passing sentence. Where a crime does not require mandatory imprisonment and it is felt both that there is a possibility of rehabilitation without incarceration and that the offender is motivated to work with the probation service, he or she may be given a suspended sentence under the supervision of a probation officer. The probation officer then offers a casework service focussed on helping the offender to understand his or her behaviour and to learn new patterns which will not conflict with the law. This may involve relationship counselling, motivating and linking this person with supporting services such as drugs clinics or retraining programmes, or giving support in finding employment. The role of the probation officer is seen as one of befriending and support.

The second category of people dealt with by the probation service are prisoners who have been refused release but have been granted permission to serve the remainder of their sentence under semi-free conditions. A prisoner wanting to join this programme must be assessed for their suitability. It is important to establish that they are motivated to work constructively to examine and take steps to change patterns of offending behaviour. When deciding whether a given prisoner is to be included in the programme, information from the following sources is taken into consideration: reports from the prison, the view of the sentencing court and assessments from psychologists, psychiatrists and other professionals. At the same time, the candidate's family and closest milieu are also assessed in detail to establish whether their degree of demoralization does not rule out possible co-operation for the good of the offender. Dangerous criminals and those who come from delinquent backgrounds which offer little support for reformation are not referred to these programmes. Re-education is intended to develop attitudes, behaviour and personality patterns which will allow an offender to function as a law abiding citizen. With this goal in view, open institutions are established where prisoners spend several weeks under the supervision of social workers in intensive groupwork programmes. For people serving a sentence, this is a concrete opportunity to make a successful return to their original social environment and, in time, to reconstruct family bonds with the support and supervision of social workers. Similar resocialization projects have been established in Great Britain, Canada and the United States.

The third statutory employer of social workers is the local housing authorities which are under the control of local government. These agencies are responsible for meeting the housing needs of the community and overcoming difficulties that result from internal migration. In recent years this has also involved migration within the European Union. Social workers provide counselling and advice to families who have difficulties in paying their rent, who have problems with neighbours, who are looking for a transfer to another area, or who are looking for housing. Social workers also act in an advocacy role for tenants and prospective tenants in their communication and negotiation with the housing authority and other government departments.

There are also specialist social workers working with travellers. These are large groups of Irish people who have led a nomadic way of life for generations.[1] Their housing needs are quite distinct. The policy for decades was to integrate this population with the settled community and efforts were made to encourage them to settle in local authority housing in specific neighbourhoods. This policy was made without consulting those concerned and it refused to recognize the unique culture of these nomads. The policy failed, meeting considerable opposition from both travelling and settled communities. It has now been recognized that another response is required. Some sites have been established where travellers can stop for short periods in the course of their seasonal migrations. Travellers themselves have now become quite vocal. Indeed, in recent years, some of them have become professional community workers. Partnerships have been established between service providers and traveller representatives and efforts are being made to develop a more responsive housing policy for this group.

Participation of Non-Government Organizations in Social Service Provision

The so-called 'third sector' of non-governmental organizations is also an important source of employment for social workers. This sector both competes with public institutions for money from the state budget and functions as an ally in the delivery of social welfare. Non-government organizations play a singular role in the Irish social security system. This is mainly the result of the model of social policy developed under the influence of Catholic social teaching and its vision of social order in the country. The principle of 'subsidiarity' (from the Latin word *subsidium* -help, support, protection) is the most important (See also the discussion by Marek Rymsza in this volume). It was put forward by Pope Pius XI in his encyclical *Quadragesimo Anno* in 1931. The principle of subsidiarity combines the idea of solidarity and the common weal, defines the proper spheres of activity of different public and non-public subjects, and states precisely to what extent particular social partners are responsible for meeting social needs. In accordance with this principle, social organizations, both formal and informal, engage in charitable activities and develop social work services to meet the social needs of the population. These bodies are not driven by a search for economic profit and any gains from commercial activities must be reinvested in the realization of their aims. This approach is based on the belief that social order and the responsibility for securing well-being rests with the smallest and most immediate social unit of which the individual is a part, whether it be family, friends, acquaintances, neighbours, the parish community or local authorities. Only as a last resort, when all of these have proved helpless, does the responsibility for maintaining social order fall to the highest agencies of public administration. The state is not relieved of its responsibility to carry out long term social policy or to engage in programmes aimed at ensuring permanent social security for its citizens. However, the fact that the legislative authority decides the basis for organizing structures independent of government means that individuals and social groups are free to choose the ways in which needs associated with participation in social life will be met. According to the principle of subsidiarity, the role of the state is to stimulate, promote, support or co-ordinate the activities of various subjects of social life. This is an incentive for citizens to be active, resourceful and helpful, and prevents them adopting claiming attitudes toward public institutions.

In building the Irish social welfare system, this strategy was not adopted purely as a result of cultural factors or Catholic teaching. It also reflected the real economic situation of the country where there was a high dependency ratio and a weak economy. Without the help of voluntary organizations the state would have been unable to develop or maintain the social security system. The active involvement of volunteers in social work makes it possible to minimize administrative costs. Regardless of the government, public organizations tend toward bureaucratization and consume more resources in administration. Salary costs are also reduced because only a proportion of the staff of non-government institutions are full-time employees.

Social policy based on the principle of subsidiarity has had several consequences for social work. Firstly it has led to the fragmentation of services and competition between organizations. This often means that there is a divided voice in policy making and makes integrated planning difficult to achieve. On the other hand, voluntary agencies have more scope for imaginative approaches to problems and for alternative solutions. On the negative side, however, may be a denial of people's rights, with the effect of placing already marginalized people in an inferior position. This is, perhaps, best exemplified by the 'charity syndrome' where disabled people are placed in a position where they are expected to be grateful for services to which they are entitled. There is a growing awareness among disabled people of the discrimination they experience. This has lead to the development of user groups seeking to control decision making about services which affect the quality of their lives.

Most social service organizations have been created on the initiative of religious communities or of people connected with the Church. For example, almost all residential care provision for children, people with disabilities, and people with learning difficulties is under the management of religious bodies. Similarly, most homes for older people were initiated and are managed by religious orders. The Irish Society for the Prevention of Cruelty to Children (ISPCC) is the oldest and best-known charity organization. It was founded in 1889 with the aim of protecting children from poverty, injustice and cruelty. Even though Ireland has the highest proportion of children of any West European country, it has the least developed network of social institutions for child welfare.[2] Ireland has also been slow to develop a legal framework for children's rights.

Barnardos is another important organization that contributed to creating an infrastructure for children's services. This charitable foundation was established in the 19th century to provide opportunities for neglected and disadvantaged children. A wide range of services are now offered. These include professional social work intervention with families who, due to some

The Irish Model of Social Work 195

current difficulties (e.g. chronic unemployment, poverty, long-term sickness, marital problems, alcoholism or drug addiction), are incapable of bringing up their own children. The strategic approach of the Barnardos foundation is expressed through a wide network of services which aid the child's development, particularly in establishing educational centres, day-centres, kindergartens, play centres, recreational-educational establishments, book and toy libraries (where toys can be borrowed), and centres specifically for single parents, or for children who have serious problems at school or who have infringed the law.

Another voluntary organization, the Brothers of Charity, was founded in Belgium in 1807. It has been operating in Ireland since the end of the 19th century. This association provides a highly professional service for disabled people, particularly children and adults with learning disabilities. The services include assessment and early intervention programmes in specialist centres which seek to support families with disabled members at a time of crisis and to provide sufficient routine support to enable children to attend ordinary school; special schools, both residential and day, for children who have been diagnosed as having moderate or severe learning needs; hostel accommodation in the community for leavers from these schools; special residential establishments for adults incapable of living in the community; and a specialist clinic for disturbed children where professionals assess the disturbance and offer therapeutic treatment programmes. Other projects have been promoted in co-operation with statutory authorities to facilitate the rehabilitation and employment of disabled people. These range from the creation of sheltered employment, where disabled people are employed in an non competitive economic situation, to vocational training programmes, which aim to enable participants to develop new skills and to improve their qualifications. For people who are unable to work, rehabilitation-recreational centres have been established with gymnasiums, occupational therapy workshops, swimming pools and sports fields. The staff employed by the association are specifically trained for the work and include educators, psychologists, social workers, psychiatrists and care personnel.

The widest range of services for families living in poverty or destitution is offered by the Society of St. Vincent de Paul. They collect large sums of money on flag days and in running charity events which they then distribute to poor families. They will support families who are having difficulties in paying their rent, electricity or heating bills. They may also provide travel tickets, help poor students to pay their fees or to buy books. They view education as very important and organize courses for women from poor and neglected areas to teach budgeting skills, so they can manage their modest allowance economically. Participants are taught how to prepare wholesome meals in spite of limited financial means, and how to care for the health and proper development of their children. The Society runs over a dozen holiday centres providing holidays for poor families and for disabled people. It also provides housing for homeless people and for lone parents. In exceptional circumstances the Society will also assist a family or co-operative escape poverty by giving a grant or loan to start a small business.

These examples illustrate the role non-governmental organizations play in meeting social needs. Social welfare tasks could not be carried out by statutory agencies alone. It is, therefore, very important for the personnel of voluntary organizations to be properly trained. Courses for volunteers who donate their time and their abilities are considered essential. Most organizations insist that volunteers undertake a preparatory course before they begin their service. Experience has shown that goodwill and good intentions alone are not enough and can, in fact, have a negative impact on service recipients. Of course, professional qualifications are required of the full-time social workers. It is, then, essential that non-statutory organizations take part in professional education. They do this through co-operation with universities and by hosting student units within their agencies. These offer students structured and supervised practice opportunities. Irish social work courses place great emphasis on the acquisition of both theoretical academic knowledge and competent practice skills. Great emphasis is laid on the ethical and normative aspects of the profession.

Notes

1. Travellers, sometimes known pejoratively as 'tinkers' or 'gypsies' may be compared with the Romany peoples found on the European mainland.
2. Children under 14 constitute 25.7 per cent of the Irish population compared with 18 per cent in Great Britain, 16 per cent in Germany and 17.4 per cent in Sweden (Lexicon of the States of the World 1993).

References

Breen, R., Hannan, D., Rottman, D.B., and Whelan, C.T. (1990), *Understanding Contemporary Ireland*, Gill and Macmillan: Dublin.

IASW (1994), *Social Work as a Career*, Draft Information Leaflet, Irish Association of Social Workers: Dublin.

Kearney, N. (1987), *Social Work and Social Work Training in Ireland: Yesterday and Tomorrow*, Occasional Paper No.1, Department of Social Studies, Dublin University:

Dublin.
Lexicon of the States of the World (1993) *Report on the Condition of 191 World States*, Harenberg Lexican-Verpag, Real Press, Dortmund, Warsaw.
Lorenz, W. (1994), *Social Work in a Changing Europe*, Routledge: London.
Report May 1995-1997, National Validation Body on Social Work Qualifications and Training, Dublin.
S.I.No.97 of 1997, *The National Social Work Qualifications Board. (Establishment) Order*, 1997.
Walker, S. (1994) *Careers in the Social Services*, University College: Dublin.

13 The Development of Social Work in Britain 1869 - 1996
Mark Lymbery

Introduction

The objective of this chapter is to outline the development of social work in Britain. Although it has been argued that the roots of social welfare are traceable to medieval times (Midwinter, 1994), most histories of social work date its origins to the late Victorian period (Young and Ashton, 1956; Woodroofe, 1962; Seed, 1973). As Seed indicates, the term social work - and the designation 'social worker' - were first used in this period (Seed, 1973, p.3). The chapter concentrates on the development of social work between 1869 and the present day. The starting date is that of the formation of the Charity Organisation Society, which is generally accepted as the precursor of modern social work (Jones, 1996). The first section briefly outlines the development of the British welfare state, to establish the political context within which social work has been located. The following section examines the emergence of social work in Britain, concentrating on four key periods in its history - the nineteenth century, 1900 - 1945, 1945 - 1970, and 1970 - 1996.

Particular themes will be explored throughout the chapter. For example, there has always been a tension within social work between the impulse to help people in need and the state's requirement that dangerous populations be effectively controlled (Adams, 1996). This duality has been expressed in many ways through the history of social work and continues to be relevant today. The relationship between social work, social injustice and poverty is also a key theme. While the origins of social work were located in concerns about the effects of poverty, social work has tended to frame this in individualistic terms and to treat the structural forces which create poverty and injustice as secondary (Jones, 1979). At various points in the history of social work, however, the link between social need and wider levels of poverty and injustice has been significant.

In addition, there has been a continued tension between different interest groups regarding the direction and control of social work. Howe has examined the way in which the power balance between different parts of the social work profession has shifted with time, concluding that, in current practice and organization, power has shifted in the direction of administrators and managers, away from practitioners, teachers and researchers (Howe, 1991).

The Evolution of the Welfare State

This section charts the key developments in British social welfare from Victorian times to the present day. Its objective is to locate the growth of social work within a broader context. Midwinter (1994) argues that modern social welfare policies have their genesis in the industrial revolution, which occurred between approximately 1770 and 1850. The industrial revolution caused three significant social changes: a massive population explosion; the rapid growth of factory-based manufacturing industry; and a shift in population from rural to urban areas (Midwinter, 1994, p.43). The growth of cities created major problems of increased poverty and crime, and poor standards of public health (Young and Ashton, 1956; Midwinter, 1994).

Towards the end of the nineteenth century, the modern pattern of local government was established. In a number of different areas - education, public health, etc. - responsibility for the development and delivery of welfare services was given to local government, with central government being limited to policy formation, advice and inspection. In many ways, this balance of responsibilities still holds today. Gradually, in a process which Midwinter (1994, p.68) terms 'creeping collectivism', the state assumed a greater responsibility for its citizens' welfare. It is important to note the limits of this: the state 'was more concerned with dousing the fires of social casualty, once ablaze, than with stopping them from breaking out originally' (Midwinter, 1994, p.72).

The *status quo* that had been established by the end of the nineteenth century continued into the early part of the twentieth, although it was severely shaken by the General Strike of 1926 and the world-wide recession of the early 1930s. These demonstrated both the continuing problems of poverty for large sections of the population and the social inequality which persisted in British society. There was an uneasy tension between competing demands for welfare from the working class and the diminished economic resources of the state (Forder, 1975; Hay, 1978). While there was a considerable amount of welfare legislation in this period, it developed in a piecemeal fashion, with no overarching aims and objectives (Brown, 1995). Although many of the foundations of welfare in Britain had been laid before the Second World War, they had not been coherently planned.

During the war, Sir William Beveridge, an academic-cum-civil servant, was asked to produce a blueprint for the reform of welfare. The subsequent report (Beveridge, 1942) has been characterized as combining 'detailed proposals for a comprehensive social insurance system and ... influential rhetoric on future social policy needs' (Hill, 1993, p.15). The most famous example of the latter describes the central purpose of post-war reconstruction; the need to slay the 'five giants' of 'Want, Disease, Ignorance, Squalor and Idleness' (Beveridge, 1942). The detail of his social insurance proposals relied on three central assumptions: the maintenance of full employment; the introduction of free health care; and the establishment of adequate systems of family allowance (Hill, 1993; Brown, 1995).

The incoming Labour government in 1945 established the basis for comprehensive welfare services through a range of social legislation (Hill, 1993; Brown, 1995). Although Beveridge made no explicit mention of social services, and most welfare legislation had no direct bearing on the development of social work, the formation of modern social work organizations is based on two pieces of legislation - the Children Act 1948 and the National Assistance Act 1948 - which will be discussed later.

The period from 1951 to approximately 1975 is traditionally treated as one of consensus around social policy issues (Hill, 1993; Midwinter, 1994), with the differences between the main political parties being matters of degree rather than of principle. However, the mid 1970s brought a number of changes which had a significant impact upon the welfare state. Several of these were economic: in the wake of the oil crisis of 1973 there was world-wide recession, which had an immediate (and long-lasting) impact on levels of employment. In turn, this increased pressure on the universalist principles of the welfare state - higher levels of unemployment increasing demand for welfare benefits (Midwinter, 1994; Brown, 1995). This meant that two of Beveridge's three prerequisites for the development of a comprehensive system of welfare - full employment and adequate family allowances - were no longer operative. In addition, the principle of free health care (which was first breached in 1951) was becoming accepted as financially impossible. The Labour government of 1974 - 1979 was forced to seek a loan from the International Monetary Fund to manage the difficult economic situation. Among the conditions on which the loan was granted were requirements that public expenditure be greatly reduced (Hill, 1993). It is ironic that the party which did most to create the welfare state was forced, under economic pressure, to institute the single biggest assault on welfare expenditure since the Second World War.

The Conservative Party were elected in 1979 and remained in office until May 1997. This provided ample time for their economic and social policy approach to become firmly embedded in place of the previous post-war consensus. Although the Welfare State was already in crisis when the Conservatives came to power, they pursued policies which further threatened some of its basic principles (Hill, 1993).

Characteristics of this period include an overriding commitment to cost controls, particularly apparent in successive reforms of social security, the incremental growth of selectivist over universalist principles in welfare, a preference for market-based solutions to welfare problems over public sector approaches, and a commitment to institutional reforms (for example, in the National Health Service and in local government) which broke up the traditional welfare state bureaucracies (Hill, 1993; Brown, 1995). The consequences for social work will be addressed in the following section.

The Emergence of Social Work

What is Social Work?

The following is a useful summary of what social workers actually do:

> All social workers have basically two functions. One is to put their clients in touch with all the services and resources ... that might be of help to them in coping with problems and to assist them if necessary in persisting with applications and appeals and understanding regulations. The other is to help clients to gain insight into the nature of their problems, to offer comfort and support in times of stress and to help clients to either adjust to their situation or move constructively to change it (Brown and Payne, 1990, pp.180-81).

The balance between the two functions is continually shifting. In particular, it is important to recognize the enduring controversy over the idea that the only appropriate role for social work is to help people adjust to their circumstances (see, for example, Jordan, 1990).

Social workers are not free agents: the majority work in large local government organizations. Their practice is defined by legislation, as interpreted by the policies and procedures of the agency, and is subject to managerial scrutiny. The practice of social workers is also scrutinized in other ways. The role of central government agencies has increased in recent years, with more explicit monitoring and inspection. In addition, there have been numerous occasions when the decision-making of social workers has been put under the microscope of the national news media, particularly over various incidents of child abuse (Aldridge, 1994). Finally, the resources available to social services agencies have been increasingly restricted (Neate, 1996). All of these create pressures on social workers, particularly in terms of their ability to feel that their work is effective and makes a difference in people's lives (Jordan, 1984).

The following sections will illustrate the progress of social work from the energy of the early pioneers, through the relatively fallow period before the second world war, to the unifying trends following 1970 and the recent assaults on social work.

The Nineteenth Century

The dominant explanations of social need in the nineteenth century were individualistic. On the whole, it was believed that, if people were destitute, this resulted from their own fecklessness. The focus on individual responsibility for poverty betrayed a lack of understanding of its structural causes (Midwinter, 1994), and ignored the needs of those people who were unable to contribute to the economic life of society. It is this latter group who were to become the people towards whom social work was to be directed.

The Poor Law Amendment Act 1834 was the main system of public relief, and has been described as 'punitive' in its effects (Parry and Parry, 1979). The workhouse - the place where many poor people were forced to live - was governed by a principle of 'less eligibility', with a level of discipline intended to discourage the 'indolent and disorderly', while being comparatively comfortable for the deserving poor (Crowther, 1981). Digby notes that many workhouses were organised on humane lines which were 'compatible with welfare' (Digby, 1978, p. 229), although this situation was not necessarily the norm throughout England. Moreover, the number of people who could be accommodated within workhouses was limited, which meant that systems of 'outdoor relief' for able-bodied paupers were still required. This aspect of relief had an explicitly moral element - the conversion of the idle pauper into a decent and productive member of the workforce - and created conditions which were in many instances harsher than the workhouse (Digby, 1978; Crowther, 1981). The ancestry of modern social services can be seen in two aspects of the Poor Law system: the development of the workhouse is a direct precursor of residential care; while the coordination of outdoor relief prefigured part of the modern social work role.

It was entirely characteristic of the late Victorian approach to welfare that voluntary organizations were felt to be the appropriate location for acts of benevolence, while the resources of the state - as distributed through the Poor Law - were both residual and minimal (Jordan, 1984). The idea of charity appealed to affluent middle class Victorians and led to a boom in charitable giving in the latter part of the century. However, this, in turn, fostered a concern that charity was 'pauperizing' the poor (Young and Ashton, 1956; Woodroofe, 1962). It was from this recognition that the Charity Organisation Society (COS) developed in 1869.

The purpose of the COS was to coordinate charitable giving, so that it could be directed towards those people who were deemed to be 'deserving'. Those who were 'undeserving' would only have recourse to help through the Poor Law. About one in three of the people investigated by the COS were felt to be 'deserving' (Jordan, 1984). In differentiating between the 'deserving' and 'undeserving' the COS established a duality which has persisted in some form or other to the present day. As Woodroofe (1962) points out, the activities of the COS were based on the working principle that charity should be directed towards promoting independence and maintaining the family, which should be seen as a whole, and that the scope of relief given should be limited. The help given should be 'adequate' - in cash or in kind - to effect a regeneration of the family and the promotion of independence (Young and Ashton, 1956; Woodroofe, 1962).

Such a systematic organization of charity required an equally systematic methodology to carry it out, in which the outlines of modern social work can be perceived (Cooper, 1983). The COS devised assessment procedures to decide if a person was worthy of help, to determine the nature of such help and - if necessary - to find forms of assistance other than financial, and to give advice on the future welfare of the client. All of this would be accomplished by visiting the individual and family in their home environment. This process of assessment resulted in the production of a written report, on which further action would be based (Woodroofe, 1962). None of this would be unfamiliar to the social worker of the late twentieth century.

As Seed (1973) has noted, other streams of social work developed around the same time: these are important in their own right, although not having such a significant impact on its future direction. In particular, Seed refers to the importance of social action in the history of social work, an example being the Settlement movement. This was based on the idea that financial support alone was insufficient for the poor and that educated men (the movement was initially confined to men and started in the universities) should combine to provide them with the means to develop education and leadership. The 'settlers' believed that environment had a major influence on character, and that a better environment would help to improve people's general ability to maintain themselves. They believed, and acted upon their belief, that people with education should live with the poor to provide them with models of an alternative way of life (Young and Ashton, 1956).

Two specific aspects of the Settlement movement are important to modern social work. The first is the recognition that poverty and destitution were not necessarily the results of individual behaviour, but were particularly influenced by environmental factors. (However, there was still no recognition of the primarily macro-economic causation of unemployment.) The second is the idealistic belief that people could be changed through a process of persuasion based on reason and example (Seed, 1973).

1900 - 1945

In the early years of the twentieth century, social work built largely on the methods, policies and practices of the pioneering voluntary and charitable organizations (Forder, 1975). The belief that social services were better not provided direct by the state still prevailed, which hampered the ability of Poor Law officers to attain a professional status (Crowther, 1981). In addition, the practice of social work was rooted in assumptions about the nature of society and the causation of social problems which clearly belonged more to the nineteenth than the twentieth century (Woodroofe, 1962). There was neither a single organizational form for social work nor a uniform governing philosophy and approach to practice. Social work was a segmented profession, with parallel associations for psychiatric social workers, hospital almoners (medical social workers) and probation officers (Younghusband, 1978a; Cooper, 1983). In all these cases, social workers/probation officers were located in subordinate structural positions - to the medical profession in the first two instances and to the courts in the third - and had a limited level of autonomy and control over their work. This fragmentation remained a feature of social work until 1970: the element of subordination to other, more established professions has arguably continued since.

The early years of the century saw attempts by Poor Law officers to improve the standards of service which they offered, and thereby to improve their low public esteem (Crowther, 1981). The National Poor Law Officers' Association, formed in 1884, reflected the professionalizing aspirations of its members, and attempted - with limited success - to apply the approaches of more established professions, including professional training and competitive examination. This represented an attempt to present the work of Poor Law officers - and particularly the relieving officers - as a form of professional social work rather than amateurish administration (Crowther, 1981). The framework of the Poor Law began to be dismantled from 1929, with the passage of the Local Government Act. This transferred the responsibility of managing the Poor Law to the direct control of local government, which has retained the core responsibility for responding to social need ever since. The relieving officers were renamed public assistance officers, and can be seen as 'the ancestors of today's social workers' (Crowther, 1981, p. 153). Modern social workers in local authority social services departments can therefore trace their roots back both to the pioneering work of the Charity Organisation Society and the rather less heralded activity of staff employed to administer the Poor Law.

In general, the development of social work can be seen as exemplifying the 'creeping collectivism' which characterised much social policy of the time. Seed (1973) has argued that the enthusiasm and hope which characterized the early years of social work had gradually decayed, to be replaced by the fragmentation of separate specialisms, which competed with each other for resources, prestige and influence. However, this period also saw the breakdown of the Poor Law, and the start of the gradual process by which social work became established within local government.

1945 - 1970

After the rigours of global conflict for 6 years and with the memory of the 1930s depression still fresh, there seems to have been a national determination to create a more equal society (Forder, 1975; Hill, 1993). The assumption that the state should take responsibility for the welfare of its citizens was a key element of this (Seed, 1973; Midwinter, 1994). The post-war years therefore saw a further transfer of responsibility away from voluntary organizations to the state (Parry and Parry, 1979). The legislation which had a direct impact on social work was clustered in 1948, with the passage of the Children Act and the National Assistance Act. Both of these created new welfare responsibilities - and increased the level of social work activity - within local government.

The Children Act was passed following the reports of the Curtis Committee, which had been set up to review the general discharge of the state's duty towards children in need of care, and of the inquiry by Sir Walter Monckton into the death of Denis O'Neil, a child in foster care. Both reports revealed great failings in the coordination of welfare services for children, and led the Curtis Committee to recommend that Children's Departments should be established in local government to oversee and coordinate welfare services for children. Although there was no specific mention of social work in the report of the Curtis Committee (Jordan, 1984), the subsequent creation of Children's Departments proved a significant boost to its status. Indeed, social work with children quickly became the dominant strand of the profession, encouraged by the 'missionary zeal' (Jordan, 1984) of many of the staff involved.

The National Assistance Act replaced the Poor Law, and transferred responsibility for the arrangement of residential care for older and 'handicapped' people onto newly formed Welfare Departments within local government. While limited in scope, the National Assistance Act established a responsibility for the needs of older people and people with disabilities which has continued and been extended. For example, the National Assistance Amendment Act of 1962 enabled local authorities to provide services to people in their own homes, establishing domiciliary care as a major element of welfare services (Holgate and Keidan, 1975). In addition, there were major increases in the budgets allocated for the care of older and disabled people throughout this period (Jordan, 1984). Social work in these areas of activity advanced more slowly (Younghusband, 1978b), but finally became a major feature of social services provision in the 1990s.

However, the fragmentation which had characterised the pre-war period still persisted. Although more social work activity now took place within local government, confirming the general direction of pre-war policy, social work could still not be described as a unified profession. There were separate professional associations for the various branches, with a plethora of different types of training course. Each branch had its own history, and tended to protect its own interests.

The element which most unified the various strands of the profession was the casework method. Although British social work had been criticised for failing to develop a coherent body of theory relevant to British society (Woodroofe, 1962), there was a considerable US literature. Much of this concentrated on the individual, using theories largely derived from psychology (Seed, 1973; Younghusband, 1978b). However, the approach used in the American tradition (of private provision with few services universally available) did not readily transfer to Britain, where there was an increasing discrepancy between casework method and the tasks which social workers actually carried out (Seed, 1973). In Brown and Payne's terms, casework theory only had a significant bearing on the attempt to enable clients to develop an insight into their problems: even then, this insight was partial, due to the relative absence of sociological theories. These became more commonly used in the 1960s as part of a radical critique of traditional social work (see, for example, Simpkin, 1983). The substantial task of creating a body of theory which was relevant to the actual practice of British social workers remained incomplete for many years.

While the social work profession became more unified in the 1950s and 1960s - through training courses, the establishment of journals, discussions between associations, etc. (Younghusband, 1978b) - many divisions still had to be overcome if the unification were to be complete (Parry and Parry, 1979). An opportunity was presented in the mid 1960s with the establishment of the Seebohm Committee with a brief to report on the most appropriate structure for social services in England and Wales. An earlier enquiry into social services in Scotland (the Kilbrandon Committee) had recommended the establishment of integrated social work departments, embracing all aspects of social work including the probation service. These were established by the Social Work (Scotland) Act 1968, the year in which the Seebohm Committee finally reported.

However, the final recommendations of the Seebohm Committee were less radical, due in large measure to the resistance of the National Association of Probation Officers, which was wary about being subsumed into large social work departments. It lobbied successfully to remain a court-based service, separate from other forms of social work (Cooper, 1983). Nevertheless, the recommended social services departments (SSDs) would unite all other aspects of social work into one large organization, located within local government (Seebohm Report, 1968). This position represented a substantial victory for social work interests, which had tirelessly pursued this goal throughout the time the Committee was in session, and which continued to campaign for the implementation of its recommendations (Cooper, 1983; Hill, 1993). After consultation, the government drew up the Local Authority Social Services Act, which became law in 1970 and was implemented from 1971.

1970 - 1996

While the creation of SSDs could be seen as a victory for the aspirations of the social work profession, other perspectives should be noted. The creation of SSDs brought most social work into local government, whose characteristic hierarchical and bureaucratic structures are fundamentally antithetical to social workers' claims to autonomous professional status (Cooper, 1983), and have been a major determinant of their failure to be ascribed this sort of recognition (Witz, 1992). There has been a constant tension between the autonomy claims of social workers and local government requirements of accountability (DHSS, 1978). The recent application of managerialist thinking to public services has led to an increased level of control, based on the presumed superiority of managerial over professional solutions (Kelly, 1991; Lawson, 1993). Finally the location in local government brings direct political control, which further erodes the claim for professional autonomy (Daniel and Wheeler, 1989; Clough, 1990). Parry and Parry argue that these tensions have created a new form of professional - a 'bureau-professional' - based on the view that neither 'autonomous professionalism nor purely bureaucratic hierarchies' emerged from the creation of SSDs (Parry and Parry, 1979, p.43).

Paradoxically, the creation of SSDs probably represented the high water mark of social work's 'professional project', but also contained many of the elements which have subsequently limited its ability to claim an undisputed professional status. This is not to underestimate the other factors which have contributed to a troubled period for social work.

Recent Challenges to Social Work

There has been much new legislation, with the Children Act 1989 and the National Health Service and Community Care Act 1990 being particularly significant. While it can be argued that the Children Act has strengthened the social work role with children and families, the National Health Service and Community Care Act constitutes a distinct threat to the social work role (Lymbery, forthcoming). In addition, recent years have brought a mass of legislation concerning criminal justice, which has markedly changed the role of the Probation Service.

In the 1970s there were attacks on the concept of state-provided social services from both ends of the political spectrum. The critique from the left included a concern that social work was overly involved in coercive, controlling functions (Simpkin, 1983), that it had become nothing more than an 'ideological state apparatus' (Althusser, 1971). There were concerns from feminists that social work's fundamental assumptions were oppressive to women, while other writers argued that its services were Anglocentric and inappropriate to the needs of Black people (Jordan, 1984).

However, while these criticisms had a significant impact on the profession the right's critique was more important because it became legitimized by central government. The Conservatives saw welfare as an economic burden, both in terms of the direct costs of providing services, and in the sense that an increasing proportion of the workforce were employed in this sector and adding nothing to the productivity of the nation as a whole (Midwinter, 1994). Welfare was thought to be overloaded with bureaucracy, dominated by the interests of the workforce and welfare professionals, and insensitive to the needs of those people who required its services. Social work was not exempt from the concerted attack on the welfare state which stemmed from this analysis.

The difficulty of providing good quality public welfare services has been exacerbated by continuing budgetary problems since the late 1970s, which have been compounded by the increased level of scrutiny which is now placed on the decisions and actions of social workers, particularly in respect of child abuse. Historically, it is interesting that the formation of Children's Departments followed the death of a child in care: since 1970, there have been numerous cases where children under the supervision of social workers have died, often directly leading to changes in policy and practice.

In addition, the years of Conservative government saw an increase in the level of injustice and inequality within British society as a direct consequence of the government's social policy (Hill, 1993). It is significant that the growth of inequality and social injustice coincided with an ideological assault on welfare: while there was increased need for social work support, these services were under constant threat.

Conclusion

There are few easy lessons to be drawn from this brief history of social work's development. It is clear that social work has always reflected the dominant social policy thinking of the day, whether this be the preference for charitable solutions to need in the 1870s, or market solutions in the 1990s. Social work rose to particular prominence in the context of the stable period of social policy following the second world war. However, recent shifts in thinking about welfare have demonstrated that the advance of social work cannot be considered as permanent, as much New Right social policy has represented an assault on the welfare systems established since the war.

Where this leaves social work as a profession is unclear: already steps have been taken to amend the requirement that Probation Officers must be qualified social workers, and SSD managers have thought in similar terms about much social work with adults. It is possible to visualize the profession contracting to a relatively small group of staff working with children and with mentally ill people, where there are statutory requirements for social work involvement. The recent history of social work represents a retreat from its successes at the time of the Seebohm Report, to the point where the profession is having to struggle for its continued survival. It is not clear that a change of government will necessarily lead to more favourable conditions for the profession. However, the existence of social work for over a century indicates that some form of social work service is needed: perhaps the most urgent debate is to clarify the nature and purpose of such a service into the twenty-first century.

References

Adams, R. (1996), *The Personal Social Services*, Harlow: Longman.
Aldridge, M. (1994), *Making Social Work News*, London: Routledge.
Althusser, L. (1971), 'Ideology and Ideological State Apparatuses', in Althusser, L. *Lenin and Philosophy and other Essays*, London: New Left Books.
Beveridge, W. (1942), *Social Insurance and Allied Services*, Cmnd. 6404, London: HMSO.
Brown, J. (1995), *The British Welfare State*, Oxford: Blackwell.
Brown, M. and Payne, S. (1990), *Introduction to Social Administration in Britain (Seventh Edition)*, London: Unwin Hyman.
Clough, R. (1990), *Practice, Politics and Power in Social Services Departments*, Aldershot: Avebury.
Cooper, J. (1983), *The Creation of the British Social Services*, London: Heinemann.
Crowther, M.A. (1981), *The Workhouse System 1834-1929: the History of An English Social Institution*, London: Batsford.
Daniel, P. and Wheeler, J. (1989), *Social Work and Local Politics*, London: Macmillan.
Digby, A. (1978), *Pauper Palaces*, London: Routledge and Kegan Paul.
Forder, A. (1975), 'Introduction', in Mays, J., Forder, A. and Keidan, O. (eds), *Penelope Hall's Social Services of England and Wales*, London: Routledge and Kegan Paul.
Hay, J. (1978), *The Development of the Welfare State, 1880 - 1975*, London: Edward Arnold.
Hill, M. (1993), *The Welfare State in Britain: A Political History since 1945*, Aldershot: Edward Elgar.

Holgate, E. and Keidan, O. (1975), 'The Personal Social Services', in Mays, J., Forder, A. and Keidan, O. (eds), *Penelope Hall's Social Services of England and Wales*, London: Routledge and Kegan Paul.
Howe, D. (1991), 'Knowledge, Power and the Shape of Social Work Practice', in Davies, M. (ed.) *The Sociology of Social Work*, London: Routledge.
Jones, C. (1979), 'Social Work Education: 1900 - 1977', in Parry, N., Rustin, M. and Satyamurti, C. (eds), *Social Work, Welfare and the State*, London: Edward Arnold.
Jones, C. (1996), 'Anti-intellectualism and the peculiarities of British social work education', in Parton, N. (ed), *Social Theory, Social Change and Social Work*, London: Routledge.
Jordan, B. (1984), *Invitation to Social Work*, Oxford: Martin Robertson.
Jordan, B. (1990), *Social Work in an Unjust Society*, Hemel Hempstead: Harvester Wheatsheaf.
Kelly, A. (1991), 'The "New" Managerialism in the Social Services', in Carter, P., Jeffs, T. and Smith, M. (eds), *Social Work and Social Welfare Yearbook 3*, Buckingham: Open University Press.
Lawson, R. (1993), 'The New Technology of Management in the Personal Social Services', in Taylor-Gooby, P. and Lawson, R. (eds), *Markets and Managers, New Issues in the Delivery of Welfare*, Buckingham: Open University Press.
Lymbery, M. (forthcoming), 'Care Management and Professional Autonomy: The Impact of Community Care Legislation on Social Work with Older People', *British Journal of Social Work*.
Midwinter, E. (1994), *The Development of Social Welfare in Britain*, Buckingham: Open University Press.
Neate, P. (1996), 'Strapped for Cash', *Community Care*, 1-7 August, pp. vi-viii.
Parry, N. and Parry, J. (1979), 'Social Work, Professionalism and the State', in Parry, N., Rustin, M. and Satyamurti. C. (eds), *Social Work, Welfare and the State*, London: Edward Arnold.
Seebohm Report (1968), *Report of the Committee on Local Authority and Allied Personal Social Services*, Cmnd. 3703, London: HMSO.
Seed, P. (1973), *The Expansion of Social Work in Britain*, London: Routledge and Kegan Paul.
Simpkin, M. (1983), *Trapped within Welfare (Second Edition)*, London: Macmillan.
Witz, A. (1992), *Professions and Patriarchy*, London: Routledge.
Woodroofe, K. (1962), *From Charity to Social Work*, London: Routledge and Kegan Paul.
Young, A. and Ashton, E. (1956), *British Social Work in the Nineteenth Century*, London: Routledge and Kegan Paul.
Younghusband, E. (1978a), *Social Work in Britain: 1950 - 1975 (Volume 1)*, London: George Allen and Unwin.
Younghusband, E. (1978b), *Social Work in Britain: 1950 - 1975 (Volume 2)*, London: George Allen and Unwin.

14 The History of Social Work in Sweden
Staffan Öberg

Sweden has always been a very sparsely populated nation. This has given rise to a form of social and political organization characterized by considerable decentralization of power, where local self-government has been more prominent than in perhaps any other country. Until the middle of the 19th century the most important local unit was the parish. This became more and more involved in non-clerical functions, some of which would later become classified as social work, such as taking care of the poor, sick and old people, dealing with alcoholism, addressing problems in the bringing up of children, and resolving conflicts within families and between neighbours.

After the Reformation, the organization of Swedish society was legitimized by principles based on Lutheran Protestantism. According to this ideology, everybody was considered to be equal before God but each individual was obliged to accept his role in society. The King was considered the father and master of the whole nation. Although the priests were supposed to be masters in their parishes, their status derived from their role as teachers of the people. Masters were obliged to take care of their servants and, in some estates and factories, they developed services such as family allowances, medical care, and pension insurance for workers and their families. Most people were not so lucky, but for most Swedes, for hundreds of years, a good society was one where the masters at different levels took good care of their subordinates, just as a father should act as a good parent.

In the middle of the 19th century, a new local government system was established. Although it was based on the old parish system, the municipalities acquired distinctive legal responsibilities in the field of social welfare. When the Swedish social democratic labour movement became a dominant political force during the 1930s, the metaphor of a good family as a model for a good society was revitalized. Like a good modern family, the new society should be characterized by democracy, social solidarity, equality and community. The individual's rights as citizens were stressed together with a belief in collective solutions to social problems and a preparedness to use the state as an instrument for this purpose. There was some inspiration from traditional European utopian ideas and a firm belief in the possibilities of rational social engineering. In social policy, this meant systematic efforts to create security for the citizens by universalist reforms. The aim was to create a safety net that would eliminate the need for what were considered to be humiliating means-tested forms of assistance (Frick, 1996).

Socio-economic development and social reforms during the 20th century brought more duties and technically more complicated tasks to the municipalities. To make it possible for them to handle these, they were restructured into larger units during the 1950s and 1960s. The number of communes was reduced from about 2500 to about 280. These new, larger municipalities were able to appoint staff with more specialized professional expertise, including social workers. However, these professionals were directed by and accountable to lay social welfare boards.

Structural Changes and Consequences for Social Work

After World War II, then, the demand for educated social workers increased rapidly. The environment in which they were asked to work also changed.

Structural changes in the pattern of trade and industry displaced many workers in traditional industries. It was difficult to re-establish these people in the labour market. These economic changes also had an uneven geographical impact. In some places, people had to move in order to get jobs, while other places grew much faster. Such trends have created a situation where preventive social work and community development have become more important tasks for social workers.

Since the 1960s, the migration of refugees to Sweden from all over the world has increased rapidly. Social workers had to meet the new demands of working with people from very different ethnic and religious backgrounds. At the same time there was a continuing process of deinstitutionalization in Sweden. Elderly people, mentally ill people and people with physical and learning disabilities were more and more integrated into the society and needed special services and care (Frick, 1996).

The situation required a new kind of legislation which provided a general framework for activities but set no detailed rules. In 1982 a new law, The Social Services Act, was implemented. This did not regulate social work in detail but allowed the municipalities considerable discretion to suit local circumstances and individual cases. The overall aims of the social services are presented in Section 1:

> Public social services are to be established on the basis of democracy and solidarity, with a view to promoting:
> economic and social security;
> equality of living conditions; and
> active participation in the life of the community.
> With due consideration for the responsibility of the individual for his own social situation and that of others, social services are to be aimed at liberating and developing the innate resources of individuals and groups. Social service activities are to be based on respect for the self determination and privacy of the individual.
> (Social Services Act, 1981, p.5)

The Social Services Act places on the municipality the ultimate responsibility for the care of people within its jurisdiction. It gives the boards of lay persons and the social workers more freedom for social planning, the organization of social programmes and social work. But it is also more demanding. The commission that proposed the new Act was also a strong advocate of more extensive social research to discover and define the needs of the population.

The Development of Social Work Education

As noted earlier, Swedish municipalities were quite small before World War II. In these small units, social work was performed by ordinary government officials, often accountants. The extensive role of the municipalities inhibited the development of charitable organizations. An important exception was the CSA (Central Association for Social Work) which, from its establishment in 1903, was an important lobby for social policy and for education in social work. This association offered the first courses in practical social work from 1910. In 1921 the CSA and the municipality of Stockholm joined forces to set up the Institute for Social, Political and Municipal Education and Research, which became Sweden's first school for training social workers. Similar schools were founded in Göteborg in 1944, Lund in 1947 and Umeå in 1962.

In the early years the programme of these schools could best be described as a general training for local government officials. Since the 1960s, however, the education of social workers has gone through two major changes. In 1964, the autonomous schools were turned into state-owned colleges and in 1977 they were integrated into the universities. At the same time, there was a huge expansion in the training facilities. By 1978, more than 1200 new social work students were admitted each year. Complete undergraduate programmes in social work are now offered in 4 universities and 3 colleges. The number of undergraduate students in each program varies from about 400 to about 700. All of these institutions are owned by the state, except for one college which is run by the Swedish church, the Sköndalsinstitutet. Postgraduate programmes up to doctoral level are offered at the universities in Stockholm, Göteborg, Lund and Umeå. Swedish universities are financed by the state and consequently the students do not pay any fees. Although they have to buy their books and pay for their subsistence students are entitled to loans and grants from the state. For almost 300 years, students at Swedish universities have been required by law to belong to a student union and to pay a membership fee.

The Organization of Social Work Education

Universities in Sweden are organized in departments. A department is responsible for courses and research within a subject such as social work, psychology, sociology, law, political science, etc. Each department has one or more full professors in charge of research and postgraduate studies. The administrative head of the entire department - budget, staff, students, etc - is a chairperson, the 'prefekt', who is appointed for three years at a time. Working with the chairperson, there is a director of studies who is responsible for the coordination of courses and the teaching within the department. From the student's perspective, programmes of study often involve course provided by more than one department.

To become a career university teacher, a doctoral degree is usually required. Once a teacher has a position at a university he or she usually can expect to stay at that position as long as he or she wants. There is no differences between teachers in social work and other disciplines in this respect. Many teachers in social work have their background in other disciplines, such as psychology, sociology, economics, law or political science, partly because it is only in the last ten years that it has been possible to complete a doctoral degree in social work. There is also a more junior category of university teachers - Lecturers and Lecturers MS.s in Social Work - who do not have doctoral degrees. Practical experience of social work is required for the field-work co-ordinators who are responsible for organizing and overseeing student placements in field-based studies and in supervised fieldwork. They also provide training for the practitioners who actually supervise the placements on a day-to-day basis.

The Study Programme

In the University of Umeå, the major activity of the Department of Social Welfare is the undergraduate programme in social work. Students must complete 140 credits, which is equivalent to three and a half years of full-time study. The programme provides a general education which prepares students to pursue a variety of occupations. Upon successful completion, graduates are awarded a baccalaureate degree in Social Work. The programme is made up from four disciplines taught by their home departments: Social Welfare, Law, Political Science and Statistics. The Department of Social Welfare is the host department for the programme and has the overall responsibility for its administration and co-ordination. The main elements of the programme are:-

Fundamentals of social science (terms 1 and 2)
The first year starts with a short introduction and a course in the use of computers and verbal communication. It then continues with foundation courses in Political Economy, Sociology, Psychology, Political Science and Law, where basic concepts and theories are presented. The year ends with a course entitled 'An Introduction to Social Work'.

Research methodology and field-based studies (term 3)
The third term is comprised of two 10-credit blocks. The first is a course in research methodology and the second course is a 10 week field-study. The two blocks are integrated in a project that is presented at the end of the term.

AB-courses in social work (terms 4 and 5)
The AB-course consists of four 10-credit theory-based courses. The first deals with children, youth and the family, the second with the changing welfare state, the third with the organizational aspects of social work and the possibilities for human adaptation, and the fourth with living conditions that place people at risk and the possibilities of intervention when individuals find themselves in difficult social situations.

Supervised field work (term 6)
This term offers students a chance to test themselves in practice under accredited professional supervision. The university uses placements in four counties in the northern part of Sweden.

C-courses in social work (term 7)
In the last term the student can choose among six alternative C-courses: social work with a focus on power and law; social work with a focus on substance abuse, criminal behaviour, and social psychiatry; social work with a focus on quality assessment and evaluation; social work with a focus on gender theory and social welfare; social work in international perspective; and social work with a focus on youth, the family and society (Student Handbook, 1996).

The Practical Organization of Placements

The field-work co-ordinators have the responsibility of arranging placements for field-based studies and supervised fieldwork. In Umeå there are four co-ordinators. Two of them meet the students in their introductory weeks and remain with them throughout the seven terms of study, so far as is possible. There are two intakes per year with about seventy students in each so that each co-ordinator will be responsible for about thirty five students. In addition, they contribute to the main academic courses in the programme.

The co-ordinators prepare the students for their field-based studies and for their supervised placements. The semester before field-based studies or supervised fieldwork the coordinators meet the students individually and in groups to explore their interests in social work practice. They then try to match students to the places where fieldwork opportunities are available, subject to the students' own, obligatory, visits in order to meet supervisors and get first-hand information about the placement sites. Supervisors receive a full briefing from the co-ordinators and the experience is monitored by a midway evaluation. All students and supervisors are visited by the field-work coordinators. A third meeting is held at the end of the period. For field-based studies, this takes the form of a seminar in small groups together with supervisors where the students' projects are examined. For students who have been carrying out a practical placement, the meeting takes place about one month before the end and is in the form of a group meeting with students and supervisors working together about how to end the practice period. They actually begin the process of ending and the evaluation of the students' learning. When students return from field-based studies and supervised fieldwork they are followed up individually and in group work, based on the students' written thoughts and reflections.

Perceived Benefits to Agency, Students and University of Practice Placements

The departments of social work have created a close partnership with the agencies of social work through the practice placements. The agencies are able to become familiar with the knowledge and skills of the students from whom they will be recruiting in the future. Indeed, for many students, their first job will be at the site where they had a placement. The agencies are kept in touch with the departments' research activities through regular seminars and joint projects such as the evaluation of service provision and other activities. The university departments have also been important providers of in-service training. In recent years, the agencies have also been actively involved in the international contacts promoted by student exchanges under the ERASMUS and SOCRATES programmes of the European Community. The impact of international students on placements has been particularly beneficial for some of the more remote counties in Sweden where the sparsity of the population makes it difficult for professionals to be challenged by different ideas and approaches to practice. There are equal benefits for students and the university departments. It is unimaginable that a successful social work programme could be run without a full integration of theory, knowledge and practice.

References

Frick, W. (1996), *Social Work Education in Sweden*, unpublished report, Department of Social Welfare, Umeå University.
Student Handbook (1996), Social Work Study Programme. Department of Social Welfare, Umeå University.

15 Social Work Education in Britain
Mark Lymbery

Introduction

Social work education has increasingly reflected the tensions between the professional aspirations of social work and a variety of direct and indirect attempts to control and regulate the production of new social workers (Howe, 1991; Webb, 1996). The focus of this chapter is more on the factors which have had a significant bearing on the structure, purpose and control of modern social work education than its detailed content. The establishment of social work education can be traced directly to the work of the nineteenth century pioneers. The early social workers did not think of themselves as professionals, nor were they perceived as such: rather, they tended to be well-to-do people charitably helping the poor (Heraud, 1981). However, as systems of social intervention became developed there was an increasing sense that education and training were needed.

Jones has argued that this training has two broad purposes. The first of these he characterizes as the 'external' dimension, the way in which the process of education is used to forge a professional identity for social work. The second of these is the 'internal' dimension, which is expressed as a concern for the qualities and skills of social workers (Jones, 1979). The first of these is central to the theme of this paper. This is not to argue that the development of a skilled workforce is a secondary issue, but rather to assert that this goal should be seen in the light of social work's struggle for professional status.

Social workers must seek both to assist those who require help and, where necessary, control those people who are defined as being troublesome to society. They are among a number of occupational groups who have the responsibility to manage the social policies of central government, and are thus directly affected by the increase in the levels of social injustice which have marked British society in the 1980s and 1990s (Hill, 1993). They have had to do this within welfare systems which have been subject to constant ideological and financial attack during the same period (Hill, 1993; Brown, 1995). They also have to practice within legally defined requirements and the policies and procedures of welfare agencies (Jordan, 1984). The way in which these problems and requirements are negotiated by the social worker has much to do with the nature and balance of control over the social work profession, which has a major impact on the levels of discretion and autonomy afforded to individual social workers.

The Early Years

There were various influences on the direction of social work education in the late nineteenth century. In common with the pattern of service delivery identified in Chapter 13, they came primarily from non-governmental sources, chief among which were the Charity Organisation Society and the Settlement movement. In both cases, the development of education for social work stemmed from a recognition that 'amateur' social workers needed to understand more about the social conditions of people with whom they were working as well as learning the skills of social work intervention. The first social work education therefore came about at the instigation of the agencies who employed social workers.

Broadly speaking, there were two main streams of development. On the one hand, the Settlement movement developed a form of in-house apprenticeship, which rapidly gave way to specialized schools of social studies based in universities, the first of which were established in Liverpool [1904] and Birmingham [1907] (Heraud, 1981). At around the same time [1903], the Charity Organisation Society established the School of Sociology and Social Economics, for the training of their own personnel (Woodroofe, 1962; Jones, 1979; Crowther, 1981). This School also offered courses of lectures and examinations for Poor Law officers, with the first examinations being held in 1906 (Crowther, 1981): it was later incorporated into the London School of Economics. The training pioneered for Poor Law officers was taken on by other universities, although it was never fully accepted that this group needed to be trained (Crowther, 1981).

Although these pioneer social work courses were developed almost a century ago, it is instructive to note some of the issues which were identified as problems at the time, which have great contemporary resonance. For example, there was concern about the relative importance of theoretical and practical learning. There were debates about the possible consequence of a

Social Work Education in Britain 223

student making a mistake while on placement, set against the need for students to prove their practical social work skills. There was tension between the need for social workers to show their ability to work within the confines of agency policy, while also demonstrating the ability to think for themselves and respond appropriately to individual circumstances (Young and Ashton, 1956). There was also a fundamental dispute about the most appropriate location for social work training, with some practice agencies believing that universities could not provide the appropriate level of practical training, while some within universities felt that practically-oriented professional training was not an appropriate function for a university (Macadam, 1945; Heraud, 1981).

Despite these concerns, Macadam argued that social work education had in fact developed a sense of unity and coherence by the second world war, based on three core principles:

... first, planned practical experience closely related to lectures and reading; second, opportunities for the observation of healthy independent working class movements; and third, specialization to follow, not to replace, a background of general study and experience (Macadam, 1945, p.54).

Even assuming that these three principles were universally held and applied, the development of social work education in the years leading to 1939 was not straightforward. The fragmented and piecemeal growth of social work (Seed, 1973) was reflected in the education of the time. The demand for social workers and, hence, the need for training courses was increased by events such as the First World War (Heraud, 1981), but the structure and content of social work education developed inconsistently in the different universities which supplied it. There was no single form of qualification, with the universities issuing their own diplomas and certificates. Although there were thematic similarities between courses (Macadam, 1945), the differences were also marked.

However, there were exceptions to this piecemeal trend. For some areas of social work, the strong development of professional associations led to their active involvement in establishing and validating courses. In this period, the Institute of Almoners was developing specific training for staff entering medical social work; on a smaller scale, the Association of Psychiatric Social Workers also established their own training courses (Younghusband, 1978b; Heraud, 1981). From 1936, the first government funded validating body appeared, the Probation Advisory and Training Board, which oversaw the development of training for Probation Officers (Cooper, 1983). The fact that these were relatively isolated attempts by social workers to control and define the nature of their work, and the structure of training required to undertake it, is an indication that the social work 'professional project' (Witz, 1992) was not far advanced by 1939. Also, in all the above cases, social work was a subordinate professional discipline, and hence dominated by longer established professions or by the legal system itself.

1945 - 1970

By the end of the Second World War, the status and significance of social work was still contested. While there were numerous universities offering training courses, social work had not established a coherent identity, being made up of heterogeneous elements, with no fixed standard and form of training (Macadam, 1945). Relatively few staff received a formal course of social work training; while there was growth in the 1950s, this proved to be slow. As late as 1970, the vast majority of people who were defined as being social workers had no relevant qualification (Younghusband, 1978b).

The first significant post-war development in the education of social workers followed the recommendations of the Curtis Committee, which introduced Children's Departments into local government. The training of child care officers (who later became known as social workers) was a source of some concern for the committee, both in terms of the shortage of qualified personnel, and in the fragmented nature of the training undertaken. This led the Curtis Committee to recommend the establishment of a Central Training Council in Child Care to oversee the quality of courses and to take a lead role in the expansion of training opportunities (Jordan, 1984). There was a subsequent increase in the proportion of child care officers who were professionally qualified, to 46.9 per cent by the end of the 1960s (Younghusband, 1978a).

While this move did increase the professional status of child care work, it also served to compound the fragmented nature of social work education, by increasing the specialist content of their training (Cooper, 1983). Although the principle of a generic base of social work had been asserted by Macadam (1945), there was little movement towards a generic form of training. The first acknowledged generic course of social work education was not started until 1954: significantly, in terms of the history of social work, this was located within the London School of Economics (Heraud, 1981).

There were also significant developments in the 1950s as regards practice learning. The growth in psychological theories for social work brought about a perceived need to manage the practice learning experience of students in a more structured way, so that students could demonstrate their ability to use complex theoretical material. Experienced and skilled practice teachers were not commonly available: one of the advances in the 1950s was the establishment of student units, where students could be taught their practice skills in a group, thus concentrating scarce staff resources (Curnock, 1975; Younghusband, 1978b). This model of practice learning - albeit in a modified form - has proved to be an enduring feature of learning for social work into the 1990s.

The Younghusband Report into the training needs of staff working in social services, which was published in 1959, represented a significant step forward for social work. The report noted the fragmented organization of education for social work, and proposed a more coherent approach where different levels of staff would receive different levels of training. It also recommended the creation of a Council for Training in Social Work to administer and plan social work education, and a National Institute for Social Work Training to take a broader developmental function in respect of social work. The Council for Training in Social Work was established in 1962. The National Institute for Social Work Training was set up in 1961: in 1973, its name was changed to the National Institute for Social Work. These bodies created a significant professional power base, which helped to influence later political decisions and secure more resources for social work. The establishment of the Council for Training in Social Work heralded a rapid increase of generic social work training courses through the remainder of the 1960s. However, it also meant that there were then three separate training councils for social work, the Probation Advisory and Training Board, the Council for Training in Child Care, and the Council for Training in Social Work. In addition, the separate training courses, validated by the professional bodies, for medical social work and psychiatric social work still persisted. Social work education remained fragmented.

The true measure of social work's success in its pursuit of professional status came with the implementation of the Seebohm Report, as outlined in Chapter 13. A key element of this was the unification of social work education with a single qualification, the Certificate of Qualification in Social Work (CQSW), under the authority of a single validating body, the Central Council for Education and Training in Social Work (CCETSW). This came about as part of the Local Authority Social Services Act 1970, which came into effect in 1971. The different social work associations (except the National Association of Probation Officers, which held on to a separate identity) united at the same time into one single body, the British Association of Social Workers. This process of unification was could also be seen in the gradual amalgamation of the various specialist social work journals into core publications, which addressed all areas of policy and practice.

Much of the evidence to the Seebohm Committee had supported the integration of social work training (Younghusband, 1978b), and indicated that the maintenance of three separate training councils was indefensible and a waste of state resources (Cooper, 1983). CCETSW was conceived as a body which was independent from direct government control, but relied on central government funding for its existence. The mission of CCETSW was to bring together all the various forms of education for social work irrespective of practice settings, to validate all the courses which offered social work training and to award the unified qualification (the Certificate of Qualification in Social Work). The task facing CCETSW was thus substantial, even without the legacy of special interests which it inherited (Cooper, 1983). In addition, as the control of government expenditure became an increasing priority through the 1980s, CCETSW's difficulty in maintaining independence from government was highlighted, with particular consequences for the independence of university-based social work courses (Webb, 1996).

1970 - 1996

The early years of the 1970s were a period of unparalleled growth in social work education, as more qualified social workers were required for the new social services departments. The social work profession appeared to have been successful in portraying social work as an intellectually complex activity (Sibeon, 1990). However, the growth of available courses happened so rapidly that it proved difficult to recruit capable staff to provide the education, leading to concerns over its quality (Younghusband, 1978b). In addition, as previously noted, the 1970s was a decade in which the nature of social work came under intense academic and political scrutiny, with pressure from various quarters both within and outside its ranks. Perhaps the most significant impact on the development of social work education was the tension between 'radicalized' social work courses, emphasizing a range of new sociological insights and committed to a professional ideology, and the expectations of employers and managers that practitioners be competent to perform the more limited tasks that agencies prescribed (Jones, 1979). Employer dissatisfaction with the type of graduate from social work courses, combined with the slower than expected growth of training opportunities for staff in residential, day and domiciliary care services, led to the development of a new form of training - the Certificate of Social Service (CSS). The dispute between the academy and employers which gave rise to the CSS is particularly interesting in terms of the continued struggle for control of social work. To borrow the terminology of Jamous and Peloille (1970), the argument can be reduced to the preference of employers for a form of training which would emphasize the 'technical' aspects of social work and which would be jointly managed and delivered by employers and educational institutions, over the existing CQSW which was felt to emphasize the 'indeterminacy' of professional autonomy and decision-making:

> A significant factor following the introduction of the CSS scheme in 1975 was the employers' realization that their ability to 'control' the new scheme enabled them to ensure it equipped newly qualified social workers with practical 'relevant' skills as defined by the employers and by senior agency administrators (Sibeon, 1990).

Initially, the CSS was intended to be a second tier qualification, which would equip staff for certain tasks related to social work, but which would not allow them to act as social workers. However, the establishment of a two-tier structure of training was never likely to be sustainable: the pressure of CSS holders to be allowed to compete for social work posts was considerable, with employers also arguing that CSS holders had demonstrated their practice competence. As a result, CCETSW changed its regulations in the late 1980s, and subsequently CSS holders could compete on equal terms with CQSW holders in the job market.

During this period, CCETSW was also engaged on a fundamental review of its strategy for social work education, which took several years to complete. The review followed public and professional concerns about the nature and quality of social work education: in particular, there was a strong employers' move to take more control of its structure and content, following their positive experience of joint management which the CSS had instigated (Sibeon, 1990). The hub of CCETSW's strategy was the desire to increase the length of social work training courses, both to ensure that students were fully prepared for the demanding nature of practice and to harmonize the two year British social work training course with the European standard of three years. However, given that the review took place within a period of public expenditure cuts, the likelihood of the government finding extra resources for a third year was never strong. When it became evident that funding for a three year course would not be made available, CCETSW had to fall back on a strategy which sought to strengthen and rationalize the existing two year structure.

It was finally decided to establish a single route to qualification, the Diploma of Social Work (DipSW), which would supersede both the CQSW and the CSS. The regulations which CCETSW issued for the DipSW required partnerships to be established between universities and employers over the delivery of the programme, to make it a joint responsibility (CCETSW, 1991, Annex 4). CCETSW did not specify the form such a partnership had to take and many different forms of partnership did arise. Payne (1994) has argued that the basis of most such partnerships has been on the 'romantic ideal' of a partnership between individuals, and therefore does not fully address the nature of partnership between organizations.

The significance of the requirement lay in the transfer of the CSS style of management arrangements to all qualifying training in social work, giving employers the opportunity to wield considerable power within social work education. This approach increased the fears of universities, as it seemed to sit uncomfortably with long-held principles of academic autonomy. More practically, universities were concerned that the joint arrangements held no legal force: in other words, if agencies defaulted on their agreements, there was no redress for universities, who were still solely accountable for the students' learning experience.

The closer involvement of employers was welcomed by many, in the belief that greater cooperation in the planning of social work education would be beneficial. In addition, it was felt that a close working relationship between universities and social work agencies would ensure that course curricula reflected the realities of practice. It was also intended that the DipSW would be more oriented towards practice, and greater attention was to be given to the management and assessment of a student's competence to practice (CCETSW, 1991). However, other perspectives also need to be considered. CCETSW's approach appeared to signal a lack of faith in the ability of universities to provide and manage a good quality of education, and significantly curtailed universities' ability to regulate themselves. Many commentators within the university sector expressed their dismay over these moves (Jones, 1996; Webb, 1996), believing that CCETSW was merely carrying out central government policies, which constituted an attack on professionalism and on the independence of the sector.

In an influential article, Brewster, a former CCETSW employee, argued that it had effectively become an arm of central government policy, affected by the climate of managerialism which has permeated the public sector (Brewster, 1992). Brewster identified close links between recent developments in social work education and the New Right agenda of central government, in which he felt CCETSW had become a willing accomplice. Far from being an independent body which was intrinsically supportive of social work's professional claims, CCETSW was seen as being under the direct control of central government, helping to carry out policies which were inimical to the professional project of social work.

Although the role of CCETSW as a validating and awarding body continues, it has been subject to increasing levels of criticism from within social work education. Jones summarizes the main area of concern:

> The creation of the CSS in 1975 through to the latest review of the DipSW ... is a story of British social work education accommodating the demands of an increasingly authoritarian state in which the role and nature of social work are being transformed (Jones, 1996, p.209).

He argues that social work should be committed to the principles of social justice and the promotion of human welfare. However, the development of social policy which is hostile to such values, when allied to the narrowed focus of social work education on competence and away from critical reflection, creates a climate where the profession may increasingly be incapable of responding to injustices within society.

In this respect, the recent decision by the Home Office that Probation Officers are no longer required to possess a social work qualification takes on additional significance. This policy is based on a presumption that probation officers do not require social work knowledge, skills or values, and was reaffirmed by the incoming Labour administration. It has broken the well-established connection of social work to the criminal justice system, and also demonstrates that the government has the power directly to control the future of social work. Such a realization could signal the demise of the professional aspirations of social work as a whole. Although a Labour administration was elected in May 1997, its intentions with regard to social work education are unclear. However, the administration has signalled its commitment to the financial spending targets which it inherited from the Conservatives, which argues that it does not plan for growth in most areas of social welfare. In addition, a review of the purpose and function of CCETSW has recently been set in hand; the result of this review will have a major impact on the future of education for social work.

Conclusion

It is instructive to review the history and development of social work education in the light of current concerns. It has been characterized by tensions between academic and practical elements since its very inception: the current emphasis on competence also demonstrates the tension between those elements of the social work task which are primarily 'technical' in nature and those which require the exercise of 'indeterminate' professional judgement (Jamous and Peloille, 1970). While the emphasis on the competence of newly qualified social workers can readily be justified - few would argue that social workers should not be competent - it appears that the concept is being treated in a reductive manner, denying the importance of independent creative thought, which has always been part of the repertoire of a skilled social worker, and which should be encouraged by a university education (Jones and Joss, 1995). Clark, in particular, has argued persuasively that the notion of competence does not fully address the complexity of social work practice, substituting ideas of the need to develop a professional discipline (Clark, 1995a; Clark, 1995b).

It is symbolically significant that some of the most worrying current developments in social work education concern two universities where social work has been longest established. It was announced in 1995 that the London School of Economics - which had run the first university-based training, and which had developed the first generic social work course - no longer intended to offer social work education. Several universities - including Liverpool University, which first established training courses for the Settlement movement - have discussed the possibility of establishing social work courses which would be disconnected from CCETSW (Froggett and Sapey, 1997), on the basis that its requirements for the DipSW are unworkable and inimical to the ethos of a university. Clearly, therefore, the future of social work education in universities is insecure. A continued over-emphasis on competence appears likely to condemn social work to a future as a highly prescribed occupation, whose members will need to be skilled at following agency policies and procedures, but where creativity is unlikely to feature as a significant part of its role. While social work education has the potential capacity to challenge this direction, it is questionable that this outcome will be achieved.

References

Brewster, R. (1992), 'The New Class? Managerialism and Social Work Education and Training', *Issues in Social Work Education*, 11, 2, pp.81-93.
Central Council for Education and Training in Social Work (1991) *DipSW: Rules and Regulations for the Diploma in Social Work (2nd Edition)*, London: Central Council for Education and Training in Social Work.
Clark, C. (1995a), 'Competence and Discipline in Professional Formation', *British Journal of Social Work*, 25, 3, pp.563-80.
Clark, C. (1995b), 'Competence, Knowledge and Professional Discipline', *Issues in Social Work Education*, 16, 2, pp.64-76.
Cooper, J. (1983), *The Creation of the British Social Services*, London: Heinemann Educational Books.
Crowther, M.A. (1981), *The Workhouse System 1834-1929: the history of an English social institution*, London: Batsford.
Curnock, K. (1975), *Student Units in Social Work Education: Central Council for Education and Training in Social Work Paper 11*, London: Central Council for Education and Training in Social Work.
Froggett, L. and Sapey, B. (1997), 'Communication, Culture and Competence in Social Work Education', *Social Work Education*, 16, 1, pp. 41-53.
Heraud, B. (1981), *Training for Uncertainty*, London: Routledge and Kegan Paul.
Hill, M. (1993), *The Welfare State in Britain: A Political History since 1945*, Aldershot: Edward Elgar.
Holgate, E. and Keidan, O. (1975), 'The Personal Social Services', in Mays, J., Forder, A. and Keidan, O. (eds), *Penelope Hall's Social Services of England and Wales*, London: Routledge and Kegan Paul.
Howe, D. (1991), 'Knowledge, Power and the Shape of Social Work Practice', in Davies. M. (ed), *The Sociology of Social Work*, London: Routledge.
Jamous, H. and Peloille, B. (1970), 'Professions or Self-perpetuating Systems? Changes in the French University Hospital System', in Jackson, J.A. (ed), *Professions and Professionalization*, Cambridge: Cambridge University Press.
Jones, C. (1979), 'Social Work Education: 1900 - 1977'. in Parry, N., Rustin, M. and Satyamurti, C. (eds), *Social Work, Welfare and the State*, London: Edward Arnold.
Jones, C. (1996) 'Anti-intellectualism and the Peculiarities of British Social Work Education', in Parton, N. (ed), *Social Theory, Social Change and Social Work*, London: Routledge.
Jones, S. and Joss, R. (1995), 'Models of Professionalism', in Yelloly, M. and Henkel, M. (eds), *Learning and Teaching in Social Work*, London: Jessica Kingsley.
Jordan, B. (1984), *Invitation to Social Work*, Oxford: Martin Robertson.
Kelly, A. (1991), 'The 'New' Managerialism in the Social Services', in Carter, P., Jeffs, T. and Smith, M. (eds), *Social Work and Social Welfare Yearbook 3*, Buckingham: Open University Press.
Lawson, R. (1993), 'The New Technology of Management in the Personal Social Services', in Taylor-Gooby, P. and Lawson, R. (eds), *Markets and Managers, New Issues in the Delivery of Welfare*, Buckingham: Open University Press.
Macadam, E. (1945), *The Social Servant in the Making*, London: George Allen and Unwin.
Payne, M. (1994), 'Partnership Between Organisations in Social Work Education', *Issues in Social Work Education*, 14, 1, pp. 53-70.

Seed, P. (1973), *The Expansion of Social Work in Britain*, London: Routledge and Kegan Paul.
Sibeon, R. (1990), 'Social Work Knowledge, Social Actors and De-Professionalization', in Abbott, P. and Wallace. C. (eds), *The Sociology of the Caring Professions*, Basingstoke: Falmer.
Webb, D. (1996), 'Regulation for Radicals: the State, Central Council for Education and Training in Social Work and the Academy', in Parton, N. (ed), *Social Theory, Social Change and Social Work*, London: Routledge.
Witz, A. (1992), *Professions and Patriarchy*, London: Routledge.
Woodroofe, K. (1962), *From Charity to Social Work*, London: Routledge and Kegan Paul.
Young, A. and Ashton, E. (1956), *British Social Work in the Nineteenth Century*, London: Routledge and Kegan Paul.
Younghusband, E. (1978a), *Social Work in Britain: 1950 - 1975 (Volume 1)*, London: George Allen and Unwin.
Younghusband, E. (1978b), *Social Work in Britain: 1950 - 1975 (Volume 2)*, London: George Allen and Unwin.

16 Delivering Social Work Education in Partnership in Britain
Tina Eadie

Introduction

This chapter discusses partnership arrangements between university social work courses and social welfare agencies in England and Wales. It focuses on the nature of partnership arrangements in relation to agencies' assessment of social work students' practice, and considers some of the costs and benefits of delivering social work education in this way.

The Diploma in Social Work (DipSW) was introduced in the late 1980s as the new professional qualification for social workers. Requirements and Regulations for the new Diploma were set out by the Central Council for Education and Training in Social Work (CCETSW) in a document known as 'Paper 30' (CCETSW, 1989a). This stipulated that higher education institutions (referred to here as universities) were to work 'collaboratively' with social welfare agencies - statutory and voluntary - as DipSW 'Programme Providers' (CCETSW, 1989a, p.5). The government made development money available to support these arrangements and to extend all social work courses to two years duration. The 'Requirements for Programmes' (CCETSW, 1989, p.22) referred to submissions for DipSW Programmes being made 'jointly', and to the need for 'active collaboration' in all decision-making aspects of the Programme. While terms such as 'collaboration' and 'partnerships' between agencies and universities were not entirely new, they had never been incorporated so *formally* into the management and delivery of social work training courses.

The chapter is in three sections; the first considers the principles underpinning partnership and the practicalities of its introduction. The second focuses on the impact of partnership requirements on practice placements, looking critically at the continuing shortage of high quality practice learning opportunities for social work students. The third section describes the process of placement provision, from identifying student learning needs through to the successful completion of a placement. The conclusion reviews the costs and benefits to both universities and agencies of delivering social work education in partnership.

Principles Underpinning Partnership

The concept of partnership between education institutions and social welfare agencies has remained a central feature of the Diploma in Social Work through two revisions of the original Paper 30 (CCETSW, 1991; 1995). 'Partnership' in this context is neither a personal relationship nor a legal contract, although it does incorporate contractual obligations: it is an agreement entered into voluntarily, offering both mutual benefit *and* mutual responsibility in relation to the training and education of social workers. By formally introducing the concept, it was hoped that agency criticisms of the former qualification, the Certificate of Qualification in Social Work (CQSW), would be addressed. A regular concern of agencies was that students were not being adequately prepared for employment because the academic teaching on courses was at an abstract, intellectual, and political level, distanced from social work practice. In response, academics argued, and continue to argue, that social work education is more than training for a job - that an ability to reflect critically on established practice with reference to theoretical analysis and research findings is an essential part of the social worker's role. In addressing these tensions, Paper 30 signalled clear support for the agency perspective, stating that the primary purpose of social work education was to prepare students for employment as professionally qualified social workers (CCETSW, 1989a, p.8), and that academic disciplines should only be assessed in relation to their relevance to social work practice (CCETSW, 1989a, p.24).

CCETSW has never been prescriptive about *how* DipSW programmes should collaborate: it remains the responsibility of the partners themselves to arrive at a working relationship which 'matches their circumstances and degree of commitment' (CCETSW, 1991, p.43). In practice, 'active collaboration' has not meant all partner agencies being involved in all areas of activity all of the time (CCETSW, 1991, p.44). What is stipulated (CCETSW, 1991, p.44) is that all parties to the programme's provision must be involved in *initial* decision-making about each of the key areas outlined in the original Paper 30 - curriculum planning and development, student selection, resource allocation for academic and practice-based learning, student assessment and the monitoring of all aspects of the programme, including equal opportunities policies and procedures (CCETSW, 1989a, p.22). The extent to which agencies have become *actively* involved with local courses has varied therefore, according to whether partnership is regarded as an opportunity to influence the education and training of future recruits, or as another demand on already stretched resources - active agency involvement in a social work programme is very time-consuming.

All DipSW programmes in England and Wales are now delivered in partnership with local social welfare agencies. Partnership agencies have entered into formal written agreements with social work courses, outlining commitment to providing teaching, agency representation on committees, task groups and selection panels, and practice placements. While not legally binding, these are based on a shared commitment to high standards of education and training. The provision of practice placements is crucial in ensuring that each student has the opportunity to demonstrate his or her competence to practice as a social worker.

Partnership in Placement Provision

It was intended that formalizing partnership arrangements between universities and agencies would address long-standing difficulties associated with practice placements - guaranteeing sufficient numbers of placements, ensuring that placement settings meet students' learning needs, making available sufficient numbers of experienced practitioners to supervise students, and securing adequate funding for placement provision. In practice, difficulties continue.

Sufficient Numbers of Practice Placements

Collaboration in the provision of practice placements is crucial in ensuring that the supply of placements meets the demand. All DipSW students are required to have two periods of assessed practice learning, one of 50 days and another of 80 days (CCETSW, 1995, p.38). A positive feature of formal collaborative arrangements is that partner agencies undertake to supply a specific number of placements each year, negotiated to meet student demand. In itself, partnership cannot compel agencies to provide the required number of placements: it is the *process* of collaboration - exchanging information, fostering good personal relationships, developing channels of communication, and negotiating levels of involvement - which promotes goodwill and results in cooperation, rather than the imposition of formal structures (Payne 1994). While applicable to all aspects of partnership, it is particularly relevant to the issue of placement provision.

Meeting Students' Learning Needs

The specific learning needs of individual students cannot be predicted from year to year. It is therefore desirable not only that there are sufficient *numbers* of placements available, but also sufficient *variety*. The learning offered by the placement should be appropriate both to the student's level of development and to stated learning needs. It is also expected that placements will be provided in settings which encourage students to reflect critically on their own practice and that of other team members. Taking these factors into account, the following sorts of questions are useful when considering settings for practice placements:

- Is the work undertaken in the setting relevant to students' overall learning?
- What will the student(s) learn and does this match stated learning needs (broken down into specific knowledge, skills and values)?
- Are practice methods used in the setting compatible with those taught on the course?
- Is office space and access to necessary equipment available for students?
- Are team members willing to share their experience and expertise with students?
- Are there opportunities for observation/joint work with practitioners?
- Will the student(s) be allowed to attend meetings/be treated as part of the team?
- Are arrangements for the supervision and assessment of the student(s) in place?

If the answer to any of these questions is no, an alternative placement setting should, ideally, be sought. Due to placement shortages, however, an alternative is rarely possible in the short term and settings which are less than ideal continue to be used. An advantage of the formal collaborative monitoring arrangements is that inappropriate placement settings are identified by programme providers. It is hoped that this will result in more suitable placements being developed in the longer term.

In addition to prescribed monitoring arrangements, CCETSW introduced with the DipSW a new system for the 'Approval of Agencies and the Accreditation and Training of Practice Teachers' (CCETSW, 1989b). This attempted to ensure that all agencies providing practice placements could guarantee a high quality learning experience in relation to both the setting and the standard of supervision and assessment. To obtain CCETSW Agency Approval, agencies must demonstrate a commitment to the provision of high quality practice learning opportunities, with associated procedures and guidelines, and evidence from universities of high standards of provision of practice placements. To be accredited, placement supervisors must either hold the CCETSW Practice Teaching Award or qualify under transitional arrangements set out by CCETSW (1989b, p.8). Whilst commendable in theory, by no means all agencies and practitioners have put themselves through the administratively cumbersome, resource-heavy, and time-consuming process of acquiring approval or accreditation - and CCETSW has no means of requiring them to do so.

Training Sufficient Numbers of Practice Teachers

While on placement in the agency, each student is individually supervised and assessed by an experienced practitioner called a practice teacher, a term designed to reflect the concept of the teaching of practice. The practice teacher is responsible for the overall management of a placement and accountable for the work of the student while he or she is in the agency. The model in Britain assumes that practice teachers will undertake some direct teaching of social work practice, provide weekly formal supervision to the student and, depending on their location, day-to-day informal supervision, and directly observe the student's practice (the current requirement is three times during each placement). Towards the end of the placement the practice teacher makes an assessment of a student's competence, based on evidence gathered throughout the placement, and submits this to the university.

Practice teaching is a complex, demanding and time-consuming task requiring specialist training. The principle that training should be available for practice teachers is well established in Britain and is generally regarded as both a good staff development and career opportunity. Training has developed from a basic 3-day course, awarding a Certificate of Attendance, to a CCETSW-Approved Practice Teacher Training Programme leading to the

Practice Teaching Award (CCETSW, 1989b, p.10). This Programme must include an education and training component of a minimum of 150 hours, extend over a period not less than three months, and include the supervision of a DipSW student (CCETSW, 1989b, pp.11-12). The resource implications are clearly substantial.

Securing Adequate Funding

Despite CCETSW's attempts to address both the quantity and quality of practice learning opportunities since the introduction of the DipSW, practice placements continue to be in short supply and their quality continues to be variable. Funding is clearly a key factor in this. The funding of practice placements has always been a contentious issue. Historically, in statutory agencies, block training grants were made to local authorities which included an amount for the provision of placements. In practice, the money often disappeared into the main budget where service delivery, not training, is prioritized. This resulted in placement provision being experienced as *additional* to normal workloads, creating dissatisfaction both from teams providing placement settings and from practitioners supervising students. A more successful method of funding placements was the payment of a fee to agencies providing placements, lasting for the duration of the placement. In the voluntary sector this was paid by CCETSW and in the probation service by the Home Office. The responsibility for managing practice placement budgets was recently passed to *Programmes*, rather than specific agencies, but with no overall increase in resources, practice learning remains under-funded.

The more explicit and predictable the funding available for practice placement provision, the more likely it is that agencies will employ staff specifically to undertake practice teaching. Specialist practice teachers supervise students on a full-time basis, often supervising several students at any one time. Semi-specialist practice teachers supervise one or two students on a regular basis in addition to managing a reduced workload. These models offer an alternative to the individual practice teacher who occasionally supervises a student and does so in addition to a normal workload. There is no doubt that these arrangements benefit both agencies and universities:

- Employing a small number of specialist or semi-specialist practice teachers reduces the high costs involved in practice teacher training.
- Supervising students on a regular basis develops practice teachers' assessment skills and broadens their knowledge of the academic

Delivering Social Work Education in Partnership in Britain 239

content of local courses.
- Regular liaison between tutors and practice teachers helps to develop trust and confidence in each other's decision-making.
- Students can be placed in different team locations whilst being supervised by a centrally-based practice teacher employed to supervise the students.
- Increased practice teacher satisfaction through receiving adequate workload relief reduces the likelihood of a high turnover of practice teachers - although their proven skill in supervision is sometimes used as a fast-track to promotion!

The Process of Providing Placements in Partnership

Having discussed the principles underpinning the concept of partnership and considered the impact of partnership on the provision of practice placements, this section outlines how partnership arrangements actually work in practice.

Identifying and Matching Learning Needs

In determining an appropriate placement for each student, university tutors help tutees identify learning needs prior to both the first and second assessed placement. This is achieved through the linking of past practice experiences, current theoretical learning and future career choices, and is detailed on a Placement Request Form. The university Placement Coordinator sends the forms to agency Placement Coordinators who, on receipt of the form, begin to identify suitable settings within the agency. For example, a student might identify the following learning needs:

- communicating with children;
- developing understanding of theories of child development;
- working with families;
- interviewing and assessment skills;
- cross-cultural understandings.

For this student, a placement in a team which specialises in nursery provision for children under school age would be very appropriate, especially if the team is based in an area of mixed ethnicity. If such a placement is not available, the Coordinator might consider placing the student in a day nursery for under fives. In either case, a practice teacher must be available to supervise the student.

The Informal Meeting

Following the identification of both placement setting and practice teacher, the student is asked to contact the practice teacher and arrange to meet with him or her for an informal discussion. This should ideally take place in the agency setting so that the student can meet other staff and see the working environment. Unless either the practice teacher or the student feels strongly that the placement setting is not going to meet the student's learning needs, the student will then inform the university Placement Coordinator that the visit has taken place and that the placement can go ahead. The Coordinator will confirm this in writing to the practice teacher and provide further information such as a course handbook and details of the assessment process.

The Agreement Meeting

Once the placement is confirmed, a formal Agreement Meeting takes place with the student, the practice teacher and the student's tutor. A standard form, provided by the tutor, is completed during this meeting, the main aim of which is to agree and confirm in writing the specific aims and objectives of the placement. These should relate explicitly to the student's identified learning needs. The Agreement should be signed by the student, practice teacher and tutor and a copy held by each as a record of the discussion.

The Induction Period

It is usual for the agency to provide a period of induction. This takes place during the first week or two, and provides students with an overview of the work undertaken within the agency, and an opportunity to discuss aspects of agency policy and practice with different members of staff. In some agencies this is arranged for the students before the placement commences. In others, students are given considerable freedom to decide for themselves which aspects of the agency they want to observe in more detail.

Direct Work

In both assessed placements, the student should undertake work for which he

Delivering Social Work Education in Partnership in Britain 241

or she has professional responsibility. Observation visits, though useful during the induction period, should not be the main focus of an assessed placement. The practice teacher is responsible for ensuring that students are undertaking appropriate work. Students are not an extra pair of hands and should not be treated as such; reading and reflection time is important, balanced with ensuring that students are learning to manage the competing demands and pressures of the job.

The Process of Assessment

The award of the Diploma in Social Work signifies that a student is competent to practice in a profession which serves a multi-racial and multi-cultural society and is extremely demanding, both intellectually and emotionally (CCETSW, 1995). The assessment procedures are necessarily rigorous and, for the practice component of the course, students must demonstrate to practice teachers that they have met the requirements of the core competences set out in CCETSW's revised Rules and Requirements for the DipSW (1995, p.24). Throughout each placement, therefore, practice teachers are required to gather evidence which demonstrates this. They use a variety of assessment methods:

- Direct observation of the student's work.
- Discussion with the student in weekly supervision about work undertaken.
- Discussion with colleagues about work undertaken by the student.
- Listening to tape recordings of the student's interviews or other work.
- Watching video recordings of interviews or other work undertaken by the student.
- Reading written work prepared by the student (including agency records and reports).
- Talking to people with whom the student has worked (including colleagues, other professionals and community groups as well as service users).

The Mid-Way Review

A review of progress must take place at the mid-point of each assessed practice placement (CCETSW, 1995, p.12). It should involve the student, the student's tutor and the practice teacher. The review provides a formal opportunity to record the progress of *all* students on placement - whatever the level of their performance. Issues concerning poor performance of a student should be discussed with the tutor at any point, not just at the review, and most Programmes have specific procedures which should be followed if a student is experiencing difficulties with any aspect of the assessment process.

The Final Report

Towards the end of the placement the practice teacher and student together review evidence gathered throughout the placement to demonstrate the student's competence to practice. Evidence must show how the practice requirements for the six core competences (CCETSW, 1995, p.25-34) have been met. These are detailed in a document known as the 'practice curriculum'. The practice teacher completes this document, including an explicit recommendation that the student passes or fails the placement, and returns it to the university Placement Coordinator.

The Practice Assessment Panel

All Diploma in Social Work Programmes are required to have mechanisms in place to monitor standards of practice assessments and are required to do this through a formally constituted Practice Assessment Panel (CCETSW, 1995, p.44). The Panel should consist of agency and university representatives. Panel members will usually read all placement reports and comment on these. They may require a practice teacher to supply more evidence to support the recommendation. The Practice Assessment Panel will prepare a written report for the Programme Assessment Board.

The Programme Assessment Board

The Programme Assessment Board, usually combined with the university examination board, consists of university social work staff members, agency representatives, and two external assessors. External assessors are appointed by Programmes from a CCETSW-approved list. Providing an overall quality control function, they are required by CCETSW to produce an annual report advising on the Programme's standards of academic and practice assessment. The Board meets annually and formally reviews all assessments, academic and practice, and makes final pass or fail decisions. The Board determines

Delivering Social Work Education in Partnership in Britain 243

whether first year students may proceed to the second year, and whether second year students have achieved an overall pass standard.

Concluding Comments

This chapter has outlined the concept of partnership between social work courses and social welfare agencies in England and Wales, focussing specifically on its impact on the provision of practice placements. In this concluding section, while acknowledging that Programmes' experience of partnership will differ, an attempt is made to balance the benefits of partnership against the costs, both for universities and agencies, in order to evaluate overall effectiveness.

For university social work courses, the active involvement of agency representatives provides opportunities for all aspects of the Programme to benefit from current practitioner and manager perspectives - from the selection of students, through teaching social work skills and methods, to supervising students on placement and assessing their practice. Set against this are the resource costs of partnership; sharing information with partner agencies and attempting joint decision-making adds a dimension to the work that academic courses without a practice component do not have to contend with. It is also alien to most university teaching and administrative systems and university social work staff, both lecturers and administrators, have to spend time explaining their accountability to CCETSW as well as to the university. Some academics have themselves struggled to acknowledge formal partnerships with agencies as an opportunity rather than as a threat - to both their academic freedom and their traditional role as final judge of students' fitness to practice.

Benefits of partnership to agencies include increased opportunities to influence the education and training of future staff, ensuring that they are adequately and appropriately prepared for practice with some of society's most disadvantaged, vulnerable and, in some cases, dangerous groups. Other potential benefits include the staff development opportunities associated with practice teaching, which have already been mentioned, and with more formal university teaching and membership of a task group or committee. Many social work students apply to work in agencies in which they have undertaken a practice placement, which can be a bonus in areas experiencing recruitment difficulties. As with university courses, the cost of staff time and energy on structures and arrangements required by CCETSW can be high.

This chapter has demonstrated that partnership is more than cooperation.

Jordan noted (1988, p.30), 'Partnership... implies some kind of pooling of resources, and fairly close integration of roles... It implies trust, and a good deal of potential or actual agreement on common goals, and the means of achieving them'. Paper 30 created legitimacy for partnerships but it did not create the climate in which real partnership could flourish: that was the task of social work staff in both agencies and universities and it has been neither easy nor straightforward. Partnership has been a developmental process, building on good relationships already in existence and negotiating the amount of 'intrusion and involvement' (Payne 1994, p.67) in each other's spheres of influence. The introduction of the Diploma in Social Work in England and Wales forced university social work departments to review their relationships with local agencies and re-establish them on a more formal basis. It has been demonstrated that partnership can be a stimulating and rewarding experience for all involved. It can also, through CCETSW's insistence on highly bureaucratic, complex policies and procedures, be a frustrating and time-consuming exercise.

References

Central Council for Education and Training in Social Work (1989a), *DipSW: Requirements and Regulations for the Diploma in Social Work*, Paper 30. London: Central Council for Education and Training in Social Work.

Central Council for Education and Training in Social Work (1989b), *Improving Standards in Practice Learning. Regulations and Guidance for the Approval of Agencies and the Accreditation and Training of Practice Teachers*, Paper 26.3. London: Central Council for Education and Training in Social Work.

Central Council for Education and Training in Social Work (1991), *DipSW : Rules and Requirements for the Diploma in Social Work*, Paper 30 Second Edition. London: Central Council for Education and Training in Social Work.

Central Council for Education and Training in Social Work (1995), *Assuring Quality in the Diploma in Social Work-1. Rules and Requirements for the DipSW Revised 1995*. London: Central Council for Education and Training in Social Work.

Jordan, B. (1988), 'What price partnerships? - costs and benefits', pp. 30-9 in James, A.L. and Scott, D.M. (eds.), *Partnership in Probation Education and Training*, London: Central Council for Education and Training in Social Work.

Payne, M. (1994), 'Partnership Between Organisations in Social Work Education', *Issues in Social Work Education*, 14, 1, pp.53-70.

17 The Development of Social Welfare in Poland
Izabela Rybka

Introduction

Social welfare is the oldest institution of public life, the means of support for people who are incapable, whether temporarily or permanently, of providing independently for their own self-subsistence. Organized forms of assistance for people in need of others' help first appeared in the period when materially differentiated societies developed. These replaced crumbling tribal communities, connected by kinship where mutual aid arose from solidarity ties within families. Social welfare has undergone subsequent stages of development through which it has taken various forms and applied different methods of activity. Its activities have been based on different grounds and performed - to a different extent - by different agents. Initially, social welfare took the form of private charity which - over centuries - was supplemented by charitable activities of a public character and, then, by organized social care. Contemporary social welfare systems are seeking to develop a range of differentiated forms of social work, in its broadest sense.

The Origins of Social Welfare in Poland

The first historical records of organized charitable activity in the territory which makes up modern Poland date from the 10th century, the period when the state was formed and adopted Christianity. In the Middle Ages, assistance to the poorest members of society was considered as an expression of Christian feelings of compassion and offered in such forms as dispensing alms or giving shelter in poorhouses. For centuries, charitable actions for the poor, the elderly, orphans and the homeless were dominated by the Roman Catholic Church - supported by foundations and donations made by the great landowners. This was a movement of private charity, inspired by religious and moral impulses and characterized by the existence of two different groups: generous donors on the one hand, and recipients stamped with a badge of poverty, on the other. Only the assistance provided by craftsmen or merchants to each other through their guilds was based on the principles of mutual aid and collective insurance. However, the close connection to particular trades or professions restricted access to a small percentage of the population.

Public authorities first addressed the problems of poverty at the end of the 15th century by adopting a law which specified the scope and methods of lawful begging. During the reign of Jan Olbracht in 1496, the Polish parliament (Sejm) approved measures which began the development of restrictive regulations under which those of the poor who were unable to work could obtain certificates entitling them to receive alms and shelter in poorhouses. Poor people thought capable of work were compelled to do so and were severely punished for any effort to beg. The application of administrative and police measures to combat poverty, beggary and vagrancy - seen as great plagues in the Middle Ages - was justified by the then dominant views on the causes of these problems. The paradigm was individualistic, disregarding the impact of the social environment and assuming that poverty resulted from defects in human nature for which people could be held responsible. The main objective of legal regulation was not to provide aid for the poor but to protect other members of society against beggars roaming around the country, appearing to threaten public safety and the existing social order.

One important development, however, was an involvement of the general public in organizing charitable aid for the poor. This process was initiated at the end of the16th century on the initiative of the famous Polish preacher and historian, Piotr Skarga. He was the author and promoter of the idea of secular charitable fraternities whose activities were designed to solicit funds for the poor, to place the homeless in poorhouses and the sick in hospitals, to visit prisoners and to seek jobs for the unemployed. Fraternities rapidly developed in both the towns and the countryside, contributing to an increased popularization and intensification of charitable activity carried out with wide participation by the rich and the co-operation of local authorities.

The position of the public authorities concerning on the question of poverty changed slightly during the reign of the last Polish king, Stanisław Augustus, at the end of the 18th century. Under his rule, the distribution of charity, although still dominated by the Church, was brought under state control. Tax exemptions were introduced to benefit of charitable institutions, and the Commission of Good Order was founded. This exercised administrative supervision over parishes, religious orders and individuals and enjoyed the

The Development of Social Welfare in Poland 247

exclusive power to approve the by-laws of foundations and hospitals. The Commission continued the state policy, of combatting beggary and vagrancy, and elaborated principles to rationalize the functioning of private sector entities, in particular the Church. This process of reform was, however, interrupted by Poland's loss of national sovereignty in 1795.

Private and Public Charity on the Partitioned Lands of Poland (1795-1918)

At the end of the 18th century, Poland was partitioned by Russia, Prussia and Austria. The further development of charity in its particular provinces depended on the policies pursued by each of the partitioning powers. The legal and actual status of those in need of help was most favourable in the area under Prussian administration, where the performance of social assistance was a duty laid on public institutions, namely municipal and provincial unions for the support of the poor. In the territories annexed by Austria, the communes' activities were limited to the provision of aid to permanent residents and then only when they were not eligible for assistance from non-public charitable sources. The communes seldom fulfilled their obligations, mostly of their limited financial resources in the economically disadvantaged rural areas. In the territories under Russian administration, the situation was also difficult. After the Polish National Insurrection of 1863, the Russian authorities took revenge by dissolving the existing network of assistance councils and replacing them by a highly centralized system of bureaucratic offices, carrying out a programme of russification, rather than any charitable activity.

If Poland's loss of statehood generally slowed down the development of public charity, it created appropriate conditions for the dynamic development of non-public charity by Poles trying to resolve the national and social questions through organizations founded outside the structures of foreign states. Private societies and social charitable organizations contributed to promoting the idea of organized social self-assistance and undertaking actions to counteract poverty. They also played an important role in founding the Polish system of health care and care for the elderly and for children. Within the framework of an 'outdoor' or community-based assistance system, they provided cash allowances, supplied fuel, clothes or cheap meals, helped to find a job, and organized home medical services and care. They also developed various forms of residential care, particularly poorhouses for elderly people and orphans, affordable housing, lodging-houses, nurseries, detention and youth custody centres, hospitals and establishments for child-bearing and convalescents.

Nevertheless, the numerous benefits and services offered by private and public sectors could not deal with the consequences of industrialisation and urbanization in the 19th century. The problem of mass poverty could not be solved unless the old views of its causes were abandoned. This finally happened when the liberal theories, which culminated in Malthusianism and Social Darwinism, were replaced by accounts of the impoverishment of entire social groups or classes as the result of external factors which were independent of an individuals behaviour. The popularization of the thesis that poverty depends on the social, political and economic system has to a changed view on the proper role of state authorities in acting to make the lives of the poor easier. The state, which had hitherto defined its tasks solely in terms of the protection of public order, found an interest in having its population free of poverty, effectively functioning and developing. This was reflected in legislation to strengthen earlier state actions related to social welfare.

Basic trends in the development of social welfare were described in the 1930s by a Polish sociologist and theoretician of social work, Konstanty Krzeczkowski (1936; 1938). He regarded the initiation of mass, obligatory social action by state authorities as a new stage in the history of social welfare. He called this *community* care, an alternative to the previous, inefficient, *individual* care. The main objective of community care is to transform existing living conditions so that they contribute to a sustainable social order instead of generating mass poverty. It involves preventive action to eliminate or considerably reduce the incidence of situations where the provision of individualized aid is necessary. Community care is directed to entire populations and contributes to an increase in everyone's living standards so that the whole population benefits, not only the people who were lagging behind. It abolishes the philanthropic aspect of individual care which results in the stigmatization of its recipients. Community care requires mass, systemic and long-term actions by state authorities. This approach was a cornerstone of the process of reconstructing and reforming the institutions of social welfare in Poland after 123 years of foreign rule.

The Polish Republic (1918-1939)

The achievements of the two decades between the First and Second World Wars made a significant contribution to both the theory and the practice of social work. The creation of a new Polish system of social care, replacing those set up by the partitioning powers, began just after the end of World War I and the restoration of Poland's independence. In Krzeczkowski's terms, the inter-war period might be defined as one establishing the foundations of *integral* (complete) care. This synthesized the prior models of individualized and community care. Integral care is implemented within the framework of the system of social security, although the majority of care and assistance is actually delivered by other institutions of social policy. The main objective of the system of social security is to provide citizens with institutional guarantees for the protection of their social rights, in particular their right to freedom from poverty and to participate in the achievements of social development. On the basis of comprehensive empirical data relating to the evolution of social welfare in Poland and other European countries, Krzeczkowski assumed that two compatible processes of development existed within this system. The first is reflected in a diminishing role for social welfare and a 'gradual withdrawal from the field'. This means the successive transfer of tasks originally fulfilled by social welfare to other spheres regulated by labour law, social insurance law or civil law. This includes, for example, the growth of social insurance, for old-age, sickness, industrial injuries, unemployment and disability, and the development of workplace-based social actions and systems of public health care and education. Examples of such transformations would include the replacement of nurseries run by religious or secular charitable fraternities by factory nurseries established at the expense of employers, inclusion of infant-feeding breaks within working time, and the transformation of various forms of institutionalized care for orphans and children from dysfunctional families into foster care by families. Simultaneously, there is a trend towards the constant extension of the scope of and access to social welfare. Having transferred some its previous tasks to other institutions, the social welfare system takes on new areas of activity and commits itself to satisfying new types of needs resulting from the development of civilization. This means that social welfare fulfils a piloting or pioneering function, identifying new, previously unknown or non-existent, social problems and providing the first response to them. Eventually, when the solution of these problems exceeds the legal and organizational capabilities of the social welfare system, it becomes the subject of action of another public institution which is better prepared to deal with it (e.g. social insurance).

This model of the state's role in resolving social problems and preventing their appearance, as well as a universal conviction about a great dynamism and prospects for the future development of social welfare, considerably influenced the 1923 Act on Social Care. Like Beveridge, its authors held that social welfare played a marginal role in a system of social security. In this sense, the Act presented itself as having a temporary character, 'in accordance with the most up to date approach, it is the task of social care to seek to replace its individual elements by social insurance (Starczewski, 1937)'. This legislation was passed during a period of uncritical belief in the omnipotence of the Polish state, now that independence had been regained. The state faced excessive and unrealistic demands substantially exceeding the capacities of its public authorities. Ultimately, a more modern measure (in terms of the then standards) was adopted, still promising a wider scope of care than that guaranteed by the legislation of other European countries, but without establishing a basis for its implementation.

Within the meaning of the 1923 Act, social care involves 'meeting, out of public funds, the essential living needs of those who are not able - permanently or temporarily - to do so by their own material means or work, as well as preventing the appearance of the above specified state.'[1] According to this approach, social care includes both meeting needs in themselves, i.e. social care in the strict sense, and preventive actions typical of social policy. Under the Act, a system of obligatory social care was introduced, organized and financed almost completely by local authorities with only a little support from central government. The main source of funds was the general revenue of the communes. However, the local authorities were not allowed to adopt additional means of raising the income to fund these services, such as using the receipts from administrative fines or introducing targeted local taxes. Nor could local authorities rely on financial support from central government, which was obliged to grant aid or subsidies only in extraordinary circumstances. Therefore, the level of communal expenditures was very low. Consequently, the 1923 Act was only implemented to a limited extent. At the same time, the hyperinflation which accompanied the Great Depression led to the devaluation of the funds available to private charitable organizations and a reduction in popular donations. The result was a decreasing trend in social service expenditure which continued for many years. Another negative aspect of the situation was the disparity between rural and urban areas, and between various regions of the country (which were coterminous with the geographical division of Poland at the time of its partition). The poor financial condition of social services is reflected by the level of expenditure in Poland compared with other European countries. In 1933/34, the average per capita expenditure from public funds in Poland for social services amounted to 2.63 zloty, as against 60.0 zloty in Germany, 101.3 in the United Kingdom, 36.6 in Switzerland and

36.4 in France (Nakoniecznikow Klukowski, 1939).

Laws, organizations and financial resources are necessary, but not sufficient, conditions for the effective functioning of a system of social service. Recognizing the role of professionally qualified personnel employed in social care units, work began during the inter-war period on establishing a system for the education of social workers and volunteers. Qualitative and quantitative changes in the tasks carried out by social welfare, and the emergence of new social security institutions, resulted in increased requirements for the knowledge and ethical standards of professional social workers. They needed to be able to view social problems within the entire context of socio-economic issues, while being able to deal directly with clients. During the intra-war period, there were no regulations specifying the level and type of formal educational requirements for practising the profession. A few vocational schools and courses were organized both for people employed in social welfare but not having appropriate theoretical qualifications and for graduates wishing to improve their professional qualifications (e.g. courses organised by the Ministry of Social Care for people in charge of care establishments). The only school of higher education, which provided comprehensive education in social work was the Social and Educational Studies of the Polish Free University. There were also three research centres which provided some education for care service personnel - the Institutes of Social Economy (IGS), Social Affairs and Social Services. They made significant scientific achievements in the analysis of different systems of social care, made in the context of a changing political system, and in studies on specific questions of social work, in particular with problems of the family, the child and young people. These institutes also conducted empirical studies aimed at identifying the needs in a particular region and the means of meeting them. These monographs were modelled on renowned foreign publications, including Smith's *The New Survey of London, Life and Labour* and the Lynds' *Middletown* studies. The institutes were also engaged in broad range of educational activity, including the publication of booklets, manuals and guide-books, the development of a periodical press, the organization of lectures and seminars, participation in the debates of the International Committee of Social Work Schools and meetings of other international bodies, like the International Social Service Conference.

The work of vocational centres and research institutes resulted in the specification of a model for the education of social workers. The basic elements included: (1) long-term professional education at a university level (MSW) and a high-school level (BSW); (2) general interdisciplinary education in such branches as social policy, sociology, psychology, pedagogy or hygiene;

(3) professional specialization as a final stage of education supplementing basic knowledge; (4) permanent education carried out by methods of regular training and courses; (5) practices and visits to model social welfare units in order to acquire practical skills and to enable an assessment of students' capability to work in the profession, based on their social maturity and personal predisposition. Even if these objectives were not achieved because of limited financial resources, their formulation and popularization in public discussions contributed to the growing prestige of the social work profession.

The Social Policy of the Socialist State

The model of social security established in Poland during the period of 'real socialism' offered a stable, even if relatively low level, system of social benefits closely related to employment. There was a gradual increase in the accessibility and scope of social insurance for that part of the population which was excluded from the labour market because of age or health status. The Constitution of the Polish People's Republic stated that work was a fundamental right and duty of all citizens, and only those who worked were entitled to other social rights. The social security system was based on a policy of full employment at low wages fixed arbitrarily by the central authorities. The social character of wages was compensated by a widely developed system of free benefits and services, mostly in the field of health care and education. Simultaneously, the State subsidized basic consumer goods and services, including foodstuff, lodgings, transport and medications. The State had an exclusive competence to organize employment and social security systems and to appropriate funds for collective consumption. The State monopoly in the social sphere deprived people of the opportunity to take individual decisions and to make independent provisions for themselves. As a consequence, individuals were relieved of any responsibility for the creation of the conditions in which they existed. This situation contributed to the rise of learned helplessness, a passive attitude towards life, together with casual and demanding social attitudes, that people had a right to help and no responsibility to avoid the need for it. Nevertheless, state dominance over most aspects of life in Poland also realised egalitarian ideals and equalized the living standards of citizens.

The very need for a social welfare system was questioned in the late 1940s. The then Minister of Labour and Social Care declared that: 'The socialist system, having eliminated economic crisis and unemployment as sources of poverty, has laid down two principles: (a) everyone has a right to work; (b) those who do not work, will not eat. These fundamental principles determine both the scope and objectives of social care - social welfare' (Quoted in Balicka-Kozłowska, 1972). The government's position was based on the conviction that an omnipotent socialist state eliminated for ever any social problems, in particular poverty, unemployment, homelessness, alcoholism and drug abuse. The category of legitimate recipients was limited to those permanently and completely unable to work, i.e. the elderly and disabled. The whole sphere of social welfare was financed from central budget sources and managed by commands and distributive methods of administration, where the State played an absolutely dominant role. The increased share of bureaucracy and statism in the system of social care was accompanied by the gradual elimination of voluntariness, reflected in the removal of volunteers from work in public institutions and the withdrawal of State subsidies for the non-government sector. The actual share of non-governmental institutions in the fulfilment of social welfare tasks had not been large, but the functioning of social organizations like the Polish Red Cross and the Polish Social Welfare Committee came to depend almost completely on grants from the State Budget.

Formally, the 1923 Act remained in force under the Polish People's Republic, but was not applied because of its inappropriateness to the new administrative structures and socio-economic relations. In practice, the legal basis of policy rested on lower-level acts and regulations including executive decrees and instructions. The stagnation of social welfare during the 1950s was reflected in the closure of training courses for social workers. Towards the end of the decade, however, there was a reconstruction of social welfare institutions and staff. In 1960, the responsibility for social welfare was transferred from the Ministry of Labour to the Ministry of Health. Functional ties between social welfare and health service were strengthened in 1973, through the creation of 'Health Care Teams' containing organizational units for care and assistance - to be called Social Services Sections. At a basic level, the idea of fundamental social and medical care provided jointly by a physician, public health nurse and social worker was realised in district health service centres. It was possible to employ social service staff with high professional qualifications and the programme was also supported by the establishment of a few post-secondary schools for social workers (BSW) and a network of training and consultation centres.

Changes in the System of Social Welfare - the Reform of 1990

The role of the social welfare system in meeting basic living and social needs changed at the beginning of the 1990s. As a result of the economic crisis, the restructuring of the economy and the implementation of market reforms, many negative social phenomena have appeared including overt unemployment, falling living standards and growing mass poverty. No uniform concept of social security has been elaborated despite the growing social costs of economic reforms. Instead, the state has withdrawn from its previous social obligations, confining itself to those protective actions which were necessary to gain public acceptance for the continuation of systemic transformation. The state's limitation of its social engagement has been reflected in changes in the structure of public expenditure. Implementation of the principles of a market economy led to the elimination of subsidies to consumer goods and services and commercialization of many services previously offered without payment. This resulted in a substantial increase in food and housing costs and growing expenses for social services. In turn, this led to a radical worsening of the material situation of medium- and low-income households. The share of expenditure for social services within the State Budget has tended to decrease.[2] This has resulted in reductions of the volume and quality of non-cash benefits provided in the field of education and upbringing, culture and arts, health protection, physical education and sport, as well as tourism and recreation. Although budgetary expenditures for social care slightly increased, the real value was maintained by decreasing investment in human capital in order to provide social protection for vulnerable groups. Decreasing expenditures for education, culture and recreation have been accompanied by rapidly growing outlays on social care to pay social welfare benefits and to carry out active and passive forms of combatting unemployment (See also the chapter by Ewa Giermanowska and Józefina Hrynkiewicz in this volume). Social welfare has become the institution responsible for easing the social consequences of economic reforms. Since the system of social welfare does not have has not have a proper legal and institutional base for this, then - despite the lack of political agreement about either the future direction of social policy or the reform of social insurance - a thorough reconstruction of the system of social welfare has begun. A new Act was adopted in 1990 to regulate the whole complex of issues connected with the functioning of social welfare. This Act specified the objective of social welfare, its general principles and detailed tasks, designated the intended recipients and a wide range of available benefits, established a new public organizational structure and fixed high qualification standards for social workers.

Within the meaning of the Act, 'social welfare is an institution of state social policy, designed to provide assistance to those individuals and families who cannot manage their life problems within their own means, capabilities and rights.'[3] Actions undertaken by public social services should strengthen the family, which is considered to be a main object of social policy actions and plays a fundamental role in the process of upbringing and socialization. The form and amounts of benefits granted by social welfare institutions should be matched in such a way as to give recipients the opportunity to live in conditions becoming to human dignity while not depriving them of motivation to make efforts to improve their living standards. In practice, it is difficult to achieve such a compromise without creating a 'poverty trap'. This is a situation where there is no substantial difference between the level of wages (earned income) and the total value of non-earned incomes (social benefits). This encourages negative attitudes in benefit recipients. If they cannot find a job with earnings significantly exceeding the amount they receive in social benefits, they stop making any effort to improve their living conditions, give up aspirations to participate in the process of social development, and are become marginalized and stigmatized. The passive adjustment of a growing part of the population to subsistence at minimal level leads to a widening and strengthening culture of poverty. In this event, social ties are broken and there is anomie, described by the classic French sociologist Emile Durkheim as a situation when fundamental values, norms and mechanisms governing social life cease to be valid. That is why the system of social security should effectively prevent the emergence of mass and structural poverty and undertake - by means of social welfare - remedial action to stimulate benefit recipients' autonomy, to support their reintegration with the community and to facilitate their return to the performance of basic social, occupational and family roles. It is impossible to achieve these objectives of social welfare without an efficient system of social insurance and appropriate social policy, particularly in respect of the labour market and the structure of wages. In such situation, the system of social welfare is overloaded, but it ought to supplement, rather than replace, employment as the basic pillar of social security.

Local authorities have the main duty to meet social welfare needs. A centre of social welfare has been established in each commune [*gmina*], and 49 social welfare teams - subordinate to government administration - have been appointed throughout the country. Public institutions are statutorily obliged to cooperate with voluntary organizations, the Roman Catholic Church and religious organizations, charitable associations, foundations and individuals.

NGOs play a significant role in the process of creating local democracy and strengthening social ties and facilitate independent citizens' initiatives contributing to the development of social solidarity. Their involvement is vital in realizing the ideal of social self-help. The State supports these activities with grants and with the development of a system of contracting for social services - designed to increase their present level and quality while reducing the cost of provision. NGOs are preferred as service providers, because - as a rule - they react more quickly and accurately to changing welfare needs and, moreover, conduct a non-profit activity based on co-operation between professionals and volunteers.

According to statistics collected by the Social Welfare Department of the Ministry of Labour and Social Policy, cash benefit is the most important form of benefits. Previously, the only people eligible for these were those who had no source of subsistence or whose per capita family income did not exceed the level of the lowest old-age (retirement) pension. Now, according to a new procedure, eligibility is calculated by relating the family income to the number and ages of people in the household. The introduction of this equivalency scale is intended to match benefit levels more precisely to the real needs of a family. From this point of view, this action seems reasonable. However, the income levels set by the amended act had the effect of withdrawing cash benefits from many people actually living in poverty, particularly families with many children and lone parent families, i.e. those especially in need of protection and support. However, one positive aspect of the change has been a shift in the basis of benefit adjustment from wage movements to price movements.[4]

The assessment of the living standards, as well as the family situation and the health status of applicants for a social welfare benefit is the responsibility of a social worker who carries out a community (family) inquiry in applicant's home. If a need for support is established, the social worker prepares a detailed plan of assistance for a given person or family. The form and scope of assistance should be appropriate to the circumstances found during the inquiry and the objectives of social welfare, particularly in making its clientele independent and in supporting ties with family and community. Because of the discretionary and individual character of benefits granted by social welfare institutions, social workers are required to have professional qualifications and to adhere to the high ethical standards. Under the 1990 Act, the profession of social worker may be practised by certified social workers and graduates of higher education in the following fields: social work, social policy, resocialization, sociology, pedagogy, psychology, as well as graduates in other faculties who have completed a specialization in social work and the organization of social welfare. The fundamental principle determining the conduct of a social worker is to respect the dignity of individuals and families applying for aid and to observe their right to self-determination. A social worker may also demand that clients cooperate in solving their living problems.

The growing pauperization of Poland's population in the 1990s has led to a gradual extension in the scope of social welfare. In 1995, aid was given to 1.8 million households including more than 6.7 million people. This means that 18 per cent of the population were not able to meet their basic social and living needs without outside help.[5] The number of beneficiaries of social welfare is expected to fall in 1997, resulting from more restrictive regulations relating to eligibility rather than improvements in the living standards of families.

Conclusion

The existence of a large number of economically dependent households has resulted from a persistently high unemployment rate and decreasing incomes of a part of the population, as well as widening social disparities. Despite a huge demand for social welfare benefits, the public funds allocated for that purpose are insufficient, even if the social welfare system is the last resort for those lacking basic means of subsistence. When considering the social costs of the transformation to a market society, it is necessary to include the effects of the recent modifications of legislation on social welfare, which have resulted in a reduced eligibility for benefits and in higher fees for residential care. In such a situation, there is a continuing need to monitor the consequences of restricting access to material assistance and social services as well as assessing the effectiveness with which the allocated funds are being used. Above all, the state should make an effort to prepare and implement a reform of the social security system, while specifying its objectives and scope of its social obligations. An analysis of the proposed changes indicates a tendency to depart from the Continental tradition in social policy to a clearly liberal Anglo-Saxon model. This means that, in the near future, social assistance will constitute the main, although ineffective, means of dealing with the problem of poverty.

Notes

1. Article 1 of the Act dated 16th August, 1923 on Social Care, Dziennik Ustaw of 1924, No. 92, item 726.
2. The share of total budgetary expenditures allocated to social services fell from 37.4 per cent in 1991 to 34.3 per cent in 1993 and 32.5 per cent in the budget for 1994. Source: 'Sfera społeczna w 1993 r. Zjawiska i tendencje'. Central Planning Office, Department of Social Development, Warsaw 1994.
3. Article 1 of the Act dated 29th November, 1990 on Social Welfare, Dziennik Ustaw of 1993, No. 13, item 60.
4. This is an advantage under current Polish conditions where prices are tending to rise more rapidly than wages. In Western parts of Europe, however, it would be a disadvantage since it excludes benefit recipients from any share in long-term economic growth, reflected in rising real wages.
5. 'Sfera społeczna w 1995 roku na tle lat 1990-1994. Zjawiska i tendencje'. Central Planning Office, Department of Social Development, Warsaw 1996.

References

Balicka-Kozłowska, H. (1972), 'Rozważania o opiece i pomocy społecznej w Polsce Ludowej', *Kultura i społeczeństwo*, No. 1-3, pp.117-37.

Hrynkiewicz, J. (1992), 'Koncepcje polityki społecznej w Polsce w latach 1989-1992', *Gospodarka Narodowa*, No. 7-8, pp.1-10.

Kuleszyńska-Dobrek, J. (1991), 'Objaśnienia do ustawy o pomocy społecznej', *Praca socjalna*, No. 1-2, pp.32-92.

Krzeczkowski, K. (1936), 'Uwagi nad drogami opieki społecznej', *Samorząd Terytorialny*, No.1-2, pp.1-25.

Krzeczkowski, K. (1938), 'O trzech etapach opieki społecznej', *Samorząd Terytorialny*, No. 3, pp.5-17.

Księżopolski, M. (1995), 'Bezpieczeństwo społeczne w Polsce', in *Raport o rozwoju społecznym Polska 1995*, Wyd.Split Trading: Warsaw, pp.167-85.

Łopato, J. (1982), 'Miłosierdzie i dobroczynność w Polsce', *Polityka Społeczna*, No. 5, pp.24-7.

Łopato, J. (1987), 'Zarys rozwoju pomocy społecznej w Polsce Ludowej', *Polityka Społeczna*, No. 11-12, pp.8-13.

Muszalski, W. (1996), *Prawo socjalne*, PWN, Warsaw.

Nakoniecznikow Klukowski, B. (1939), 'Przegląd najbardziej aktualnych zagadnień z zakresu polityki opiekuńczej', *Praca i Zabezpieczenie Społeczne*, No.1, pp.18-26.

Polityka społeczna i warunki społeczne w Polsce w latach 1989-1993 (1994), Raport Instytutu Pracy i Spraw Socjalnych, No.5: Warsaw.

Polityka społeczna w latach 1993-1994 na tle przemian okresu transformacji (1995), Raport Instytutu Pracy i Spraw Socjalnych, No.8, Warsaw.

'Sfera społeczna w 1995 roku na tle lat 1990-1994. Zjawiska i tendencje' Centralny Urząd Planowania (1994), Departament Rozwoju Społecznego: Warsaw.

'Sfera społeczna w 1993 roku. Zjawiska i tendencje.' Centralny Urząd Planowania (1994), Departament Rozwoju Społecznego: Warsaw.

Starczewski, J. (1937), Ustawodawstwo o opiece społecznej', *Opiekun Społeczny*, No. 4, pp.1-6.
Szurgacz, H. (1993), *Wstęp do prawa pomocy społecznej*, Wyd. Uniwersytetu Wrocławskiego, Wrocław.
Ustawa z dn. 16.08.1923 r. o opiece społecznej, Dziennik Ustaw z 1924 r., nr 92, poz. 726.
Ustawa z dn. 29.11.1990 r. o pomocy społecznej, Dziennik Ustaw z 1993 r., nr 13, poz. 60.